BUSINESS AND SUSTAINABLE DEVELOPMENT IN AFRICA

The book offers new critical insights into the relationship between corporate social responsibility (CSR) and sustainable development in Africa.

The extent to which CSR initiatives can contribute to sustainable development in Africa remains debatable. This book examines in a very clear structure how, when, and whether CSR initiatives are able to contribute to the realization of the sustainable development goals, peace, and environmental sustainability at the micro levels of society. It also explores some macro-level issues such as the relationship between taxation and CSR, CSR and human rights, and CSR and public governance and, in so doing, challenges existing CSR dogmas.

With themes aligned with the UN Sustainable Development Goals (SDGs), this book provides useful practical guidance for policymakers and business leaders seeking to better understand the strength and limitations of CSR as a vehicle for advancing sustainable development in Africa. It will also appeal to scholars, researchers, and students of African studies, development studies, international business, strategic management, and business and society.

Uwafiokun Idemudia is a professor and chair of the Department of Social Science at York University, Canada. He teaches in the Business and Society, Development Studies, and African Studies programmes.

Francis Xavier Dery Tuokuu is a lecturer in sustainability at Bournemouth University, UK.

Tahiru Azaaviele Liedong is an associate professor of strategy and international business at the School of Management, University of Bath, UK.

BUSINESS AND SUSTAINABLE DEVELOPMENT IN AFRICA

Medicine or Placebo?

Edited by Uwafiokun Idemudia, Francis Xavier Dery Tuokuu, and Tahiru Azaaviele Liedong

LONDON AND NEW YORK

Cover image: © Getty Images

First published 2022
by Routledge
4 Park Square, Milton Park, Abingdon, Oxon OX14 4RN

and by Routledge
605 Third Avenue, New York, NY 10158

Routledge is an imprint of the Taylor & Francis Group, an informa business

British Library Cataloguing-in-Publication Data
A catalogue record for this book is available from the British Library

Library of Congress Cataloging-in-Publication Data
Names: Idemudia, Uwafiokun, editor. | Tuokuu, Francis Xavier, editor. | Liedong, Azaaviele Tahiru, editor.
Title: Business and sustainable development in Africa : medicine or placebo? / edited by Uwafiokun Idemudia, Francis Xavier Tuokuu and Tahiru Azaaviele Liedong.
Description: Abingdon, Oxon ; New York, NY : Routledge, [2022] | Includes bibliographical references and index.
Identifiers: LCCN 2021048102 | ISBN 9780367481186 (pbk) | ISBN 9780367481179 (hbk) | ISBN 9781003038078 (ebk)
Subjects: LCSH: Social responsibility of business--Africa. | Sustainable development--Africa.
Classification: LCC HD60.5.A35 B87 2022 | DDC 361.765096--dc23
LC record available at https://lccn.loc.gov/2021048102

ISBN: 978-0-367-48117-9 (hbk)
ISBN: 978-0-367-48118-6 (pbk)
ISBN: 978-1-003-03807-8 (ebk)

DOI: 10.4324/9781003038078

Typeset in Times New Roman
by Deanta Global Publishing Services, Chennai, India

CONTENTS

CONTRIBUTORS

About the Editors

Uwafiokun Idemudia is a full professor and chair of the Department of Social Science, in the Faculty of Liberal Arts and Professional Studies at York University, Toronto, Canada. He teaches in the International Development Studies and African Studies program. His research interests are in the area of business and development, natural resource governance and conflict and development. His recent book is titled *Africapitalism: Sustainable Business and Development in Africa* (2019), and other works have appeared in journals such as *Business Strategy and Environment*, *Environmental Science and Policy*, *Organization and Environment*, and *Natural Resources Forum.*

Francis Xavier Dery Tuokuu is a lecturer in sustainability at Bournemouth University in the UK, having completed two postdoctoral fellowships at Keene State College in the United States and York University in Canada. Over the past decade, Francis has lived and worked in the United States, Canada, the UK, and Ghana. His research and professional interests include; environmental and energy policy, extractive sector governance, sustainability and clean energy, and corporate social responsibility. His peer-reviewed papers have appeared in prominent journals such as *Energy Research and Social Science*, *Environmental Science and Policy*, *Journal of Cleaner Production*, *Journal of Environmental Policy and Planning*, *The Extractive Industries and Society*, *Resources Policy*, *Natural Resources Forum*, *Journal of Sustainable Mining*, *Journal of Global Responsibility*, *Journal on Migration and Human Security*, and *International Journal of Energy Sector Management.* Francis has consulted for the Government of Sierra Leone, Environmental and Energy Technology Council of Maine (E2TECH), New-Takoradi Community, and Campaign for Female Education (CAMFED-Ghana). He holds a PhD in environmental studies from Antioch University, New Hampshire, preceded by two masters: an MSc in interdisciplinary environmental studies from Antioch University and another MSc. in corporate social responsibility and energy from the Robert Gordon University in Aberdeen, UK. He also has a bachelor's degree in geography and resource development with philosophy from the University of Ghana, Legon.

Tahiru Azaaviele Liedong is an assistant professor of strategy and international business and head of research ethics at the University of Bath School of Management, UK. He is also an external examiner at Southampton Business School, UK, and previously taught at Kings College London and the University of Buckingham, UK. Prior to joining academia, Tahiru held various professional and management positions in UK and Ghana. His experience spans treasury, investment banking, development banking, strategy consulting, and project management. He was a professional associate at the World Bank where he was a member of the senior management team responsible for developing the Bank's strategy and overseeing its operations in Ghana, Liberia, and Sierra Leone. Prior to this, he worked as a treasury officer at Ecobank (one of the largest banks in Africa), as treasury chairperson at Silsoe Aid for Appropriate Development (SAFAD-UK), and as an investment and research officer at First Atlantic Bank Ghana. His research focuses on strategic management, corporate governance, corporate social responsibility, institutional entrepreneurship, and international business. He wrote an award-winning PhD dissertation, and his work has appeared in books and reputable refereed journals such as the *British Journal of Management*, *Journal of World Business*, *Long Range Planning*, *Group & Organization Management*, *Management International Review*, *Strategic Change*, and *Africa Journal of Management*. Tahiru was Emerald's 2015 Outstanding Reviewer for *Journal of Strategy & Management* and Wiley's best reviewer for *Business Ethics: A European Review*. He holds a BSc in banking and finance from the University of Ghana, an MSc in finance and management, MRes. in management research, and a PhD in strategy and finance from Cranfield University, UK. Tahiru was also a visiting doctoral researcher at the University of Warwick, UK. He is a fellow of the UK Higher Education Academy (FHEA) and a member of the Chartered Management Institute, UK.

Contributors

Raymond A. Atuguba is a professor and currently the dean of the University of Ghana School of Law, where he has taught since 2002. He has been a visiting professor of law and the Henry J. Steiner visiting professor of human rights at the Harvard Law School (2018–2019) and has taught 37 related courses at several universities in Africa, Europe, the United States of America, and Australia. His research interests are in constitutional and administrative law in the global south, law and development in Africa, and human rights and community lawyering. A graduate of the University of Ghana and of Harvard Law School, where he obtained a master of law degree and did doctoral studies. Professor Atuguba has also worked in the public sector (he was one time the executive secretary to the president of Ghana); the private sector (he was the team leader of Law and Development Associates (LADA) and Atuguba and Associates); and the non-profit sector (he is co-founder and former executive director and former board chair of the Legal Resources Centre). Prof. Atuguba has over 100 publications, been engaged in over 100 research and advocacy projects, produced over 100 Research and Technical Reports, and delivered over 300 papers and presentations on all continents of the world. He has consulted for many African governments (Gambia, Ghana, Lesotho, Liberia, Sierra Leone, Uganda, Zimbabwe, etc.) and major international development agencies and NGOs (The UN and UNDP, The World Bank, IOM, AU, ECOWAS, USAID, DFID, GIZ, DANIDA, OXFAM, IBIS, IIED, ActionAid International, Human Rights Watch, CARE International, Plan International, OSI/OSIWA, etc.) and led or co-led over 30 training programmes and workshops. He has also chaired or sat on over 50 boards and committees.

François Lenfant is a researcher at the University of Amsterdam Business School, and lecturer at the Centre for International Conflict Analysis and Management at the Radboud University in Nijmegen, The Netherlands. His areas of expertise are in multi-stakeholder partnerships in Africa, corporate social responsibility, sustainable development, and the economic dimensions of peace processes. His PhD thesis "On business, conflict and peace: Interaction and collaboration in Central Africa" explored business interaction with peace and conflict in Central Africa, mostly Rwanda and the Democratic Republic of Congo. He has published articles in different journals ranging from the *Journal of Business Ethics* to *Development in Practice*. François also carries out research and evaluation assignments in Africa for governments, NGOs, and multilateral institutions such as UNICEF. François holds an M.A. in international development from the American University in Washington, DC, and a PhD from the University of Amsterdam. For more information and an overview of his publications, see www.lenfant-research.com

Marcellinus Essah is a PhD student in human geography at the University of Toronto, Canada. His current research focus on the political economy/ecology of food policies and agrarian reforms. Marcellinus is also passionate about gold mining, CSR, sustainability, and community development in Ghana. He has published in *Resources Policy: A Journal Devoted to the Economics and Policy Issues Related to Mineral and Fossil Fuel Extraction, Production and Use.*

Emmanuel Graham is a PhD student at York University's Department of Politics in Toronto, Ontario, Canada. In terms of research interest, Graham's focus is on the political economy of the extractive sector and energy politics in Ghana and West Africa, his research has been on the role of civil society in escaping the resource curse in Ghana, oil exploration, and production in sub-Saharan Africa. He is also interested in electoral politics, political vigilantism, and democratic consolidation in Ghana and West Africa. He has some publications in international peer-reviewed journals such as *Extractive Industry and Society*, *Africa Review*, *Insight on Africa*, and *Journal of African Elections*.

Adaeze Okoye is a senior lecturer at the University of Brighton, UK, and a visiting professor at the Coal City University, Enugu, Nigeria. She holds a PhD from the University of Hull, UK, and a master's degree in environmental law and policy from the University of Dundee, Scotland. Dr. Okoye is also a barrister and solicitor of the Supreme Court of Nigeria and an associate academic fellow of the Honorable Society of the Inner Temple (Inn of Court, London). She was a visiting fellow at the Institute of Advanced Legal Studies, the University of London from 2015 to 2016. She is a 2010 alumni of the Institute for Global Law and Policy (IGLP) workshop, Harvard Law School. Her monograph, *Legal Approaches and Corporate Social Responsibility* (2016), explores legal approaches to law and the corporate social responsibility relationship. She has also written about corporate governance, law and development, joint development agreements, and environmental management systems in the oil industry.

Olushola Emmanuel Ajide is the head of partnership development/CSR at RCCGUK's Scotland Provincial Headquarters, Fountain of Love, Aberdeen, UK. Also, he is the RCCG Scotland social action officer overseeing over 55 branches of social action activities. He researches on CSR, community engagement, climate change, sustainability, renewable energy, and circular economy. He has publications in refereed journals.

Oluyomi Abayomi Osobajo is a lecturer in operations management and project management at Robert Gordon University, UK. He researches climate change, sustainability, CSR, renewable energy, circular economy, and waste management. He has authored and co-authored papers, which are published in refereed journals.

Prince Amoah holds a PhD from Massey University, Auckland Campus in New Zealand. Prior to this, he was a visiting research scholar at North Carolina State University and a lecturer at the University of Ghana. Prince's current research focuses on CSR, business ethics, and sustainability practices and governance within the mining industry. He is a research associate with the sustainability and CSR research group – a multidisciplinary team of researchers from Massey Business School and an Adjunct Faculty member of the Nobel International Business School (NiBS) – a graduate school offering academic and professional doctoral qualifications. Prince has published in international academic journals, including in *Business Strategy and the Environment* and *Social Business*, and has presented his empirical research findings at international conferences.

Gabriel Eweje is a professor of responsible and sustainable business at the School of Management, Auckland Campus, Massey Business School, Massey University, New Zealand. He is also director of the CSR and Sustainability Research Group – a multi-disciplinary team of researchers from Massey Business School. He is the editor-in-chief of *Corporate Governance – An International Journal of Business in Society*. Gabriel's current research interests are ethical decision-making in public and private organizations, CSR, conscious and responsible organizations, sustainable supply chain management, and sustainability, including the UN Sustainable Development Goals (SDGs). He has published his work in international academic journals such as *Journal of Business Ethics, Business & Society, Business Strategy and the Environment, International Journal of Operations and Production Management, International Journal of Human Resource Management, Business Ethics: A European Review, Australasian Journal of Environmental Management, Journal of Business Logistics, Marketing Intelligence and Planning, Sustainable Development Journal*, and *Corporate Social Responsibility and Environmental Management Journal* and has presented his research findings at international conferences.

Uwem E. Ite holds a PhD in geography from Cambridge University, UK. He is currently the head of Community and Government Relations at Oriental Energy Resources Limited, an oil exploration and production company operating in Nigeria. He has more than 20 years of working experience in sustainability and CSR issues in the Nigerian oil and gas industry. The views expressed in this chapter are personal and not necessarily shared by the company.

FIGURES

TABLES

INTRODUCTION

The Nexus of Business, Corporate Social Responsibility, and Sustainable Development in Africa

Uwafiokun Idemudia, Francis Xavier Dery Tuokuu, and Tahiru Azaaviele Liedong

The fact that Africa is behind all other regions of the world in the push to achieve sustainable development goals (SDGs) is hardly contentious (Njoh, 2016). For example, one in three Africans, equating to about 422 million people, live below the poverty line. The region is home to 70% of the world's poorest people.[1] Of the 54 countries in Africa, 42 are highly impoverished. Among the 28 poorest countries in the world, 27 are in sub-Saharan Africa. According to the World Bank, even though the share of Africans living in extreme poverty fell from 54% in 1990 to 41% in 2015, the actual number of poor people increased from 278 million to 413 million within the same period due to population growth.[2] With poverty affecting agricultural productivity, the threat of hunger is on the rise. In 2020, the Food and Agriculture Organization (FAO) estimated that 256 million Africans were hungry, an increase of 44 million people from 2014.[3] Moreover, the state of healthcare in Africa is deplorable. Though accounting for only 11% of the world's population, Africa records 60% of all HIV/AIDS cases. Of all malaria cases in the world, 90% occur in Africa. Similarly, of the 20 countries with the highest maternal mortality rates in the world, 19 are African.[4] While there is an abundance of natural resources in Africa, this rich resource endowment has not necessarily translated into a positive developmental dividend for its people (Idemudia, 2012). In 2019, sub-Saharan Africa's budget deficit was about 4.2% of GDP, and it is expected to worsen in the coming years. This will be exacerbated by the COVID-19 pandemic which is projected to wipe US$115 billion off the economies of sub-Saharan African countries and cause the region's first recession in 25 years.[5] Unsurprisingly, African countries are highly indebted. As of 2021, 44 out of the 54 countries in the region participated in the Debt Service Suspension Initiative (DSSI) – a World Bank/IMF initiative aimed to provide temporal debt-service relief to poor countries.

DOI: 10.4324/9781003038078-1

Given that business has been central to Africa's development for centuries (Visser et al., 2006), there is now a growing consensus that businesses have a role to play in any efforts geared towards arresting and reversing the problem of underdevelopment within the African continent (Knorringa & Helmsing, 2008) It is therefore not surprising that since the 1990s, concerted efforts have been made by national and international development agencies to add 'development' to the list of business social responsibilities (Sharp, 2006; Idemudia, 2014). The idea that business enterprises have a social responsibility to society is as old as commerce (Holmes, 1976). However, the conception of this idea in terms of corporate social responsibility (CSR) is a recent occurrence in both social development thinking and corporate business culture. Yet, the emergence of CSR has been shrouded in controversy that has often taken the form of a polemic debate (i.e. stakeholder versus stockholder theory debate). The issue in most of the earlier debates is disagreements about the nature and scope of the responsibilities encapsulated under the umbrella of CSR, and the differences in perceptions and understanding of the role and purpose of the corporation in society (see Sohn, 1980; Smith, 2003). However, contemporary realities such as the bifurcation of world politics, the process of globalization, information technology revolution, and incidences of corporate misdemeanours have all ensured that CSR is both not a passing phase of a business–society relationship and a core societal expectation of business–society relationships. Consequently, analysis of business–society relationship in Africa has shifted from concerns over whether corporations would imbibe the principles of CSR or not; to the extent to which CSR principles actually influence corporate decisions and practices (see Davis, 1960; Frederick, 1983; Mintzberg, 1983; Buchholz, 1991; Smith, 2003). For example, a majority of transnational corporations (TNCs) and even local businesses in Africa now publicly declare their commitment to the socio-economic development of the region, which they demonstrate through adherence to CSR principles and the implementation of social interventions. This commitment is now often captured in business sustainability reports (Kolk & Lenfant, 2010; Kühn, Stiglbauer, & Fifka, 2018). Yet, the extent to which this kind of corporate commitment to CSR principles have been translated into responsible behaviour on the ground in Africa remains debatable (Idemudia, 2007, 2010a; Egbon et al, 2018). Consequently, the onus is still often on businesses operating in Africa to demonstrate the substance of their sociability (see Moon, 2001). For example, Utting and Margues (2010) have suggested that while business might have the potential to contribute to 'hard development' through CSR, a major blind spot in CSR practices is in the area of 'soft development', i.e. issues of distributional justice and equity. Similarly, Ireland and Pillay (2010) have also suggested that while it is likely true that the earlier idea of socially responsible corporation might have had a genuinely transformative edge and therefore good for development, contemporary CSR practices have essentially become ameliorative in purpose seeking to enshrine and secure corporate legitimacy and shareholder value (see Idemudia, 2010b).

At any rate, contemporary emphasis in CSR debates in the African context seems to have also evolved from the extent to which corporate rhetoric of CSR matches CSR practices, to how well CSR practices and interventions can contribute to sustainable development (see Idemudia, 2014; Idemudia & Ite, 2006a). This shift in the analytical lens within business–society relationships has led to a number of positions being taken by critics and proponents of the CSR-development relationship. At one end of the divide is the 'greenwash' school versus the ecological modernization school. The greenwash school argues that there continues to be a huge gap between corporate rhetoric and CSR practices in Africa (see Corporate Watch, 1996; Friends of the Earth, 2004). In contrast, the ecological modernization school argues that significant progress is being made in terms of how businesses are responding to their social and environmental responsibility (see Dryzek,1997; WBCSD, 1999). For example, Wilenuis (2005) has argued that only a small minority of the business world has sustainability in their core values and even fewer really put their values and principles into action. In contrast, based on over 60 case studies, Holliday, Schmidheiny, and Watta (2002) argued that significant change in business practices was already underway. It is therefore not surprising that in recent years, despite the role of business in the colonization of Africa, business has increasingly recast itself as no longer part of the problem of underdevelopment in Africa, but now a part of the solution (Idemudia, 2014). Initially, for decades, most Transnational Corporations (TNCs) in Africa tended to resist the demands to meet their social responsibility obligations and contribute to sustainable development. They instead argued that addressing developmental challenges in the continent was largely the prerogative of governments. However, the combinations of global and local pressures have changed this trajectory. African societies have increasingly become aware of business complicity in the development problems they face, and have come to expect that businesses behave responsibly and actively contribute to developmental efforts (Eweje, 2006). These demands often manifest in the forms of demand for corporate accountability such that businesses in Africa now increasingly see their ability to secure their social legitimacy as being tied to the quality and nature of their corporate citizenship practices (Amaeshi, Adegbite, & Rajwani, 2016b; Claasen & Roloff, 2012; Gifford, Kestler, & Anand, 2010).

Today, the CSR initiatives of most business enterprises in Africa cover a wide range of issues such as health and HIV/AIDS, community development, economic and enterprise development, education and scholarships, human rights, poverty alleviation, peacebuilding, and sports (van Alstine & Afionis, 2013; Bagire & Namada, 2013). However, efforts to examine the extent to which CSR initiatives actually contribute or fail to contribute to sustainable development in Africa remain limited. Consequently, our understanding of the changing role of business in development within Africa and its impact on local people is still fragmented and relies too heavily on anecdotal evidence. Idemudia (2014) attributes these issues to three reasons. First, the literature on the relationship between CSR and development in Africa is only just emerging, and as such, it is still largely uneven. Second, while some extant analysis of the CSR–development nexus in Africa has been particularly insightful, there is often the lack of sufficiently grounded systematically accumulated empirical evidence to suggest whether CSR is good or bad for Africa's development. Third, as Blowfield (2012) has pointed out, a core challenge at the centre of the CSR and development debate remains the failure to clarify whether a business is expected to be simply a tool or an agent of development. This has meant that the expectations around the developmental role of business can often depend on the views of the analyst rather than on rigorous analysis.

As such, it is still not clear whether CSR practices can be part of the medicine for underdevelopment in Africa or if it is just simply another placebo. For instance, there is some recognition that CSR has some potential to make important contributions towards alleviating the developmental challenges in Africa (Eweje, 2006; Idemudia, 2008, 2014). Specifically, some researchers have shown how CSR could contribute to the achievement of the United Nation's sustainable development goals (SDGs) in the region (Selmier II & Newenham-Kahindi, 2021; Yakovleva, Kotilainen, & Toivakka, 2017). However, several challenges such as the lack of coordination, disjuncture between CSR priorities with community needs, the skewed nature of CSR practices that seems to emphasize the social dimension of sustainable development over its environmental dimensions appear to limit the potential of CSR to tackle sustainable development challenges facing the continent (Idemudia, 2014; Kumi, Yeboah, & Kumi, 2020). Consequently, there is weak evidence to support claims that businesses are engaging with and contributing to addressing important sustainable development challenges in Africa (Malan, 2016). The apparent ineffectiveness of CSR practices in terms of its contributions to sustainable development could also be linked to the superficial nature of social interventions of business that resonate more with 'ticking boxes' rather than substantive efforts to address SDG goals in the continent. This perhaps explains why Idemudia (2010b, 2011) argued that CSR practices in Africa suffer from both structural and systemic deficiencies in the way CSR is conceived and implemented. However, it is also clear that given the prevalence of weak institutions, a high incidence of corruption, and governance failure, governments alone are unable to drive and ensure that the SDGs can be met in Africa. This unpleasant prevailing situation has led Ite (2004) to argue that the institutional environment in Africa can present formidable challenges and, in some cases, a hostile environment for CSR policies and practices (Naor, 1982). Consequently, unpacking the changing role of business in development in the African context requires us to examine the extent to which businesses in Africa recognize their developmental role and have developed the capacity to facilitate and support sustainable development. Crucially, there is a need to re-examine the areas where CSR initiatives might have a more tremendous impact and understand how to better position CSR initiatives to strengthen local institutions and support local livelihoods.

Given the neglect of sub-Saharan Africa in the debate on CSR and development, this book takes seriously the role of business in development and seeks to move the CSR-development debate in Africa forward. Indeed, there is a need to go beyond the question of whether CSR is good or bad for development and instead focus on the different ways in which CSR is implicated in both the processes and the multifaceted nature of development outcomes associated with CSR practices in Africa (Idemudia, 2008, 2014). Hence, this book contains chapters that explore how CSR can be used to advance developmental challenges related to SDGs. Focusing on themes ranging from poverty alleviation to institutional strengthening, the chapters probe the conceptualization of CSR as it relates to development, critique current CSR approaches and initiatives, and proffer recommendations for harnessing the potential of CSR for Africa's socio-economic development. While this book acknowledges some of the strides that CSR has made in the improvement of social welfare in African countries, it also recognizes that several CSR initiatives in the region are irrelevant to the real challenges that African people face. The overall sense is that while CSR has some ability to contribute to addressing Africa's development problems, it is yet to achieve its full potential due to how it is often conceived and practiced. Therefore, one of the aims of this book is to provide a road map for turning 'placebo CSR' in Africa into possible 'medicinal CSR'.

Against this backdrop, Chapter 1 of this book examines the literature on the relationship between corporate social responsibility (CSR) and development in Africa. It argues that the literature is only just emerging and characterized by a wide range of diverse perspectives. Idemudia shows that while the analyses of the CSR-development nexus in Africa have been particularly insightful, it often lacks sufficient grounding in systematically accumulated empirical evidence. However, central to the CSR-development nexus debate in Africa is the disagreement over the reimagining of the role of business from being the cause to becoming a part of the solution to the problem of underdevelopment in the region. The chapter lays bare the controversies that have so far emerged around the CSR-development nexus in Africa. The chapter engages with the drivers of CSR, its dynamics, and nature within Africa. It then examines the debate of whether or not contextual factors matters for CSR and its relationship with development. Crucially, it identifies differences between proponents of CSR are good for development and those that share opposing views at the conceptual, practical, and discourse levels. The chapter concludes by considering the emerging issues and their implications for future research agendas.

Given the high incidences of human rights violations associated with resource extraction within rural communities (Idemudia, Kwakyewah, & Muthuri, 2020), in Chapter 2, Atuguba explores the connection between CSR and fundamental human rights obligations of corporate entities. He challenges the popular yet misleading notion that CSR is only made up of voluntary humanitarian assignments that corporate bodies may perform if they are minded to. He postulates that CSR is not an entirely philanthropic endeavour and that the primary value of CSR requires corporate bodies to act in the best interest of stakeholders of community development. Focusing on the case of Ghana, the chapter demonstrates that contrary to the popular conception of CSR as a voluntary initiative, there are mandatory elements of CSR interspersed within Ghana's laws. However, given that most of these laws are often not explicitly couched as CSR laws, the extent to which they directly impact corporate behaviours on the ground remains limited.

Furthermore, despite the prevalence of both low and high-intensity conflict in the region that undermine sustainable development, research on the role of the private sector in conflict resolution and peacebuilding in Africa is only just emerging (Idemudia, 2017, 2018). Indeed, most extant works have largely focused on how conflict affects firms, or the strategies firms can adopt to minimize the negative impact of conflict on their business. However, there is a paucity of works on how firms contribute to the fires of conflicts in Africa (Idemudia, 2017, 2010b) or how they might contribute to resolving conflicts. Chapter 3 addresses this gap in the CSR literature on Africa by examining where, when, and how international business can contribute to peace in the Democratic Republic Congo (DRC). Lenfant argues that CSR standards in the extractive sector fall short of delivering on their sustainable development and conflict reduction promises because they are based on a technical, 'check the box' exercise and ignore the messy and complex institutional context in the Democratic Republic of the Congo. This chapter highlighted the potential, and the limitations of business initiatives geared towards supporting the emergence of accountable, fair, and just institutions in fragile institutional contexts. The chapter contributes to our understanding of the challenges of contributing to SDG 16 as well as promoting accountable institutions in a complex environment marked by historical injustice and predatory state authorities.

In Chapter 4, Idemudia, Tuokuu, Essah, and Graham explore the relationship between CSR and community development in Africa. At its core, the chapter contends that if CSR is to become a more effective vehicle for promoting sustainable community development in rural communities in Africa, business would have to become more of a development agent and less of a development tool by shifting their CSR policies and practices geared towards community development (CD) from an emphasis on an imposed/directed community development framework to an emphasis on enabling self-help community development projects. Crucially, therefore, is the need to rethink CSR practices through the lens of community development rather than framing community development through the lens of CSR. In addition, firms would need to develop their community development capabilities if their CSR efforts are to go beyond tokenism. The development of these community development capabilities would enhance the ability of CSR to make a more effective contribution to community development.

Crippled by budget deficits, illicit financial flows, and high levels of debt, African countries have limited capacity to address the development problems that plague them. This makes corporate taxes and taxes on goods and services, the biggest revenue source for African countries, which has over time become a central issue within development studies. Yet analysis of the relationship between CSR and taxation in Africa remains limited. Hence, in Chapter 5, Okoye analyses the relationship between the ethics of taxation and corporate social responsibility, to reveal the complex and sometimes contradictory objectives that underpin the relationship in an African context. This chapter critically engages with mainstream analysis of the relationship between CSR and tax and considers its implication for the African context. Okoye examined the possibility of experimenting with different tax regimes to further CSR objectives but also highlights the limitations of such an approach. Focusing on the Mauritian case where there is a direct reference to CSR within its tax system, she makes important recommendations on how to contextually integrate CSR frameworks into tax systems that can help to support CSR initiatives and CSR contributions to sustainable development.

Africa is the world's most vulnerable region to climate change, despite being the smallest contributor to global warming. Recognizing how climatic variations impact several millions of people in the region, Liedong, Osobajo, and Ajide in Chapter 6 explore how CSR can be used to mitigate the effects of climate change in Africa. Positioning climate change as a business issue, this chapter also delineates how global warming poses challenges for the private sector and critiques the sector's 'business-as-usual' response as problematic, especially in Africa where the resources capabilities and innovations required to turn environmental problems into business opportunities are lacking or far-fetched for most businesses. Consequently, this chapter calls for businesses to move away from an instrumental approach towards an altruistic perspective in the way CSR is conceived and deployed to tackle environmental issues, and draws from the four dimensions of corporate citizenship to present climate change as a core CSR issue. In doing so, this chapter presents suggestions about how corporations' fulfilment of their economic, legal, ethical, and philanthropic responsibilities can help to protect the natural environment, reduce global warming, and support climate change mitigation while also creating conditions that enhance their profitability and competitive advantage. Drawing from Carroll (1979, 1998), Liedong and colleagues delineate how CSR can attend to climate change if it fulfils the fundamental responsibilities expected of corporate citizens. Among several recommendations, they outline the potential role of CSR in helping governments fight climate change. On the one hand, like Okoye in Chapter 5, they argue that the social responsibility to pay taxes would allow governments to support environmental initiatives. On the other hand, they propose that the buffering of legal institutions to strengthen climate change mitigation is a potential CSR activity for businesses in Africa. This proposal does not only call for firms to engage in corporate political activity (CPA) – i.e. attempts to influence public policy (Hillman & Hitt, 1999; Rajwani & Liedong, 2015) but it also underscores political CSR

– i.e. 'movement of the corporation into the political sphere to respond to environmental and social challenges such as human rights, global warming, or deforestation' (Scherer & Palazzo, 2011: 914). While regulation and policy-making may be the reserve of the State, there is a role that businesses, through CSR, can play to either advocate for action or engage in self-regulation to fill regulatory voids. This chapter, therefore, connects to and joins conversations in the CSR, political CSR, climate change, and CPA literature from an African perspective.

The actions that firms take to address human rights violations contribute to community development or mitigate climate change explored in the preceding chapters may not be able to yield sustainable benefits if those actions are not built and leveraged on strong institutions. Indeed, this issue is implicit in most of the chapters as they highlighted how weak institutional contexts directly or indirectly limit the ability of CSR to serve as an effective vehicle for addressing the SDGs. In this sense, the ability of CSR to unlock Africa's potential depends, to a large extent, on the presence or absence of efficient institutions that can ensure effective public governance. Liedong, in Chapter 7, explores the complicity and role of business in corruption. He also critiques the private sector's response as an array of superficial, transactional, and symbolic efforts that gloss over the fundamental causes of the corruption problem. Consequently, he highlights the untapped promise of CSR to strengthen anti-corruption institutions through de-institutionalization, disembeddedness, and buffering. This chapter presents a RARE model to show how CSR can foster institutional change and promote anti-corruption through regulatory, archetypal, reinforcement, and enforcement channels. It champions the need for firms to act as change agents in Africa's political and social arenas and highlights how CSR could be used to wield institutional entrepreneurship. This chapter, therefore, draws from and joins the conversation about business and institutional change (Battilana, Leca, & Boxenbaum, 2009; Garud, Jain, & Kumaraswamy, 2002; Greenwood & Suddaby, 2006; Liedong, 2017; Maguire, Hardy, & Lawrence, 2004). It adds to the literature by unpacking the specific mechanisms, channels, and activities through which firms' social interventions can have a lasting and positive impact on the fledgling and weak regulatory institutions of Africa. It highlights that such impact must start from within, in the sense that firms must first change internally before they can push for external changes in society. Therefore, the RARE model presented in this chapter addresses both the internal and external channels for realizing institutional change via CSR. To a large extent, the central argument of the chapter straddles corporate political activity (CPA) and political CSR. Its proposals for CSR to advocate regulations for combatting and mitigating corruption as well as those for regulatory enforcement are political in nature, which is reflective of the blurring boundaries between the political, social, and economic spheres of society (Scherer & Palazzo, 2007; Wettstein & Baur, 2016). One of the main takeaways from this chapter is that there is potential for CSR to not only address corruption through singular and ad hoc actions but there is also the potential for carefully designed social initiatives to strengthen the institutional root causes of systemic and pervasive corruption in Africa.

In Chapter 8, Amoah and Eweje focused on the question of environmental sustainability risks in mining that remain a major concern in most developing countries. This chapter provides insights into the environmental CSR practices of large-scale mining companies with regards to promoting sustainability and sustainable mining in a challenging and non-enabling institutional context of Ghana. It is argued that while environmental responsibility remains a regulatory compliance issue, anecdotal evidence suggests that some corporate managers of large-scale mining companies have embraced an industry-led voluntary institutionalized process based on perceived ethical obligation. However, Amoah and Eweje argue that environmental issues and impacts require managers of large-scale mining projects to refocus their sustainability efforts from impact mitigation to prevention strategies, especially during the development, production, and closure stages of mining. Consequently, CSR practices should consider impact mitigation and prevention practices during the development and production stages as part of concurrent mine closure strategies. The chapter suggests that the implementation of environmental CSR and sustainability initiatives can be beneficial to large-scale mining companies in terms of managing both regulatory and community pressures. The chapter concludes that beyond compliance, environmental CSR practices based on global standards and continuous improvement are positive steps towards sustainable mining in Ghana.

Chapter 9 provides guidance on how the Nigerian oil and gas industry can contribute across all SDGs through CSR strategy and programs. Given that the SDGs are frequently interlinked and indivisible, they require approaches that ensure synergies and manage trade-offs. Hence, effective collaboration and partnership between the oil and gas industry and other relevant stakeholders would be a step in the right direction for achieving the SDGs through the CSR strategy and program of the Nigerian oil and gas industry. In this chapter, Uwem argued that while the upstream oil and gas industry has played a pivotal role in the Nigerian economy for over four decades, accounting for a predominant proportion of Nigeria's export earnings and driving economic activity at various levels of government and society, its operations and products have also had negative impacts on a range of areas covered by the SDGs, including communities, ecosystems, and economies. As such, there is ample opportunity for Nigerian oil and gas companies to fully integrate SDGs into their CSR strategy even though the primary responsibility for the implementation of SDGs rests with the government. As such, the chapter concluded that oil companies are expected to be proactive in understanding the priorities of their various host nations and seek to align with the priority SDGs they feel they can make strong and meaningful contributions.

Across the chapters in this book, the contributors acknowledge that even though CSR has some potential to contribute to Africa's development, there continue to remain significant gaps between advertised CSR objectives and concrete sustainable development outcomes for local people on the ground. As such, Muthuri (2013) has previously argued that there is still a need to better understand the impact of CSR policies on development and how CSR can be used to foster transformative change in Africa. In response to this challenge, the contributors to this volume shared a common concern with not only the need to better understand the strengths and limitations of CSR as a vehicle for fostering sustainable development (Idemudia, 2011, 2014) but also the often neglected questions of how to make CSR initiatives more relevant and effective to address Africa's developmental problems. On this basis, the recommendations and suggestions the contributors proffer share two commonalities. First, they highlight the fact that given that regulatory institutions in Africa are weak (Liedong, 2017; Nana & Beddewela, 2019; Williams-Elegbe, 2018; Zoogah, Peng, & Woldu, 2015), and are thus largely ineffective in monitoring business behaviour and ensuring adherence to principles that advance socio-economic development, CSR policies of most business in African then tend to rest more on ethical or moral framing and less on legal. For instance, while in Chapter 2, Atuguba recognizes regulatory shortcomings and its negative impact on the responsibility of business to respect human rights, Amoah and Eweje in Chapter 8 suggested managers of large-scale mining relied more on global standards to drive their CSR policies. Similarly, in Chapter 5, Okoye hints at the presence of loopholes in tax regulations in Africa that allow businesses to evade and avoid taxes. It is thus apparent that doing CSR within a weak institutional context often means that moral rather than legal arguments tend to serve as a major driver of CSR policies and practices. This turn to morality as a driver of CSR policies in Africa is reflected in Chapter 6 as Liedong et al. discuss the ethical (moral) dimension of CSR and how it pertains to climate change mitigation. Businesses must hold themselves to higher standards than those prescribed by law. This way, their CSR would more likely resonate with the aspirations of African societies. It is this turn to ethical arguments for CSR that perhaps explains why CSR initiatives in Africa have largely tended to simultaneously contribute and undermine different aspects of sustainable development, some of the time and in some places (see Newell, 2005). Indeed, Uwem did not only highlight this issue in Chapter 9, but it also led Idemudia, Essah, and Graham to argue that if CSR is to make an effective contribution to community development in rural African communities then CSR must become less of a piecemeal effort to address development challenges often in silos and become a tool for driving sustainable social transformation.

Consequently, the second commonality is the need for CSR to shift from a focus on philanthropy to institutional works (Amaeshi et al., 2016a) if CSR is to achieve its full potential in addressing important developmental problems in Africa. Much of the CSR done in Africa is philanthropic and centred on material and monetary donations (Amaeshi et al., 2016a; Kühn et al., 2018), which to some extent is tokenism. Most donations are consumables that address immediate and short-term needs without fixing the fundamental issues that give rise to those needs. For instance, a business may donate money to a local clinic, but this donation does not resolve the root causes of the financial difficulties experienced by the local clinic, such as corruption or mismanagement (Idemudia, 2009). The socio-economic development of Africa will remain a fleeting illusion unless Africa's formal institutions are strengthened (Liedong, 2017). Essentially, championing development efforts amid weak institutions is like building castles on sand. Therefore, it is imperative that CSR shifts towards strengthening the institutional capacity of African countries. In Chapter 7, Liedong posits ways CSR could foster institutional entrepreneurship and strengthening. Crucial here is the need to be sure there is alignment between a firm's CSR and CPA (Idemudia, 2018). This is captured by the call for businesses to not only follow existing climate change regulations but also that they should lobby and advocate for new regulations and initiatives that will improve climate change outcomes.

In a nutshell, the plethora of issues addressed, and the recommendations proffered in this book provide a clear picture of the state of the CSR and development in Africa and move the debate forward by also focusing on how CSR can become a driver of sustainable social change in a weak institutional context. Collectively, the chapters in the book shed new insights into the nature and outcomes associated with the CSR-development relationship in Africa. Written for a broad audience, this book contains new insights for academics, practitioners, students, and others who are interested in, or curious about business, CSR, and development in Africa.

Notes

1 https://www.brookings.edu/blog/future-development/2019/03/28/poverty-in-africa-is-now-falling-but-not-fast-enough
2 https://www.worldbank.org/en/region/afr/publication/accelerating-poverty-reduction-in-africa-in-five-charts
3 http://www.fao.org/documents/card/en/c/ca7343en
4 https://www.who.int/bulletin/africanhealth/en/
5 https://www.worldbank.org/en/region/afr/overview

References

Amaeshi, K., Adegbite, E., Ogbechie, C., Idemudia, U., Kan, K. A. S., Issa, M., & Anakwue, O. I. J. (2016a). Corporate social responsibility in SMEs: A shift from philanthropy to institutional works? *Journal of Business Ethics, 138*(2), 385–400.

Amaeshi, K., Adegbite, E., & Rajwani, T. (2016b). Corporate Social Responsibility in Challenging and Non-enabling Institutional Contexts: Do Institutional Voids matter? *Journal of Business Ethics, 134*(1), 135–153.

Bagire, V. A. & Namada, J. (2013). Managerial skills, financial capability and strategic planning in organizations. *American Journal of Industrial and Business Management, 3*, 480–487.

Battilana, J., Leca, B., & Boxenbaum, E. (2009). How actors change institutions: Towards a theory of institutional entrepreneurship. *Academy of Management Annals, 3*(1), 65–107.

Blowfield, M. E. (2012). Business and development: making sense of business as a development agent. *Corporate Governance: International Journal of Business and Society, 12*(4), 414–426.

Buchholz, A. R. (1991). Corporate responsibility and good society: From economics to ecology. *Business Horizon*, July-August, *34*(4), 19–31.

Carroll, A. B. (1979). A three-dimensional conceptual model of corporate performance. *Academy of Management Review. Academy of Management, 4*(4), 497–505.

Carroll, A. B. (1998). The four faces of corporate citizenship. Business and Society Review. John Wiley & Sons, Ltd, *100–101*(1), 1–7. doi:10.1111/0045-3609.00008.

Claasen, C., & Roloff, J. (2012). The link between responsibility and legitimacy: The case of de beers in Namibia. *Journal of Business Ethics, 107*(3), 379–398. doi:10.1007/s10551-011-1045-0.

Davis, K. (1960). Can business afford to ignore social responsibility? *California Management Review, 2*(3), 70–76.

Dryzek, J. (1997). *The politics of the earth: Environmental discourses.* Oxford: Oxford University Press.

Egbon, O., Idemudia, U., & Amaeshi, K. (2018). Shell Nigeria's Global Memorandum of Understanding and corporate-community accountability relations: A critical appraisal. *Accounting, Auditing & Accountability Journal, 31*(1), 51–74.

Eweje, G. (2006). The role of MNEs in community development initiatives in developing countries: Corporate social responsibility at work in Nigeria and South Africa. *Business and Society.* SAGE Publications Inc, 45(2), 93–129. doi:10.1177/0007650305285394.

Frederick, W. C. (1983). Corporate social responsibility in the Reagan era and beyond. *California Management Review, 25*(3), 145–157.

Garud, R., Jain, S., & Kumaraswamy, A. (2002). Institutional entrepreneurship in the sponsorship of common technological standards: The case of Sun Microsystems and java. *Academy of Management Journal. Academy of Management, 45*(1), 196–214. Retrieved from http://search.ebscohost.com/login.aspx?direct=true&db=bth&AN=6283620&site=ehost-live.

Gifford, B., Kestler, A., & Anand, S. (2010). Building local legitimacy into corporate social responsibility: Gold mining firms in developing nations. *Journal of World Business, 45*(3), 304–311. Retrieved from https://www.sciencedirect.com/science/article/pii/S1090951609000686.

Greenwood, R., & Suddaby, R. (2006). Institutional entrepreneurship in mature fields: The big five accounting firms. *Academy of Management Journal. Academy of Management, 49*(1), 27–48. Retrieved from http://search.ebscohost.com/login.aspx?direct=true&db=bth&AN=20785498&site=ehost-live.

Hillman, A. J., & Hitt, M. A. (1999). Corporate political strategy formulation: A model of approach, participation, and strategy decisions. *Academy of Management Review, 24*(4), 825–842. Retrieved from http://search.ebscohost.com/login.aspx?direct=true&db=bth&AN=2553256&site=eds-live.

Holliday, C. O. Jr., Schmidheiny, S., & Watta, P. (2002). *Walking the talk. The business case for sustainable development.* Sheffield, UK: Greenleaf Publishing Limited.

Holmes, L. S. (1976). Executive perceptions of corporate social responsibility. *Business Horizons, 19*(3), 34–40.

Idemudia, U. (2007). *Corporate social responsibility and community development in the Niger Delta, Nigeria: A critical analysis* (Doctoral dissertation), University of Lancaster.

Idemudia, U. (2008). Conceptualising the CSR and development debate: Bridging existing analytical gaps. *Journal of Corporate Citizenship.* Greenleaf Publishing (29), 91–110. Retrieved from http://www.jstor.org/stable/jcorpciti.29.91.

Idemudia, U. (2009). Oil extraction and poverty reduction in the Niger Delta: A critical examination of partnership initiatives. *Journal of Business Ethics, 90*(1), 91–116.

Idemudia, U. (2010a). Corporate social responsibility and the rentier Nigerian state: Rethinking the role of government and the possibility of corporate social development in the Niger Delta. *Canadian Journal of Development Studies/Revue canadienne d'études du développement, 30*(1–2), 131–151.

Idemudia, U. (2010b). Rethinking the role of corporate social responsibility in the Nigerian oil conflict: The limits of CSR. *Journal of International Development, 22*(7), 833–845.

Idemudia, U. (2011). Corporate social responsibility and developing countries: Moving the critical CSR Research agenda in Africa forward. *Progress in Development Studies, 11*(1), 1–18.

Idemudia, U. (2012). The resource curse and the decentralization of oil revenue: The case of Nigeria. *Journal of Cleaner Production, 35*, 183–193.

Idemudia, U. (2014). Corporate social responsibility and development in Africa: Issues and possibilities. *Geography Compass*. Chichester: John Wiley & Sons, Ltd, *8*(7), 421–435. doi:10.1111/gec3.12143.

Idemudia, U. (2017). Business and peace in the Niger Delta: What we know and what we need to know. *African Security Review, 26*(1), 41–61.

Idemudia, U. (2018). Shell–NGO partnership and peace in Nigeria: Critical insights and implications. *Organization and Environment, 31*(4), 384–405.

Idemudia, U., & Ite, U. E. (2006). Corporate–community relations in Nigeria's oil industry: Challenges and imperatives. *Corporate Social Responsibility and Environmental Management, 13*(4), 194–206.

Idemudia, U., Kwakyewah, C., & Muthuri, J. (2020). Mining, the environment, and human rights in Ghana: An area of limited statehood perspective. *Business Strategy and the Environment, 29*(7), 2919–2926.

Ireland, P., & Pillay, R. G. (2010). Corporate social responsibility in a neoliberal age. In: Utting, P. and Marques, J.C. (eds), *Corporate social responsibility and regulatory governance* (pp. 77–104). London: Palgrave Macmillan.

Ite, U. (2004). Multinationals and corporate social responsibility in developing countries: A case study of Nigeria. *Corporate Social Responsibility and Environmental Management, 11*(1), 1–11.

Knorringa, P., & Helmsing, A. H. J. (2008). Beyond an enemy perception: Unpacking and engaging the private sector. *Development and Change, 39*(6), 1053–1062.

Kolk, A., & Lenfant, F. (2010). MNC reporting on CSR and conflict in Central Africa. *Journal of Business Ethics, 93*(2), 241–255.

Kühn, A.-L., Stiglbauer, M., & Fifka, M. S. (2018). Contents and determinants of corporate social responsibility Website reporting in sub-Saharan Africa: A seven-country study. *Business and Society, 57*(3), 437–480. Retrieved from http://10.0.4.153/0007650315614234.

Kumi, E., Yeboah, T., & Kumi, Y. A. (2020). Private sector participation in advancing the Sustainable Development Goals (SDGs) in Ghana: Experiences from the mining and telecommunications sectors. *Extractive Industries and Society*, 7(1), 181–190. Retrieved from https://www.sciencedirect.com/science/article/pii/S2214790X18303253.

Liedong, T. (2017). Combating corruption in Africa through institutional entrepreneurship: Peering in from business-government relations. *Africa Journal of Management*. Routledge, *3*(3–4), 310–327. doi:10.1080/23322373.2017.1379825

Maguire, S., Hardy, C., & Lawrence, T. B. (2004). Institutional entrepreneurship in emerging fields: HIV/AIDS treatment advocacy in Canada. *Academy of Management*

Journal, 47(5), 657–679. Retrieved from http://search.ebscohost.com/login.aspx?direct=true&db=bth&AN=14574632&site=eds-live.

Malan, D. (2016). Corporate support for the SDGs. *Journal of Corporate Citizenship*. Greenleaf Publishing, *64*, 98–120. Retrieved from http://www.jstor.org/stable/90003794.

Mintzberg, H. (1983). The case for corporate social responsibility. *Journal for Business Strategy, 4*(2), 3–16.

Moon, J. (2001). Business social responsibility: A source of social capital? *Reason in Practice: Journal of Philosophy of Management, 1*(3), 385–408.

Nana, R. K. H. M., & Beddewela, E. (2019). The politics of corporate social responsibility in the mining industry in Burkina Faso. *Africa Journal of Management, 5*(4), 358–381. Retrieved from http://10.0.4.56/23322373.2019.1676099.

Naor, J. (1982). A new approach to multinational social responsibility. *Journal of Business Ethics, 1*(3), 219–225.

Newell, P. (2005). Citizenship, accountability and community: The limits of the CSR agenda. *International Affairs, 81*(3), 541–557.

Njoh, A. J. (2016). *Tradition, culture and development in Africa: Historical lessons for modern development planning*. London: Routledge.

Rajwani, T., & Liedong, T. A. (2015). Political activity and firm performance within nonmarket research: A review and international comparative assessment. *Journal of World Business, 50*(2), 273–283.

Scherer, A. G., & Palazzo, G. (2007). Toward a Political Conception of Corporate Responsibility: Business and Society seen from a Habermasian Perspective. *Academy of Management Review, 32*(4), 1096–1120. Retrieved from http://search.ebscohost.com/login.aspx?direct=true&db=bth&AN=26585837&site=eds-live.

Scherer, A. G., & Palazzo, G. (2011). The new political role of business in a globalized world: A review of a new perspective on CSR and its implications for the firm, governance, and democracy. *Journal of Management Studies*. Chichester: John Wiley & Sons, Ltd, 48(4), 899–931. doi:10.1111/j.1467-6486.2010.00950.x.

Selmier II, W. T., & Newenham-Kahindi, A. (2021). Communities of place, mining multinationals and sustainable development in Africa. *Journal of Cleaner Production, 292*, N.PAG-N.PAG. Retrieved from http://10.0.3.248/j.jclepro.2020.125709

Sharp, J. (2006). Corporate social responsibility and development: An anthropological perspective. *Development Southern Africa, 23*(2), 213–222.

Smith, C. N. (2003). Corporate social responsibility: Whether or how? *California Management Review, 45*(4), 52–76.

Sohn, F. H. (1982). Prevailing rationale in the corporate social responsibility debate. *Journal of Business Ethics, 1*(2), 139–144.

Utting, P., & Marques, J. C. (2010). Introduction: The intellectual crisis of CSR. In Utting, P and Margues J.C. (ed.), *Corporate social responsibility and regulatory governance* (pp. 1–25). London: Palgrave Macmillan.

Van Alstine, J., & Afionis, S. (2013). Community and company capacity: the challenge of resource-led development in Zambia's 'New Copperbelt'. *Community Development Journal, 48*(3), 360–376.

Visser, W., McIntosh, M., & Middleton, C. (2006). Corporate citizenship in Africa: lessons from the past; paths to the future. In: Visser, M., McIntosh, M. and Middleton, C. (eds.), *Corporate Citizenship in Africa: Lessons from the Past; Paths to the Future* (pp. 1–17). Sheffield: Greenleaf Publishing.

WBCSD (1999). *Corporate social responsibility: Meeting changing expectations*. Geneva, Switzerland: World Business Council for Sustainable Development (WBCSD).

Wettstein, F., & Baur, D. (2016). 'Why Should We Care about Marriage Equality?': Political advocacy as a part of corporate responsibility. *Journal of Business Ethics*. Springer Nature, *138*(2), 199–213. Retrieved from http://10.0.3.239/s10551-015-2631-3.

Wilenius, M. (2005). The age of corporate social responsibility? Emerging challenges for the Business. *World Futures*, *37*(2–3), 133–150.

Williams-Elegbe, S. (2018). Systemic corruption and public procurement in developing countries: Are there any solutions? *Journal of Public Procurement*, *18*(2), 131–147. Retrieved from http://10.0.4.84/JOPP-06-2018-009.

Yakovleva, N., Kotilainen, J., & Toivakka, M. (2017). Reflections on the opportunities for mining companies to contribute to the United Nations Sustainable Development Goals in sub – Saharan Africa. *Extractive Industries and Society*, *4*(3), 426–433. Retrieved from https://www.sciencedirect.com/science/article/pii/S2214790X16301526.

Zoogah, D. B., Peng, M. W., & Woldu, H. (2015). Institutions, resources, and organizational effectiveness in Africa. *Academy of Management Perspectives*. Academy of Management, *29*(1), 7–31. Retrieved from http://10.0.21.89/amp.2012.0033.

1

CORPORATE SOCIAL RESPONSIBILITY (CSR) AND DEVELOPMENT IN AFRICA

A Critical Overview

Uwafiokun Idemudia

Introduction

Berle and Means's (1932) explication of the implications of the divorce of property ownership from control, which used to be inseparable in the dominant neo-classical understanding of the business enterprise, provided the impetus for questioning the idea that the corporation should be run by prioritizing the interest of the stockholder (Jones, 1996). For example, Stokes (1996) and Beasley and Evans (1978) argued that with the separation of property ownership from control, it no longer made sense for the corporation to be run solely in the interest of the stockholders. Rather it was argued that business should now be run in the interest of stakeholders (Freemen, 1984). Hence, the issue of corporate social responsibility (CSR) actually began as a concern for the role of the corporate managers and their ability to consider the interest of stakeholders in decision-making processes (Whitehouse, 2003; Jones, 1996). Nevertheless, the 'social responsibility' of business has been a recurring theme within the discourse of business–society relations for many years (Doane, 2005; Carroll, 1999). For example, Cicero in 44 BC wrote about unscrupulous business practices, while European social thinkers in the seventeenth and eighteenth centuries routinely engaged in a lively debate over the relationship between self-interest and the greatest good (Ciulla, 1991). Historical evidence, therefore, suggests that societal concerns for business social obligations are not new and that such concerns have continually ebbed and flowed at various times (Monsen, 1972; Cuilla, 1991; Jenkins, 2005). However, the latest manifestation of this concern within the concept of CSR (Smith, 2003; Blowfield and Frynas, 2005; Jenkins, 2005) appears to defy conventional pattern, as CSR seems to have taken on a life of its own and is unlikely to disappear any time soon (Doane, 2005; Eilbirt and Parket, 1973; Economist, 2005). Yet, the concept of CSR lacks a consensual definition and it

DOI: 10.4324/9781003038078-2

is now seen as an essentially contested concept (Okoye, 2009; Gond & Moon, 2011). Nonetheless, the idea of CSR presupposes that business has obligations to society that go beyond profit-making to include helping to solve 'hard' social and ecological problems (Fredrick, 1960; Lodge, 1970, Idemudia, 2008). In other words, the CSR thesis suggests a shift from government to business enterprise as a source of social improvement and a means to promote specific items of social welfare (Beesley & Evans, 1978). However, Cash (2012) has argued that Transnational Corporations (TNCs) are not development agencies and therefore must not be viewed as such or called to lead a development agenda (see also Freidman, 1970; Levitt, 1958; Henderson, 2001).

Nevertheless, a key part of the contemporary debate has been the shift from whether business can or cannot contribute to development to how best to maximize business contribution to sustainable development (see Blowfield & Dolan, 2014). For example, Fox (2004) has argued that there is an urgent need to develop a better understanding of not only where the drivers for responsible business practices exist in the south, but also ways to build, broaden, and sustain them where they currently do not exist. This requires the identification of local CSR drivers and constraints in the south, the development of the human and institutional capacity to respond to these drivers, and the reorientation of CSR tools to address southern stakeholders' developmental concerns (Fox et al., 2002; Fox, 2004). It is against this background that this chapter seeks to:

1. Critically examine the drivers, dynamics, and nature of CSR practices in Africa
2. Consider whether business is a tool or agent of development in Africa
3. Examine the emerging issues for CSR and development relationship in Africa

Corporate Social Responsibility in Africa: Issues and Drivers

The notion of CSR is not new to Africa. Indeed, Hönke (2012) showed that there are continuities between the paternalistic nature of corporate-community intervention pursued by mining companies during the colonial and the postcolonial period within the Democratic Republic of the Congo (DRC). Similarly, Noyoo (2010) points to how Anglo-American Corporation as early as 1929 was responsible for providing housing and hygiene for its employees in Zambia but with racial bias. Nonetheless, the literature on CSR in Africa is only just emerging and continues to be dominated by the works undertaken in South Africa and Nigeria (Visser, 2006; Muthuri, 2013). Although, in recent years, the scope (i.e. geographic focus within Africa) and scale (i.e. issues or themes covered) in the literature has steadily widened and deepened respectively. For example, while Ragodoo (2009) and Gokulsing (2011) have expanded the scope of CSR studies in Africa by exploring CSR practices in Mauritius, Kolk, and Lenfant (2010, 2013) have deepened the literature by examining CSR within a conflict context in Central African countries. This steady growth of the CSR literature in Africa is due to the interdisciplinary approach to the study of CSR that has allowed for contributions from other disciplines like geography, political sciences, anthropology, and sociology. For example, Hamilton (2011) provides a comprehensive analysis of the contributions of geographers to the CSR debate.

At any rate, given the role of TNCs in the process of colonial domination and exploitation in Africa, the notion of CSR for some scholars is just a euphemism that has recently re-emerged to 'sugar coat' the pillage of Africa by TNCs that has lasted for hundreds of years (see Orock, 2006; Noyoo, 2010; Bagire et al., 2013). Hence, CSR is seen by them as a new form of corporate colonialism (Malan, 2005; Banerjee, 2008; Fougere & Solintander, 2009; Vertigans, 2011). For example, Orock (2006) argues that TNCs have failed to adequately respond to social needs in Africa. He argued that while TNCs are generating significant profits on a daily basis from their investment in Africa, they are failing to make a plausible case for their social relevance in such a way as to be directly felt by most people at the grassroots. Indeed, rather than alleviating poverty, most TNCs are rendering Africans poorer and contributing to the widening of income inequalities. In contrast, Visser, McIntosh, and Middleton (2006) have noted that since the late 1990s, there is now a general consensus that the private sector via CSR is well placed to make significant positive contributions towards improving social, economic, and environmental conditions in Africa. For example, Garcia-Rodriguez et al. (2013) argued that their research findings in Angola suggest that despite the absence of an enabling environment in developing countries for CSR activities of oil TNCs, small actions such as the introduction of the environmental management system (EMS) using a bottom-up approach can generate important impacts in terms of strengthening the institutional context and helping to develop structures and institutions that contribute to social justice, environmental protection, and poverty eradication.

Hence, it is the practical and discursive implications of the reimagining of the role of business from being the cause to becoming a part of the solution to the problem of underdevelopment in the region (Idemudia, 2010, Rajak, 2011) that lies at the centre of the CSR debate in Africa. This is because the question of whether Africa lags behind all other regions on every established indicator of development is no longer necessarily contentious (Njoh, 2006), but what remains a subject of disagreement is what to do about it. Consequently, CSR is seen to be deeply enmeshed in the debate about the future of Africa's development (Visser et al., 2006; Gokulsing, 2011). This is particularly the case given that the process of globalization for Africa has largely been contradictory and thus characterized by instances of collaborations and contestations as well as domination and resistance. For example, while the process of globalization ensured the opening of new markets and business opportunities especially for TNCs in Africa, revolution in information and communication technology has also meant corporate misdemeanours, incidents of human rights violations, and conflict between local communities and TNCs, which are now often broadcasted globally in real time with consequences for these TNCs (Kapelus, 2000; Smith, 2003). As a result, TNCs operating in Africa have not only had to respond to different forms of external pressures (i.e., from local communities, government, and non-governmental organizations, for them to address their social responsibility) but also TNCs have also sort to shape, define, and control the emerging CSR agenda in Africa. Thus, the 'double movement' approach suggested by Utting (2005) as opposed to Zadek's (2001) conception of CSR as a business unilateral response to external pressure, best captures the nature and the dynamics of CSR evolution in Africa. This is because the corporation influences the institutional context within which it operates, just as the institutional context within which a company operates influences its social, economic, and environmental performance (Amaeshi et al., 2006; Muthuri, 2013). For example, Egels (2005) demonstrated how Asea Brown Boveri (ABB) effort to define its CSR agenda in its rural electrification project in Tanzania was based not simply on the CSR definitions offered by local stakeholders or on ABB's preferred CSR definition. Rather, it was a joint formulation of a local definition of CSR through a myriad of translation processes, but in which the TNCs played a key role by actively determining who would become a stakeholder.

Furthermore, the drivers of CSR practices in Africa can usefully be categorized into three dimensions: internal factors (e.g. local social movements, corporate–community conflict), external factors (e.g. spread of global norms such as the United Nations Global Compact; international reputational concerns; shareholder activism), and transnational factors (e.g. collaboration between African NGOs and Western NGOs) (see also Mzembe and Meaton, 2013). However, the relative effectiveness of each of these different CSR drivers is likely to vary across regions and between countries. This explains Cash's (2012) observation that there are lower levels of CSR activities undertaken by oil TNCs in Chad compared to say Nigeria. Nonetheless, three principal arguments have often been put forward to explain why businesses operating in Africa should adopt CSR and contribute to development. The first is the governance deficit argument (see Fitzpatrick, Fonseca & McAllister, 2011). Proponents of the governance deficit argument assert that a combination of government failure and neoliberal policies foisted on African states has meant that African governments have been unable to both deliver positive political and economic goods for their people and effectively regulate the activities of TNCs operating within their border. Hence, TNCs have been both victims and benefactors of governmental failure. TNCs are victims in the sense that governmental failure has meant certain responsibilities previously assumed by governments are increasingly now being demanded of them (see Blowfield, 2010; Alstine & Afions, 2013; Campbell, 2012). On the other hand, governmental failure has also meant that TNCs are able to exploit their weak regulatory environment in a manner that allows them to externalize the cost of production and exploit cheap labour at great profits to TNCs, but with huge social and environmental costs for the local population. Hence, it is argued that TNCs as powerful actors[1] in the region have an obligation to voluntarily adopt CSR principles to ameliorate problems associated with the weak governance environment within which they operate and pursue CSR practices to compensate for governmental failure (see Okafor, 2003). The second argument for CSR in the African context is the business case argument (Staff, 2013; Garcia-Rodriguez, Garcia-Rodriguez, Gutierrez, & Major, 2013). The business case argument suggests that by adopting CSR, TNCs operating in Africa will generate win–win outcomes for themselves and their host society. This is especially the case in certain sectors such as the extractive industries, where there are limited opportunities for competitive advantage. For example, Wiig and Kolstad (2010) pointed out that oil companies use CSR strategically to improve their chances of winning licenses and contracts in Angola (see also Frynas, 2005). Similarly, Kamlongera (2013) noted that mining companies in Malawi used CSR as a means of securing and legitimizing huge tax breaks it receives from the government. The implication is that the pursuit of CSR by business in Africa has instrumental value in terms of tangible (e.g. increase in market share) and intangible benefits (e.g. a boost of employee morale) for the corporation as well as developmental benefits for the society at large. The third is the changing societal expectation argument. This position suggests that TNCs are part of (and not separate from) the host society within which they operate (see Davis, 1960; Elbing, 1970). As a result, TNCs have an obligation to respond to changing societal expectations if they are to maintain their legitimacy as well as benefit from societal goodwill (Tavis, 1982; Mzembe & Meaton, 2013). The failure of TNCs to meet societal expectations might result in a legitimacy crisis that might undermine business as a useful societal institution and the loss of the 'social license to operate' for each company (Eweje, 2006; Idemudia, 2007).

In contrast, critics argue that the idea that business via CSR can contribute to development in Africa is misguided as business contribution to development at best will always be inconsequential for three reasons. First, critics point out that it is the weak regulatory context and governance failure in Africa that makes the region attractive for TNCs' investments and partly makes it possible for a huge Return on Investment (ROI) (see Leys, 1996; Orock, 2006). Hence, TNCs will always be constrained by the logic of capitalist production and profitability as they are more likely to choose profitability over contributing to development that might incur costs not compensated for in profit (Blowfield & Frynas, 2005, Idemudia, 2011a). Second, critics point to the limit of the business case arguments by suggesting that a business case argument cannot often be made for most development problems (Jones, 1996; Smith, 2003; Blowfield & Frynas, 2005; Egbon et al, 2018). In other words, not all development problems can be converted into business opportunities. Hence, by implication, most development problems are likely to be left unaddressed (see also Hamilton, 2011). Finally, the idea that CSR can contribute to development in Africa tends to be ahistorical, informed by a depoliticized understanding of development, and has thus allowed business to appropriate the meaning of development by making business rationality the predominant basis for development thinking and practice in the region. (Blowfield, 2005; Rajak, 2011).

Corporate Social Responsibility Practices in Africa: Nature and Strategies

While most TNCs in Africa initially resisted the demands for social responsibility,[2] the majority now publicly declares their commitment to CSR principles on their websites and some even include their African operations in their annual sustainability reports. Today, the CSR initiatives of most business enterprises in Africa cover a wide range of issues such as health and HIV/AIDS, community development, economic and enterprise development, education and scholarships, human rights, and sports (Muthuri, 2013; Alstine & Afionis, 2013; Bagire et al., 2013). Consequently, Hayes (2006) has argued that social issues, as opposed to environmental ones, are overwhelmingly at the top of the CSR agenda in Africa. In addition, CSR practices in Africa have largely taken the form of philanthropy or social investment. For example, while Visser (2006) and Ameashi et al. (2006) identified corporate philanthropy as the dominant CSR practice of firms in South Africa, and Nigeria respectively, Kivuitu, Yambayamba, and Fox (2005) and Muthuri (2013) confirmed this was also the case in Kenya and Zambia. As a result, Rossouw (2000) has argued that CSR practices in Africa are still largely rudimentary and yet to fully mature, and Bagire et al. (**2013**) empirical research in Uganda suggests that the problem might lie in the fact that CSR is still not well understood. In any case, the predominance of philanthropy as a CSR strategy in Africa might be due to weak local pressure from government and NGOs (Julian & Ofori-Dankwa, 2013), and the exceptional capacity of TNCs to actively shape, control, and lead CSR agenda in Africa via a strategy of accommodation and legitimization.[3] This strategy allows TNCs to pursue CSR on their own terms, make public criticisms of them difficult, and legitimize their claims that real progress in the pursuit of sustainable development objectives are being made (Hamann & Acutt, 2003; Rajak, 2011).

Corporate Philanthropy (CP), the dominant CSR practice of TNCs in Africa, is corporate charitable contribution to address economic, environmental, and social problems as part of a business overall strategy for implementing CSR initiatives (BSR, 2004). Philanthropic ideals have been said to be deeply entrenched in religious beliefs. However, over the years, philanthropy has become a tool for responding to civic obligations and as such has been gradually institutionalized (Burke, Logsdon, Mitchell, Reiner, & Vogel, 1986). CP has evolved from ad hoc philanthropy to social investment and then into strategic philanthropy (Porter & Kramer, 2002). These changes correspond to changing business emphasis from just a concern or a need to give to laying more emphasis on effective grant marking (Burke et al., 1986). Burke et al. (1986) asserted that corporate philanthropy to meet social needs generally takes one of three forms: (1) donation of funds either directly or through associated foundations, (2) contribution of goods and services, and (3) volunteerism, with a large proportion of these contributions often going to the communities in which the facilities of the corporation are located. However, according to Zadek (2001), philanthropy represents the first of three phases in the evolution of CSR practices, because it allows business to respond to the clamour for it to be socially responsible without changes to how it conducts its core business operation. Zadek (2001) thus characterized philanthropy as largely a defensive tool based on a bolt-on CSR strategy.[4] It is therefore not surprising that philanthropy in Africa has often been criticized for failing to address the core social and environmental issues at the heart of businesses' day-to-day operations. Besides, while charitable donations are very useful for public relations purposes, philanthropy very rarely addresses the problem that it is supposedly expected to solve as most of the developmental problems are not amenable to its quick-fix nature. Similarly, Fig (2005) has also suggested that corporate contribution to social issues via philanthropy is often modest, especially when corporate charity is pitched against corporate profits. This criticism was confirmed by Ragodoo (2009) in the context of Mauritius.

Furthermore, there is a tacit consensus in mainstream CSR literature that the meaning attached to CSR and therefore CSR practices will vary from region to region and even within a region (Idemudia, 2011a). This is because CSR is inescapably underpinned by such notions as morality, ethical responsibility, and responsive action that vary across place, time, and circumstances (Pratt, 1991). For example, in a global stakeholder dialogue held in different countries by World Business Council for Sustainable Development (WBCSD), a core finding was that while there was widespread acceptance of the notion of CSR, there was however considerable difference in terms of emphasis on what it means in different parts of the world (WBCSD, 2000). Similarly, Julian and Ofori-Dankwa (2013) empirically demonstrated that in contrast to the developed world where an increase in financial resources is generally believed to lead to an increase in CSR activities, in Ghana the reverse was the case. Consequently, the regional CSR agenda is generally often a product of historical and cultural factors, and it often continues to mature according to the prevailing economic and political priorities of the country (Idemudia & Ite, 2006). For example, Visser (2005) and Hamman et al (2005) showed that CSR in South Africa has been influenced largely by the historical events of apartheid, injustices, and inequalities. In Nigeria, Okafor (2003) has argued that the pursuit of CSR initiatives as a business strategy is an emerging concept as various corporations constantly seek to tailor their CSR strategy to meet the demands of their environment. However, there continues to be disagreement about the extent to which contemporary CSR agenda in Africa is shaped by Western values and priorities or by indigenous African values. For example, Visser (2005) argued that the values-based traditional philosophy of African humanism underpins much of the modern conception of CSR in Africa (see also Philips, 2006; Muthuri, 2013). In contrast, Ameashi et al. (2006) suggested that the CSR agenda in Africa is more of a product of Western mimicry than indigenous influence. They attribute this to the fact that foreign firms and the local ones modelled after them are not embedded within African society and culture. The problem with both perspectives might be the tendency to use totalizing discourses that homogenizes the factors that shape the CSR agenda in Africa. For example, Kuada and Hinson (2012) in their empirical study that compared the CSR practices of foreign firms with that of local firms in Ghana suggested that the rationale guiding the CSR behaviour of foreign and local firms is different. They stated that while the CSR activities of foreign firms are triggered mainly by legal obligations and anticipated economic gains that of local firms are driven more by moral and ethical considerations. Consequently, they argued that while their findings do not in any way suggest that CSR activities of local firms are superior to that of foreign firms, what it shows is that the two groups of firms place different degrees of emphasis on legal and moral/ethical expectations in their CSR decisions.

Similarly, the debate over whether or not cultural and socio-economic factors influence CSR policies and practices in Africa remains unresolved. For example, Ameashi et al. (2006), Muthuri and Gilbert (2011), and Visser (2006) in their works on CSR in Nigeria, Kenya, and South Africa respectively found evidence of cultural and socio-economic influence on CSR practices in these countries. Similarly, Mzembe and Meaton (2013) in their study of CSR in Malawi suggested that socio-cultural factors are a key driver of CSR in the country. In contrast, Lindgreen, Swaen, and Campbell (2010) did not find any such influence in Botswana and Malawi. Nonetheless, available evidence suggests that the sociocultural and economic contexts of Africa do shape societal expectations of the social responsibility of business and therefore what should ideally constitute CSR priorities of businesses operating in the region. For instance, in rural areas where there is limited social infrastructure and where poverty can be endemic; especially around extractive sites, local communities tend to expect TNCs to provide social infrastructure and contribute to poverty reduction (Idemudia, 2007). Bagire et al. (**2013**) empirical result in Uganda confirmed the influence of socio-cultural context on CSR undertaking, as 62% of their respondents identified community demands as a core CSR driver in the country. Unfortunately, the extent to which CSR initiatives have been able to meet the expectations of local communities or positively contributed to sustainable development (SD) in Africa remains highly contested.

Corporate Social Responsibility in the African Context: Is CSR Good or Bad for Development?

The disagreements about CSR-development relations in Africa manifest on three main levels: conceptual, practical, and discourse. Conceptually, the assumptions underpinning the propositions that business can contribute to SD in Africa via CSR are often rooted in two key concepts i.e. *stakeholder theory* and the *social license to operate* (SLO). Yet, critics argue that the assumptions that inform these two concepts upon which CSR is based, suffers from what has been described as the tyranny of borrowed paradigms, in which the particularities of the African context are either dismissed or ignored in theoretical discussions, while African realities are forced to fit into Western concepts. Consequently, Banerjee (2008) argues that the stakeholder theory is too simplistic and fails to recognize the inability of the framework to represent different realities and the effect of using a single lens to view issues of legitimacy and responsibility. For instance, Boyle and Boguslaw (2007) pointed out that the poor and impoverished communities in Africa and elsewhere are typically not named as stakeholders (i.e. stakeholders with power, legitimacy, and urgency (see Mitchell, Agle, & Wood, 1997)) that warrant due consideration by managers in corporate decision-making. As such, TNCs are often more likely to neglect the developmental needs of the poor and local communities in Africa than the stakeholder theory would like us to believe. Besides, in instances where the poor are considered stakeholders, it is often to regulate their behaviour and those that do not toe the corporate line is either marginalized or co-opted (Banajee, 2008). In addition, given the significant power differential between TNCs and poor local communities on the one hand, and the close nature of the relationship that often exists between TNCs and governments in Africa on the other hand (see Idemudia, 2010), the ability of local communities to enforce the SLO in most cases in Africa has so far been marginal. Hence, Owen and Kemp (2013) have argued that contemporary application of the SLO has been more about reducing overt opposition to business activities than it is about stakeholder accountability for long-term development.

At the level of practice, proponents of CSR as a vehicle for development point to corporate social investments in education, health, social infrastructures, micro-credits schemes, and employment opportunities which stimulate economic growth and thus allow for poverty reduction (World Bank, 2001). Indeed, empirical works by Idemudia (2009), Muthuri (2007), Kamlongera (2013), and Alstine et al. (2013) have all cited examples of such investments in Nigeria, Kenya, Malawi, and Zambia, respectively. For instance, Muthuri (2007) notes that Magadi Soda Company via its Corporate-Community Involvement (CCI) projects remains the dominant social welfare provider in the region and the community has benefited from the company's benevolence through donation and philanthropy. Similarly, Borzel, Hönke, and Thauer (2012) point to significant investments by the automotive and mining industry in the fight against HIV/AIDS in South Africa. However, critics have responded by arguing that in most cases such corporate social investments often have minimal to no effect in terms of improving the lives of its intended beneficiaries because of issues of poorly executed projects, misplaced priorities, and lack of project sustainability. For example, Idemudia (2009) points to boreholes provided by oil TNCs that were not functional, school structures that were built but with no teachers or students and a litany of other abandoned CSR projects in local communities due to the non-involvement of community members in CSR decision-making process. Others point to a significant disjuncture between CSR rhetoric and reality (Utting, 2007; Slack, 2012; Kamlongera, 2013). For example, communities in the Niger Delta frequently complain of broken promises by oil TNCs (Idemudia, 2007). Similarly, some scholars have argued that since corporate social investment is often driven by the business case logic, it often does not address core community needs (Watts, 2005; Blowfield & Frynas, 2005; Idemudia, 2008; Emel et al., 2012). In contrast, proponents of 'CSR is good for Africa's development' respond by pointing to the difficult and sometimes hostile environment within which CSR initiatives are being implemented as responsible for the limited impact of CSR initiatives in the region (Noar, 1982). For example, Maria and Devuyst (2011) argue that while mining companies in the DRC seek to promote enlightened CSR and focus on individual rights, the paternalistic mindset of local communities' clashes with, and undermined such enlightened approach. In addition, some CSR advocates also cite changes in corporate policies and CSR strategies as evidence of business contribution to SD because it shows that business is actively seeking to better respond to the needs of its stakeholders. For example, Ite (2007) notes that Shell in Nigeria has over the years changed its CSR strategy from Community Assistance (CA) to Community Development (CD) and then to Sustainable Community Development (SCD) so as to better address the community development needs of its host communities. Similarly, Muthuri (2007) argued that the CCI strategy of Magadi Soda has evolved from a paternalistic approach motivated by the need to be 'good neighbour' to the current practice of multi-sector collaboration seeking to achieve sustainable livelihoods in the Magadi division in Kenya. However, critics argue that the extent to which such changes in CSR strategies have led to significant improvements on the ground remains limited and at best fragmented (Hamann, 2004). Besides, Blowfield (2010) points out that the issue is not whether change happens but how, and for whose benefit. Indeed, Aaron (2012) showed that while the turn to Global Memoranda of Understanding (GMOU) by Shell and Chevron in Nigeria is a radical departure from their previous CSR strategies, the GMOU is still being plagued by old challenges and as such has failed to deliver sustainable development benefits for the people in the Niger Delta. Similarly, the suggestions by Maria and Devuyst (2011) that community mindset is the problem is not only ahistorical but also lack empirical grounding. For example, Idemudia (2011b) showed that the emergence of such dependency mentality in Africa is often a product of decades of top-down CSR strategies adopted by TNCs that have undermined the local culture of self-help. Besides, it is not clear what Maria and Devuyst (2011) mean by enlightened CSR as SGM (i.e. the mining company in their study) focused mainly on the provision of minimal social infrastructures while issues of capacity building and empowerment were completely neglected. Indeed, a number of scholars have argued that while CSR tends to contribute in a fragmented manner to the substantive aspects of development such as road construction and building schools that are useful tools for public relations, CSR tends to neglect the process aspect of development such as social protection, empowerment, equality and redistribution (Utting, 2007; Utting & Margues, 2010). For example, Lompo and Trani (2013) confirmed this is the case in Nigeria where oil TNCs seem to have contributed to access to basic capabilities like water, electricity, and shelter but have actually undermined human development. Similarly, Renouard and Lado (2012) argued that while the CSR activities of oil TNCs have somewhat contributed to the improvement of the material well-being of some of the people living close to production sites, inequalities, or 'relational capabilities' has deteriorated (see also Le Mare, 2008).

Furthermore, proponents of 'CSR is good for development' in Africa see governmental failures as the *raisons d'être* for CSR, and a means via which business can complement governmental efforts (Moon, 2007; Perks, 2012). In contrast, others have argued that CSR activities are essentially allowing the government in Africa to abandon their developmental responsibilities and CSR is thus diverting attention away from the real structural political and economic reform needed in Africa to address the challenges facing the continent (Frynas, 2005, Ite, 2005; Campbell, 2012; Alstine & Afionis, 2013). Hence, Okoye (2012) has argued that business contribution to development must occur alongside governmental efforts and cannot entail the wholesale transfer of developmental responsibilities to business. Underpinning this particular disagreement is the tendency of CSR proponents and critics to see CSR as a domain of shifting responsibility (Crane et al., 2008). Yet, empirical research by Idemudia (2010, 2011b) has shown that the CSR activities of oil TNCs in Nigeria neither necessarily complement nor allow the government to abandon their development responsibilities. Instead, CSR is a domain of contestation in which both the government and oil TNCs seek to actively pass on the cost associated with community development to the other. This contestation is conceptualized by Idemudia (2011b) as the *politics of development*, which undermines the prospect of community development. This example supports Hamilton's (2011) argument that the role of the state in CSR is a far more complicated one than often assumed, and that there is a need to move beyond seeing it as unproblematic. While the foregoing debates have been insightful, Blowfield (2012) has pointed out that a core challenge remains the failure to clarify whether business is expected to be simply a tool or an agent of development. This is particularly important given that it would help clarify the expectations analysts have of business with regard to CSR–development relationship. For instance, as a tool of development, business has no responsibility beyond just contributing to development, while as a development agent, business consciously strives to deliver, and be held accountable for its developmental roles and impacts (Blowfield, 2010; Okoye, 2012). For Blowfield (2012), by addressing this expectation issue, analysts and policymakers would be better able to determine under what circumstances business are likely to be development agent as opposed to being just a development tool (see idemudia, 2008).

At the level of CSR discourse, Rajak (2011) has argued that while the debate about whether CSR is good or bad for African development has been insightful, it obscures the discursive capacity of CSR to reshape development agendas according to corporate values and interests. She then points to how poverty is recast within a depoliticized framework due to lack of market opportunities or capital. Consequently, a key business solution to poverty has been the adoption and promotion of micro-credit schemes. The danger here lies in the power of CSR rhetoric to validate a particular form of ideology along with accompanying epistemological and ontological assumptions while excluding alternative views and in the process institutionalize a particular form of corporate rationality that despite its emancipatory intent serves to marginalize a large group of people (Banerjee, 2008). For example, Rajak (2006) has shown how the CSR practices of mining companies in South Africa inspired deference and dependence as opposed to autonomy and empowerment that such CSR initiatives promised to deliver. Similarly, Akpan (2009) has shown that instead of being a tool of poverty reduction, CSR initiatives of oil TNCs in the Niger Delta tend to foster inter and intra-community violence. However, Blowfield (2010) drawing on the works of post-development theorists, argued that elements of business response to development issues such as the tendency to reduce complex social, cultural, and economic issues into technical problems are characteristic of contemporary development itself. Hence, it is harder to argue that business might co-opt development thinking and practice than to make the case that business as development actors mirror the established norms of the predominate development discourse.

Emerging Issues and the Way Forward

There are two main emerging issues with implications for future research agendas. Firstly, the role of socio-economic and socio-cultural factors as drivers of CSR in the African context means that if CSR is to be meaningful in Africa, it must engage with developmental objectives (Okoye, 2012). Yet, the lack of sufficient systematically accumulated empirical evidence means that disagreements over the actual effectiveness and impact of CSR initiatives in Africa remain a major problem that continues to undermine our ability to reach a reasoned conclusion about the usefulness of CSR in Africa. In addition, it also partly explains why CSR continues to hold alluring possibilities for development in Africa despite strong misgivings about its ability to deliver for the poor and marginalized. This lack of empirical evidence can be attributed to at least two reasons. The first is that CSR as a discipline lacks established methodologies that capture its effect (Prieton-Carron et al., 2006; Hamann, 2007) and the dearth of empirical research on the relationship between CSR and development in Africa. Hence, there is a need to move beyond the present polemic debate of whether CSR is good or bad for Africa's development and instead take a more nuanced perspective to the analysis of the CSR-development nexus and its contradictions in Africa. The debate should be expanded to include not only a focus on whether there is a link between CSR and development but also how such a link might be made to function more effectively. A key first step would be the need to study and analyze CSR from the perspective of Africans whose voices are often either neglected or ignored in mainstream CSR discourse. This would entail rich empirical studies that are based on how local people experience CSR, how socio-cultural factors shape local population expectations and perceptions of CSR, and a comparative analysis of different CSR processes and their associated outcomes within and between regions. At stake here is the need to better understand the circumstances and forms under which CSR is most likely to contribute to development in Africa.

Second, the available evidence and controversies surrounding the CSR-development nexus in Africa suggest that business at present is more of a development tool than a development agent. This is largely because business engages with issues of development predominantly via the eradication of development problems through a profit lens (Boyle & Boguslaw, 2007). Consequently, the developmental record of big business in Africa is at best mixed (Vissser et al., 2006). Hence, there is a need for the analysis of CSR-development nexus in Africa to move beyond the business case perspective and begin to explore the factors that drive and constrain CSR initiatives and their ability to contribute to development. For example, how do historical, contextual, and institutional factors drive and constrain CSR and what are the implications for the possibility of corporate social development in Africa? In addition, the role and impact of the CSR initiatives of non-Western TNCs on Africa's development remain poorly understood. This is particularly problematic given the significant increase in Chinese investment in Africa. Although Pegg (2012) have suggested that Chinese oil companies have embraced mainstream CSR agenda and thus there are no qualitative differences between the CSR initiatives of Chinese companies and their Western counterpart, there is the need to explore under what circumstances are the CSR initiatives of Chinese companies different and what this might mean for the impact of CSR on development in Africa.

Notes

1 According to Davis (1960) and Frederick (1983) the idea that power and responsibility go hand in hand is as old as civilization, and appears to have its origin in logic.
2 What Orock (2006, 256) has called an 'escapist' culture.
3 While accommodation occurs primarily in explicit interaction of interest, and legitimization at the level of discourse (Hamann and Acutt, 2003).
4 The second generation focuses on whether CSR can underpin or at the very least be an integral part of business' long-term strategy for success. The third generation focused on whether CSR can make contribution to poverty, exclusion, and environmental degradation.

Bibliography

Aaron, K. K. (2012). New corporate social responsibility models for oil companies in Nigeria's delta region: What challenges for sustainability? *Progress in Development Studies*, *12*(4), 259–273.

Akpan, W. (2009). When corporate citizens 'second-class' National Citizens: The antimonies of corporate mediated social provisioning Nigeria's Oil province. *Journal of Contemporary African Studies*, *27*(1), 105–118.

Alan, H. R. (1999). Transnational corporations and their regulation: Issues and strategies. *International Journal of Comparative Sociology, 40*, 1–16.

Alstine, J. A., & Afionis, S. (2013). Community and company capacity: The challenge of resource-led development in Zambia's 'New Copperbelt'. *Community Development, 48*(3), 360–376.

Amaeshi, K. M., Adi, B. C., Ogbechie, C., & Amao, O. O. (2006). Corporate social responsibility in Nigeria: Western mimicry or indigenous influences. *Journal of Corporate Citizenship, 24*, 83–99.

Bagire, V. A., Tusiime, I., Nalweyiso, G., & Kakooza, J. B. (2013). Contextual environment and stakeholder perception of corporate social responsibility practices in Uganda. *Corporate Social Responsibility and Environmental Management, 18*(2), 102–109.

Banaerjee, S. B. (2008). Corporate social responsibility: The good, the bad and the ugly. *Critical Sociology, 34*(1), 51–79.

Beesley, M. E., & Evans, T. (1978). *Corporate social responsibility: A reassessment.* London: Croom Helm.

Berle, A. A., & Means, G. C. (1932). *The Modern Corporation and Private Property.* New York: Harcourt Brace.

Blowfield, M. (2005). Corporate social responsibility reinventing the meaning of development. *International Affairs, 81*(3), 515–524.

Blowfield, M. (2010). Business, corporate responsibility and poverty reduction. In P. Utting & J. C. Marques (Eds.), *Corporate social responsibility and regulatory governance: Towards inclusive development?* (pp. 124–150). New York: Palgrave MacMillan.

Blowfield, M., & Frynas, J. G. (2005). Setting new agenda: Critical perspectives on corporate social responsibility in the developing world. *International Affairs, 80*(3), 499–513.

Blowfield, M. E. (2012). Business and development: making sense of business as a development agent. *Corporate Governance: International Journal of Business and Society, 12*(4), 414–426.

Blowfield, M. E., & Dolan, C. S. (2014). Business as a development agent: evidence of possibility and impossibility. *Third World Quarterly, 35*(1), 22–42.

Borzel, T. A., Hönke, J., & Thauer, C. R. (2012). Does it really take the state? *Business and Politics, 14*(3), 1–34.

Boyle, M. E., & Boguslaw, J. (2007). Business, poverty and corporate citizenship: Naming and the issues and framing solutions. *Journal of Corporate Citizenship, 26*, 101–120.

Buchholz, A. R. (1991). Corporate responsibility and good society: From economics to ecology. *Business Horizons, 34*(4), 19–31.

Burke, L., Logsdon, M. J., Mitchell, W., Reiner, M., & Vogel, D. (1986). Corporate community involvement in the San Francisco Bay area. *California Management Review, 28*(3), 122–141.

Business for Social Responsibility (BSR) (2004). Philanthropy investment in CED. *BSR Issue Briefs.* Retrieved from http://www.bsr.org/print/printThisPage.cfm (accessed 19 July 2004).

Campbell, B. (2012). Corporate social responsibility and development in Africa: Redefining the roles and responsibilities of public and private actors in the mining sector. *Resources Policy, 37*(2), 138–143.

Carroll, A. B. (1999). Corporate social responsibility: Evolution of a definitional construct. *Business and Society, 38*(3), 268–295.

Cash, A. (2012). Corporate social responsibility and petroleum development in Sub-Saharan African: The case of Chad. *Resources Policy, 37*(2), 144–151.

Ciulla, B. J. (1991). Why is business talking about ethics?: Reflection on foreign conversations. *California Management Review, 34*(1), 67–86.

Crane, A., Matten, D., & Moon, J. (2008). *Corporations and Citizenship.* Cambridge: Cambridge University Press.

Davis, K. (1960). Can business afford to ignore social responsibility? *California Management Review, 2*(3), 70–76.

Doane, D. (2005). Beyond corporate social responsibility: Minnows, mammoths and markets. *Futures, 37*(2–3), 215–229.

Dunn, P. C. (1991). Are corporations inherently wicked. *Business Horizons, 34*(4), 3–6.

Economist (2005). The good company: A survey of corporate social responsibility, January.

Egels, N. (2005). CSR in electrification of rural Africa: The case of ABB in Tanzania. *Journal of Corporate Citizenship, 18*, 75–85.

Egbon, O., Idemudia, U., & Amaeshi, K. (2018). Shell Nigeria's Global Memorandum of Understanding and corporate-community accountability relations: A critical appraisal. *Accounting, Auditing & Accountability Journal, 31*(1), 51–74.

Eilbirit, H., & Parket, R. I. (1973). The practices of business: The current state of corporate social responsibility. *Business Horizons*, 5–14.

Ekeh, P. (1990). Social anthropology and two contrasting uses of tribalism in Africa. *Comparative Studies in Society and History 32*(4), 660–700.

Elbing, A. O. Jr. (1970). Value issue of business: The responsibility of businessmen. *Academy of Management Journal, 16*, 79–89.

Emel, J., Makene, H. M., & Wangari, E. (2012). Problems with reporting and evaluating mining industry community development projects: A case study from Tanzania. *Sustainability 4*, 257–277.

Eweje, G. (2006). The role of MNEs in community development initiatives in developing countries: Corporate social responsibility at work in Nigeria and Southern Africa. *Business and Society, 45*(2), 93–129.

Fig, D. (2005). Manufacturing amnesia: Corporate social responsibility in South Africa. *International Affairs, 31*(3), 599–617.

Fitzpatrick, P., Fonseca, A., & McAllister, M. L. (2011). From Whitehorse mining initiative towards sustainable mining: Lesson learned. *Journal of Cleaner Production, 19*(4), 376–384.

Fox, T. (2004). Corporate social responsibility and development: In quest of an agenda. *Development, 47*(3), 26–36.

Fox, T., Ward, H., & Howard, B. (2002). *Public Sector Roles in Strengthening Corporate Social Responsibility: A Baseline Study.* Washington DC: World Bank.

Fougere ,M., & Solintander, N. (2009). Against corporate responsibility. Critical reflections on thinking and practice, content and consequences. *Corporate Social Responsibility and Environmental Management, 16*(4), 217–227.

Frederick, W. C. (1960). The growing concern over business responsibility. California Management Review, 12(4), 54–61.

Freeman, R. E. (1984). *Strategic management: A stakeholder approach.* Boston, MA: Pitman.

French, A. P. (1979). The corporation as a moral person. In T. Donaldson & H. P. Werhane (Eds.) (1993), *Ethical issues in business: A philosophical approach* (4th ed., pp. 120–129). Englewood Cliffs, NJ: Prentice Hall.

Friedman, M. (1970, September 13). The social responsibility of business is to increase its profits. *New York Times Magazine, 33.*

Frynas, J. G. (2005). The false development promise of corporate social responsibility: Evidence from multinational oil companies. *International Affairs, 81*(3), 581–598.

Garcia-Rodriguez, F. J. G., Garcia-Rodriguez, J. L., Gutierrez, C. C., & Major, S. A. (2013). Corporate social responsibility of oil companies in developing countries: From altruism to business strategy. *Corporate Social Responsibility and Environmental Management, 20*(6), 371-384.10.1002/csr.1320

Gokulsing, R. D. (2011). CSR matters in the development of Mauritius. *Social Responsibility Journal*, 7(2), 218–233.

Gond, P. J., & Moon, J. (2011). *Corporate Social Responsibility in Retrospect and Prospect: Exploring the Life-Cycle of an Essentially Contested Concept, Research Paper Series International Centre for Corporate Social Responsibility*, ISSN 1479-5124, Nottingham University: Nottingham University Business School.

Goodpaster, E. K., & Matthews, B. J. (1982). Can a corporation have a conscience? *Harvard Business Review, 60*, 132–141.

Greenfield, W. M. (2004). In the name of corporate social responsibility. *Business Horizons, 47*(1), 19–28.

Hamann, R. (2004). Corporate social responsibility, partnership, and institutional change: The case of mining companies in South Africa. *Natural Resources Forum, 28*(4), 278–290.

Hamann, R. (2007). Is corporate citizenship making a difference? *Journal of Corporate Citizenship, 28*, 15–29.

Hamann, R., & Acutt, N. (2003). How should civil society (and Government) respond to 'Corporate Social Responsibility'? A critique of business motivations and the potential for partnerships. *Development Southern Africa, 20*(2), 255–270.

Hamann, R., Kapelus, P., Sonnenberg, D., Mackenzie, A., & Hollesen, P. (2005). Local governance as a complex system: Lessons from mining in South Africa, Mali and Zambia. *Journal of Corporate Citizenship, 18*, 61–73.

Hamilton, T. (2011). Putting corporate responsibility in its place. *Geography Compass, 5*(10), 710–722.

Hayes, K. T. A. (2006). Grounding African corporate responsibility: Moving the environment up the agenda. In M. Visser, M. McIntosh, & C. Middleton (Eds.), *Corporate citizenship in Africa: Lessons from the Past; paths to the future* (pp. 93–104). Sheffield: Greenleaf Publishing

Henderson, D. (2001). *Misguided virtue: False notion of corporate social responsibility.* New Zealand Business Roundtable, The Terrace, Wellington, New Zealand.

Honke, J. (2012). Multinationals and security governance in the community: Participation, discipline and indirect rule. *Journal of Intervention and Statebuilding, 6*(1), 57–73.

Idemudia, U. (2007). Community Perceptions and Expectations: Reinventing the Wheels of Corporate Social Responsibility Practices in the Nigerian oil Industry. *Business and Society Review, 112*(3), 369–405.

Idemudia, U. (2008). Conceptualising the CSR and development debate: Bridging existing analytical gaps. *Journal of Corporate Citizenship, 29*, 1–20.

Idemudia, U. (2009). Oil extraction and poverty reduction in the Niger Delta: A critical examination of partnership initiatives. *Journal of Business Ethics, 90*(1), 91–116.

Idemudia, U. (2010). Corporate social responsibility and the rentier Nigerian State: Rethinking the role of government and the possibility of corporate social development in the Niger Delta. *Canadian Journal of Development Studies, 30*(1–2), 131–152.

Idemudia, U. (2011a). Corporate social responsibility and developing countries: Moving the critical CSR Research agenda in Africa forward. *Progress in Development Studies, 11*(1), 1–18

Idemudia, U. (2011b). Oil companies and sustainable community development in the Niger Delta, Nigeria: The issue of reciprocal responsibility and its implications for corporate citizenship theory and practice. *Sustainable Development*, 1–11. 22(3), 177-187 doi:10.1002/sd.538

Idemudia, U., & Ite, U. E. (2006). Corporate-community relations in Nigeria's oil Industry: Challenges and imperatives. *Corporate Social Responsibility and Environmental Management Journal*, *13*(4), 194–206.

Ite, U. E. (2005). Poverty reduction in resources-rich developing countries: What have multinational corporations got to do with it? *Journal of International Development*, *17*(7), 913–929.

Ite, U. E. (2007). Changing times and strategies: shell's contributions to sustainable community development in the Niger Delta, Nigeria. *Sustainable Development*, *15*(1), 1–14.

Jenkins, R. (2005). Globalisation, corporate social responsibility and poverty. *International Affairs*, *81*(3), 525–540.

Jones, T. M. (1996). Missing the forest for the trees: A critique of the social responsibility concept discourse. *Business and Society*, *35*(1), 7–41.

Julian, S. D., & Ofori-Dankwa, J. C. (2013). Financial resources availability and corporate social responsibility expenditures in sub-Saharan economy: The institutional difference hypothesis. *Strategic Management Journal*, 34(11), 1314-1330 doi:10.1002/smj.2070

Kamlongera, P. J. (2013). The mining boom in Malawi: Implications for community development. *Community Development*, *48*(3), 377–390.

Kapelus, P. (2002). Mining, corporate social responsibility and the 'community': The case of Rio Tinto, Richards Bay minerals and the Mbonambi. *Journal of Business Ethics*, *39*(3), 275–296.

Kivuitu, M., Yambayamba, K., & Fox, T. (2005). How can corporate social responsibility deliver in Africa? Insights from Kenya and Zambia. In *Perspectives on corporate responsibility for environment and development*. International Institute for Environment and Development. Retrieved from http://www.csr-weltweit.de/uploads/tx_jpdownloads/Mumo_Kivuitu_How_can_Social_Responsibility_deliver_in_Africa.pdf

Kolk, A., & Lenfant, F. (2010). MNC reporting on CSR and conflict in central Africa. *Journal of Business Ethics*, *93*(S2), 241–255.

Kolk, A., & Lenfant, F. (2013). Multinationals, CSR and partnerships in Central African conflict countries. *Corporate Social Responsibility and Environmental Management*, *20*(1), 43–54.

Kuada, J., & Hinson, R. E. (2012). Corporate social responsibility (CSR) practices of foreign and local companies in Ghana. *Thunderbird International Business Review*, *54*(4), 521–536.

Ladd, J. (1970). Morality and the ideal of rationality in formal organisations. In T. Donaldson & H. P. Werhane (Eds.) (1993), *Ethical issues in business: A philosophical approach* (4th ed., pp. 130–142). Englewood Cliffs, NJ: Prentice Hall.

Le Mare, A. (2008).The impact of fair trade on social and economic development: A review of the literature. *Geography Compass*, *2*(6), 1922–1942.

Levitt, T. (1958). The danger of social responsibility. *Harvard Business Review*, *36*(5), 41–50.

Leys, C. (1996). *The rise and fall of development theory*. Bloomington, IN: Indiana University Press.

Lindgreen,A., Swaen, V., & Campbell, T. (2010). Corporate social responsibility practices in developing and transitional countries: Botswana and Malawi. *Journal of Business Ethics*, *90*(S3), 429–440.

Lodge, G. C. (1970). Top priority: Renovating our ideology. *Harvard Business Review* (September-October), 43–55.

Lompo, K., & Trani, J. J. (2013). Does corporate social responsibility contribute to human development in developing countries? Evidence from Nigeria. *Journal of Human Development and Capabilities: a Multi-Disciplinary Journal of People-Centered Development, 12*(2), 241–265.

Malan, D. (2005). Corporate citizens, colonialists, tourists or activists? Ethical challenges Facing South African Corporations in Africa. *Journal of Corporate Citizenship, 18*, 49–60.

Maria, J. F., & Devuyst, E. (2011). CSR and development: A mining company in Africa. *Journal of Management Development, 30*, 955–967.

Mitchell, R., Agle, B. R., & Wood, D. J. (1997). Towards a theory of stakeholder Identification and Salience: Defining the principle of who and what really counts. *Academy of Management Review, 22*(4), 853–886.

Monsen, J. R. (1972). Social responsibility and the corporation: Alternatives for the future of capitalism. *Journal of Economic Issues, 6*(1), 125–141.

Moon, J. (2007). The contribution of corporate social responsibility to sustainable development. *Sustainable Development, 15*(5), 296–306.

Moore, D. (2001). Neoliberal globalization and the triple crisis of modernization in Africa: Zimbabwe, the Democratic Republic of Congo and South Africa. *Third World Quarterly, 22*(6), 909–929.

Muthuri, J. N. (2007). Corporate citizenship and sustainable community development: Fostering multi-sector collaboration in Magadi Division in Kenya. *Journal of Corporate Citizenship, 28*, 73–84.

Muthuri, J. N. (2013). Corporate social responsibility in Africa: Definition, issues and process. In T. R. Lituchy, B. J. Punnett & B. B. Puplampu (Eds.), *Management in Africa: Macro and micro perspective* (pp. 90–111). New York and London: Routledge

Muthuri, J. N., & Gilbert, V. (2011). An institutional analysis of corporate social responsibility in Kenya. *Journal of Business Ethics, 98*(3), 467–483.

Mzembe, A. N., & Meaton, J. (2013). Driving corporate social responsibility in the Malawian mining Industry: A stakeholder perspective. *Corporate Social Responsibility and Environmental Management, 21*(4), 189–201. doi:10.1002/csr.1319

Naor, J. (1982). A new approach to multinational social responsibility. *Journal of Business Ethics, 1*(3), 219–225.

Newell, P. (2001). Managing multinationals: The governance of investment for the environment. *Journal of International Development, 13*(7), 907–919.

Njoh, A. J. (2006). *Tradition, culture and development in Africa: Historical lessons for modern development planning*. Aldershot: Ashgate.

Noyoo, N. (2010). Linking corporate social responsibility and social policy in Zambia. In P. Utting & J. C. Marques (Eds.), *Corporate social responsibility and regulatory governance: Towards inclusive development?* (pp. 105–123). New York: Palgrave MacMillan

Okafor, L. (2003). *Enhancing business-community relations: The role of volunteers in promoting global corporate citizenship: National research report*. New Academy of Business and United Nations Volunteers. Retrieved from http://www.new-academy.ac.uk/research/businesscommunity/unvpages/ (accessed 17 July 2004).

Okoye, A. (2009). Theorising corporate social responsibility as an essentially contested concept: Is a definition necessary. *Journal of Business Ethics, 89*(4), 613–627.

Okoye, A. (2012). Exploring the relationship between corporate social responsibility, law and development in African Context: Should government be responsible for ensuring corporate responsibility? *International Journal of Law and Management, 54*(5), 364–378.

Omeje, K. (2006). Extractive economies and conflicts in the global south: Re-engaging rentier theory and politics. In K. Omeje (Ed.), *Extractive economies and conflict in the global south: Multi-regional perspectives on rentier politics* (pp. 1–25). Aldershot: Ashgate

Orock, R. T. E. (2006). An overview of Corporate Globalization and non-globalization of corporate citizenship in Africa. In M. Visser, M. McIntosh & C. Middleton (Eds.), *Corporate citizenship in Africa: Lessons from the Past; paths to the future* (pp. 250–260). Sheffield: Greenleaf Publishing.

Owen, J. R., & Kemp, A. (2013). Social license and mining: A critical perspective. *Resources Policy, 38*(1), 29–35.

Pegg, S. (2012). Social responsibility and resource extraction: are Chinese oil companies different? *Resource Policy, 37*(2), 160–167.

Perks, R. (2012). How can public-private partnerships contribute to security and human rights policy and practice in the extractive industries? A case study of the Democratic Republic of Congo. *Resources Policy, 37*(2), 251–260.

Philiips, F. (2006). Corporate social responsibility in an African context. *Journal of Corporate Citizenship, 24*, 23–28.

Porter, E. M., & Kramer, R. M. (2002). The competitive advantage of corporate philanthropy. *Harvard Business Review, 80*(12), 57–68.

Pratt, C. B. (1991). Multinational corporate social policy process for ethical responsibility in sub-Saharan Africa. *Journal of Business Ethics, 10*(7), 527–541.

Prieto-Carron, M., Lund-Thomsen, P., Chan, A., Muro, A., & Bhushan, C. (2006). Critical perspective on CSR and development: What we know, what we don't know and what we need to know. *International Affairs, 82*(5), 977–987.

Prno, J., & Slocombe, S. D. (2012). Exploring the origins of 'social license to operate' in mining sector: Perspectives from governance and sustainability theories. *Resources Policy, 37*, 346–357.

Ragodoo, N. J. F. (2009). CSR as tool to fight against poverty: The case of Mauritius. *Social Responsibility Journal, 5*(1), 19–33.

Rajak, D. (2006). The gift of CSR: Power and the pursuit of responsibility in the mining Industry. In M. Visser, M. McIntosh, & C. Middleton (Eds.), *Corporate citizenship in Africa: Lessons from the Past; paths to the future* (pp. 190–200). Sheffield: Greenleaf Publishing.

Rajak, D. (2011). Theaters of virtue: Collaboration, consensus, and the social life of corporate social responsibility. *Journal of Global and Historical Anthropology, 60*, 9–20.

Renourard, C., & Lado, H. (2012). CSR and inequality in the Niger Delta (Nigeria). *Corporate Governance, 12*(4), 472–484.

Rossouw, G. J. (2000). Out of Africa: An introduction. *Business Ethics: A European Review, 9*(4), 225–228.

Slack, K. (2012). Mission Impossible?: Adopting a CSR based business model for extractive industries in developing countries. *Resources Policy, 37*(2), 179–184.

Smith, C. N. (2003). Corporate social responsibility: Whether or how? *California Management Review, 45*(4), 52–76.

Staff, F. (2013). Africapitalism: Purposeful thinking for African business. Retrieved from http://finweek.com/2013/08/13/africapitalism-purposeful-thinking-for-african-business/ (accessed 1/8/13).

Stokes, M. (1996). Company law and legal theory. In W. Twining (Ed.), *Legal theory and the common law* (pp. 155–183). Oxford: Oxford University Press.

Tavis, L. A. (1982). Multinational corporate responsibility for third world development. *Review of Social Economy, 40*(3), 427–437.

Utting, P. (2005). Corporate responsibility and the movement of business. *Development in Practice, 15*(3&4), 375–388.

Utting, P. (2007). CSR and equality. *Third World Quarterly, 28*(4), 697–712.

Utting, P., & Marques, J. C. (2010). Introduction: The intellectual crisis of CSR. In P. Utting & J. C. Marques (Eds.), *Corporate social responsibility and regulatory governance: Towards inclusive development?* (pp. 1–25). New York: Palgrave MacMillan.

Vertigans, S. (2011). CSR as corporate social responsibility or colonial structures return? A Nigerian case study. *International Journal of Sociology and Anthropology, 3,* 159–162.

Visser, W. (2005). 'Is South Africa World class in Corporate Citizenship?'How do South African companies measure up? In A. Freemantle (Ed.), *The good corporate citizen* (pp. 118–123). Trialogue: Johannesburg.

Visser, W. (2006) .Research on Corporate Citizenship in Africa: A ten year Review (1995–2005). In M. Visser, M. McIntosh, & C. Middleton (Eds.), *Corporate citizenship in Africa: Lessons from the Past; paths to the future* (pp. 18–28). Sheffield: Greenleaf Publishing

Visser, W., McIntosh, M., & Middleton, C. (2006). Corporate citizenship in Africa: Lessons from the Past; Paths to the Future. In M. Visser, M. McIntosh, & C. Middleton (Eds.), *Corporate citizenship in Africa: Lessons from the past; paths to the future* (pp. 1–17). Sheffield: Greenleaf Publishing.

Visser, W., Middleton, C., & McIntosh, M. (2005). Corporate citizenship in Africa. *Journal of Corporate Citizenship, 18,* 18–20.

Watts, M. (2005). Righteous oil?: human rights, the oil complex and corporate social responsibility. *Annual Review of Environment and Resources 30,* 9.1–9.35.

WBCSD (2000). *Corporate social responsibility: Making good business sense.* Geneva: World Business Council for Sustainable Development (WBCSD).

Wiig, A., & Kolstad, I. (2010). Multinational corporations and host country institutions: A case study of CSR activities in Angola. *International Business Review, 19*(2), 178–190.

Whitehouse, L. (2003) Corporate social responsibility, corporate citizenship and the global compact: A new approach to regulating corporate social power. *Global Social Policy, 3*(3), 299–318.

World Bank. (2001).*World Development Report 2000/2001: Attacking Poverty.* Oxford: Oxford University Press.

Zadek, S. (2001). *Third generation corporate citizenship: Public policy and business in society, A Foreign Policy Centre/accountability report.* London: Foreign Policy Centre.

2

CORPORATE SOCIAL RESPONSIBILITY AND HUMAN RIGHTS

Raymond A. Atuguba

Introduction

Corporate entities target private economic benefits. However, their money-making objectives could reflect well on society. For example, corporations offer jobs to the working force of every nation and this enables individuals to earn a living. In some industries, corporations are mandated to adhere to local content and local participation rules to accommodate local inclusion into their businesses. They are also demanded by governments to pay heavy taxes. We cannot deflate the immense contributions of corporate services that are beneficial to economic and social growth, even if they are merely incidental to their business survival.

In the past, corporations were criticized for being unconcerned about the collective good of the people. Now, the growing practice is that corporate bodies set business objectives that spawn community development, and more corporate bodies are active actors in the direct human rights growth of the community. This has positively influenced corporate bodies that were formerly nonchalant about community impact and has led to a heightened public interest in promoting Corporate Social Responsibility (CSR) at both national and international levels.

Under the garment of CSR, corporate bodies undertake to support the developmental goals of communities where they operate. An inspection of the CSR initiatives adopted by these corporate bodies uncloaks either a proactive CSR corporate policy or a reactive corporate CSR policy to repair the broken or diminishing parts of State economies.

With this in clear view, it is expected that African economies would fully capitalize on CSR as a factor implicit in economic arrangement, development, and sustainability by producing an all-inclusive, robust CSR Policy. However, African countries continually exhibit a taciturn attitude towards the

DOI: 10.4324/9781003038078-3

comprehensive regulation of CSR. There is law, but because of the absence of a CSR structure, corporations are led to adopt a limited perception of CSR – as an act of philanthropy. It is dreaded that, in Africa, CSR may not reach its fullest potential owing to the absence of a comprehensive policy regime to piece the elements of human rights and CSR together. The concept of CSR may have been borne out of philanthropic inclinations; however, CSR's reach has expanded, and its development in the twenty-first century must and should be deliberate, and streamlined according to a country's development targets and human rights needs.

In this chapter, I evaluate the connection between CSR and the fundamental human rights obligations of corporate entities. I challenge the popular yet misleading notion that CSR is only made up of voluntary humanitarian assignments that corporate bodies may perform if they are minded to. I postulate that CSR is not an entirely philanthropic endeavour and that the primary value of CSR requires corporate bodies to act in the best interest of stakeholders of community development. Using Ghana as a case study, I seek to establish that mandatory elements of CSR are interspersed in Ghana's laws, except that they are not as straightforward and operational as they should.

In the first part of the chapter, I deconstruct the limited perception of CSR by explaining the wide net of the concept. Second, I lay out the CSR environment in Ghana and assess its competence in achieving human rights goals. I proceed to delve significantly into the human rights elements of CSR in Ghanaian law, through three main headings: Community Involvement; Environmental Stewardship; and Sustainable Development. Finally, I analyze the merits of a mandatory regulatory system to effectively mobilize Corporate Social Responsibility as a tool to ensure the respect and protection of human rights in Africa.

Scope of CSR in Ghana

Corporate Social Responsibility is perceived by many as the charitable service of corporate bodies out of sheer benevolence. This is not exactly wrong. However, this skewed understanding is bad business for national development because firms would regard CSR as a solely discretionary moral obligation. Unless corporations are convinced that there is a legal backing to CSR, they will not attach much significance to it.

Contrary to popular belief, the CSR mechanism is broad indeed. It is incorporated into domestic laws and CSR objectives have proven to comprise a major part of the ideals and successes of a corporation. It is not totally divorced from the basic precepts of donations which remain, but it must be acknowledged that CSR has transcended donations; it requires corporate devotion to the community and compliance with the rules of corporate ethics.

Whichever way one looks at it, CSR is about the relationship of corporations with society as a whole, and the need for corporations to align their values with societal expectations in order to avoid conflicts and reap tangible benefits

(Atuguba & Dowuona-Hammond, 2006; Idemudia, 2007). Beyond philanthropy, CSR is associated with the responsiveness of corporate bodies to existing social conditions and issues. It requires that a company considers the impact of its activities on all CSR stakeholders (the immediate environment, shareholders, employees, customers, the community, organizations, and the local and national government) when making decisions (Idemudia, 2008). This means that at the centre of CSR, there is a balancing act of the interests of the stakeholders of CSR against the business policies of the corporation. Philanthropy is not discounted in the CSR framework, but a holistic approach to CSR implementation, with stress on human rights objectives, is imperative in achieving maximum human rights and development results.

The wider net of the CSR framework therefore covers:

1. Community involvement, relations, and engagement;
2. Environmental stewardship;
3. Sustainable development;
4. Proper treatment of workers, including regard for safety and good working conditions, retirement benefits, and health insurance;
5. Avoiding or mitigating defective or faulty products;
6. Disclosure of relevant information;
7. Ethical business practices;
8. Observation of human rights standards;
9. Avoiding discriminatory practices and instituting anti-discrimination policies;
10. Protecting interests of minorities and active service to minorities;
11. Service to women, children, and other traditionally disadvantaged groups;
12. Avoiding misleading advertising;
13. Proper customer relations;
14. Setting and ensuring compliance with minimum standards;
15. Public policy roles of business; and
16. Good corporate governance.

The tall list of CSR elements is reflective of the human rights role of CSR. It clears the misconception that CSR is merely a voluntary act of giving to the poor or needy. In building up regulations for CSR, we are called to consider the entirety of the rights of CSR stakeholders and to construct CSR to promote those rights.

The CSR Environment in Ghana

There are regulatory laws, practices, and fragmented policies that are somewhat linked to CSR in Ghana. The problem is, there is no exhaustive document or policy that expresses one complete thought towards the CSR initiative. In 2016 the Government of Ghana launched the National Policy for CSR, under the auspices of the Ministry of Trade and Industry, to optimize the socio-economic impact of CSR. However, there is no source that indicates that further steps were taken to ensure its realization as an effective policy in Ghana. The policy never saw the light of day, and consequently there is still no cogent policy framework on CSR in Ghana. This is confirmed by Ansu-Mensah et al., who take the position that:

> There is no full package of CSR policies or regulations in Ghana, however there are a range of regulations, rules, procedures and programs that direct CSR programs in Ghana and the government seeks to encourage CSR by adopting regulation that establishes basic standards of business efficiency, like statutes, local authority regulations and environmental impact evaluation criteria found in a parliamentary statute.

The absence of a clear and enforceable policy and a complete bundle of law may suggest an unguarded and uncertain environment for CSR in Ghana. Thus, we lack an approved ethical or moral standard for all CSR initiatives and the borders of CSR have not been well demarcated. Whilst CSR policies, laws, and practices exist in Ghana, they are unorganized, divergent, and conflicting.

The Companies Act of 2019 (Act 992)[1] is the main legislation that regulates corporate bodies in Ghana. Essentially, the Act prescribes what corporate transactions are permissible and those that offend the law; it defines the liabilities of companies towards their shareholders and third parties and holds the officers of companies accountable for their actions and inactions.

Act 992 was passed in 2019 to effectively repeal the Companies Act of 1963 (Act 179).[2] The old Act did not explicitly capture or mention the term CSR, although one could glean dribs and drabs of CSR references from its provisions. The implied allusion to CSR was not helpful. The idea of CSR back then was keenly contested by companies themselves and the enforcement of CSR was hampered by the lack of properly designated institutions. In 1963, when the old Companies Act was passed, we concede that it did not make much sense to insist on CSR guidelines because Ghana was focused on building its basic corporate scheme and CSR was neither desirable nor fashionable.

Post 1963, and with the expansion of the presence of multinational companies on the corporate scene in Ghana, the corporate system in Ghana began to look more favourably on CSR and showed its solidarity towards CSR by implementing social projects. It was conceivable, therefore, that the new Act, Act 992, seized with the corporate history of Ghana and, having developed a culture of 'philanthropic CSR', would have plugged the wide-gaping hole of CSR once and for all. Sad to say, Act 992 maintained almost the same corporate governance rules of the old Act in this regard. It did not overtly address the fundamental human rights and public policy role of companies within the CSR scheme. As it stands, CSR, within the latitude of corporate governance, continues to be disfigured by indefiniteness. The saving grace then is to resort to fishing for CSR principles from the host of provisions in the new Companies Act.

The drafters of the new Act may counter-argue that, since there are different business sectors, the current Companies Act cannot or should not take up the overwhelming responsibility of picking and assembling all CSR laws across the sectors. The quick rebuttal is, general guidelines for CSR could have been prescribed in an enactment of this special nature regulating all companies, by capturing the basic substantive and procedural rules of CSR. This would have served as the standard for all companies in Ghana irrespective of the industry.

Owing to the lack of a CSR policy and the deficiency of precise laws on CSR, individuals, the community, advocacy groups, and government agencies seeking to hold corporations accountable for socio-economic engagement will be confronted by an enforceability block; and be forced to have recourse to sectoral laws that provide faint but manageable references to CSR. Also, companies seeking to meet their corporate social responsibilities are in doubt about the scope of CSR in Ghana. Until our policy makers and the legislature ponder on the failures of our floating CSR system and create a sustainable CSR environment in Ghana, we have no other choice but to rely on the scattered laws available.

These laws, although flawed by dis-unification and the lack of a CSR cutting edge, represent the foundations for managing CSR in Ghana. The ethics of businesses is managed under the Companies Act, 2019 (Act 992). Tax mobilization from companies is supervised by the Income Tax Act[3] for direct income taxes from business, investment and employment, and the Value Added Tax Act[4] caters for the regulation of indirect taxes on taxable services and supplies. The Revenue Administration Act[5] deals with tax revenue administration. In the area of employment, there is the Labour Act[6] which addresses wages and salaries, employment leave, unlawful termination of employment, amongst others. The labour laws have been expounded in case law by our Ghanaian courts and the Labour Commission. Health and Safety is manned under the Labour Act, in conjunction with the Factories, Offices and Shops Act.[7] Environmental compliance is under various environmental protection laws and various sectoral laws, such as the Minerals and Mining Act[8] and its accompanying regulations. The Ghanaian legal framework provides for specific laws regulating particular industries and sectors of the economy such as banking,[9] insurance,[10] telecommunications,[11] energy and power,[12] which have bearing on CSR.

A number of International Conventions[13] that Ghana has ratified are also applicable to Ghana and have a bearing on CSR. The government also facilitates CSR by providing incentives to companies undertaking activities that promote the CSR agenda and drive social and environmental improvements. The role of the government here is basically catalytic, secondary, or supportive.

The Relationship between CSR and Human Rights

As stated early on, CSR cannot be fully appreciated without recognizing its human rights affiliations. CSR plays a big role in the economic, social, and cultural scene and carries mammoth human rights obligations, exercised through third-party corporations on behalf of the government.

The core of our submission is that, much as CSR is subtly woven into Ghanaian laws, there is a weak recognition by society that CSR and human rights instructions are bedfellows. This is why it is problematic to accept the proposition that the role of corporations in leavening development through CSR should be voluntary and discretionary.

Using the principal elements of the Human Rights–CSR relationship, namely Community Engagement, Environmental Stewardship and Sustainable Development, we would unravel the whole gamut of CSR, detailing how corporations must align their business strategies to respond to the human rights needs of stakeholders of CSR under the existing but dispersed CSR laws.

a. Community Involvement, Relations, and Engagement

Companies blossom on the strength of public image and branding. The road to accomplishing their business targets is a multilayered one, and community involvement is one of the distinct strata in the business image ecosystem.

As a corollary for the fulfilment of the right to development, companies, in their capacity as juristic persons, have a mandate to collaborate with the authorities of the Nation-State in setting up a base for community consultation in business matters generally, more especially where the actions of the company have the potential to invade current and inter-generational rights and equity.

Community involvement connotes a collaborative and mutually beneficial relationship between the community and the corporate body. It is driven by the corporation's business objective to maintain a healthy bond between it and the surrounding community of people in order to comfortably facilitate and promote its business mission and vision. The people, whose validation has to be sought, become the centre of attention in this equation, and consequently, enjoy the fruits of the company's business. With community engagement, the company secures its position in the lives of the people and the people in turn experience some degree of economic growth relevant to their circumstances.

Community involvement in CSR can be examined in two folds: Community engagement antecedent to the introduction of developmental projects; and community engagement subsequent to the incorporation of the company and its projects.

On the first path, there is law that enjoins the state to consult the inhabitants of an area where a community-impacting project is in the offing. It would seem that in the interest of both the company and the community, there ought to be direct and effective correspondence between officials and the people until common ground is established. This participatory and inclusive requirement is firmed up in the right to development. The right to development in Ghana can be gleaned from articles 35, 36, 37, 38, 39, and 40 under the belt of the Directive Principles of State Policy in Chapter 6 of the 1992 Constitution. In the African Legal System, the right to development is etched in Article 22(1) of the African Charter on Human and Peoples' Rights which provides that:

> All peoples shall have the right to their economic, social and cultural development with due regard to their freedom and identity and in the equal enjoyment of the common heritage of mankind.

Implicit in the right to development is the aforementioned community participation. The Office of the High Commissioner for Human Rights has declared that 'The right to development entitles all people to free, active and meaningful participation in the development decisions that affect them' (OHCHR *Fact Sheet No. 37*, p. 3). As such, development is not only pegged at improving the quality of lives of the people, it is also hinged firmly on the concept of participation and involvement of the people whose lives will be under the direct impact of development decisions.

The Right to Development (RTD) was affirmed by the African Commission on Human and Peoples' Rights in *Democratic Republic of Congo v Burundi & Ors*,[14] and subsequently upheld in the *African Commission v. Kenya* (Endorois case)[15] where the Commission noted that RTD requires fulfilling five main criteria: it must be equitable, non-discriminatory, participatory, accountable, and transparent (Yeneabat, 2015).

As stakeholders in development, the community deserves to be consulted by prospective business entities on the use of their land or neighbouring or adjoining lands for business activities. Under Ghana's decentralization policy, there are Municipal and District Assemblies,[16] and at the minute level, there are kingship systems in most localities in Ghana with representatives who protect the interests of the people. Companies have a duty to seek the consent of the people, through their representatives, before implementing environmentally augmenting projects such as mining and petroleum exploration.

In the mining sector of the Ghanaian economy, the consent of the inhabitants cannot be discounted. By Article 257(6) of the Constitution:

> every mineral in its natural state in, under or upon any land in Ghana, rivers, streams, water courses throughout Ghana, the exclusive economic zone and any area covered by the territorial sea or continental shelf is the property of the Republic of Ghana and shall be vested in the President on behalf of, and in trust for the people of Ghana.

Although Article 257(6) of the 1992 Constitution vests the ownership of mineral resources in the President for and on behalf of the people of Ghana, Article 1(1) of the same Constitution provides that sovereignty resides in the people, hence, it would follow that in the exercise of its trusteeship, the government must guarantee the rights of citizens to participate adequately in natural resource governance decisions (Niber, Owusu-Koranteng, Owusu-Koranteng & Greenspan, 2015).

This argument is, however, not an impenetrable one. The High Court of Ghana, in *Adjaye and Others v. Attorney-General and Others*,[17] relying on the English decision of *Tito v. Waddell*[18] held that the trust relationship created in Article 256(7) of the 1992 Constitution is a higher-order trust, and is unenforceable by the beneficiaries. The effect of this ruling is that the government cannot be held accountable for how it manages the mineral interests of the people. It would seem that this prevailing state of the law absolves mining corporations from holding consultations with the indigenes of the place of mining excavation. However, a synthesis and deductive reasoning of other provisions of the Constitution and all the relevant mining laws in Ghana would reveal otherwise.

The 1992 Constitution guarantees the right of every person to own property either alone or in association with others in Article 18(1). Further, Article 18(2) provides that no person shall be subjected to interference with the privacy of her property. The only exception permitted is interference in accordance with law and as may be necessary for public safety or the economic well-being of the country, for the protection of health or morals, for the prevention of disorder or crime, or for the protection of the rights or freedoms of others.[19] In property law, despite the fact that a person, and in this case, the project-affected persons, may have full possession and complete interest in land, it is conceded that by Article 18(2), the rights of an individual to land is subject to certain constitutional restrictions, such as that imposed under Article 257(6) of the Ghana Constitution. Land in the country can therefore be made the subject of an application for a mineral right according to Section 3 of the Minerals and Mining Act, 2006 (Act 703).

Notwithstanding, the state's supra overriding interest in minerals in private land, Section 72 of the Mining and Minerals Act of Ghana is to the effect that mineral rights are exercised subject to the surface rights of the owner or lawful occupier of the land and any further limitation determined by the Minister. The surface rights of the lawful owner are retained and run concurrently with the mining lease granted to the corporation by the state. Again, the law provides in Section 71(3) that the lawful occupier of land within an area subject to a mineral right shall retain the right to graze livestock upon or to cultivate the surface of the land if the grazing or cultivation does not interfere with the mineral operations in the area. This rule affirms the rights of the landowner and protects his interests from being trammelled upon by the corporation. This law is rooted in judicial thinking.

The case of *Asare v. Ashanti Goldfields and Co*[20] illustrates the principle of law that the rights of the owner of land are not extinguished by a mining concession. In this case, Plaintiff's land was the subject of a mining lease granted the first Defendant. Upon entry by the first defendant onto the land, an assessment of all the plaintiff's crops was made, recorded, and signed by him and the plaintiff received compensation. Subsequently, Plaintiff sued the first defendant and the government to be compensated for the acquisition of the land. The court dismissed his claim on the reasoning that the land had not been compulsorily acquired. In the court's application of the law to the facts, it was of the firm view that on the acquisition of mining rights under the Mineral and Mining Law then in force, the rights of the owner were not completely divested, but limited by the rights conferred on the mineral concessionaire. The court indicated that the rights retained by the owner or occupier under the law to graze livestock and cultivate and even mine building or industrial minerals, alongside the mineral rights conferred on the concessionaire, were rights which were inconsistent with rights under compulsory acquisition.

There might be no law in Ghana which instructs community consultation in respect of procedural steps to be taken in the acquisition of mining leases. However, the direction of the law in the Minerals and Mining Act informs corporations with mineral rights to take the initiative of conferring with inhabitants of land subject to the acquired mineral rights, because by the dictates of enactment and case law, the grant of mineral rights by the Minerals Commission is not to be interpreted as an unlimited right to the use of the land, unless the land has already been compulsorily acquired by the State. The right is enjoyed subject to the surface rights of the owner of the land. It will be in the financial interest of a corporate body desirous of obtaining a mining lease over a tract of land which is not vested in the State to negotiate with the community to avoid potential conflicts in future.

The law equally restricts the landowner from undertaking acts that defeat the purpose of the mining lease. Under Section 72(4) of the Minerals and Mining Act of Ghana, in the case of a mining area, the owner or lawful occupier of the land within the mining area shall not erect a building or a structure without the consent of the holder of the mining lease, or if the consent is unreasonably withheld, without the consent of the Minister. Section 72(6) of the Minerals and Mining Act of Ghana contains the law that the owner or lawful occupier of land shall not upgrade to a higher value crop without the written consent of the holder of the mining lease, or if the consent is unreasonably withheld, without the consent of the Minister.

The prescription of these rules invites community involvement to clarify any doubts in the minds of the people and to settle controversies stirring up from people who are likely to be unaware of these legal stipulations. This answers the question that corporate bodies by implication of the law, are not absolved from consulting the community and seeking their consent.

A compensatory duty is also thrust on mining corporations under the law. The Minerals and Mining Act of Ghana itemizes that, the holder of the mineral right has to compensate the owner or lawful occupier of the land for the disturbance. Section 73(1) of the same Act, therefore, provides that the owner or lawful occupier of any land subject to a mineral right is entitled to and may claim from the holder of the mineral right compensation for the disturbance of the rights of the owner or occupier, in accordance with Section 74. The law, in section 75(1), permits the owner or lawful occupier of the land affected by a mineral right to apply to the High Court where dissatisfied with the terms of compensation offered by the holder of the mineral right or as determined by the Minister.

Demonstrably, it is appropriate for the Company, in the process of obtaining licenses for mining and upon its approval, to include the community folks in decision-making and to consider their opinions and concerns. There is the need for that face-to-face interaction with the people through consultative meetings to discuss these adverse social, legal, and moral complications which, when unattended to, could eventually ground the company's operations.

A clean dichotomy lies between consultation before the projects and consultation in the course of the corporation's business life. The former is what has been discussed and elaborated on in the preceding paragraphs. The main difference between both streams, we argue, is that the former is compulsory CSR whilst the other straddles between both compulsory and voluntary CSR, depending on the special facts of each situation.

In respect of the voluntary CSR aspect, upon establishment of the corporation and during the currency of its projects, companies, with the aim of strengthening their existing relationship with the community, decide voluntarily to mend or build from the ground up, the basic amenities that a community is lacking. These are usually manifested by bountiful charity donations, academic scholarships, need-based financial aid, construction of schools and healthcare facilities, construction of community centres, amongst others. This type of CSR is what the truncated notion of CSR as a concept represents.

A flock of these voluntary CSR initiatives are present in Ghana and all corporate bodies decide what direction their CSR moral obligation should take. A 2019 comprehensive report (Avance Media, 2019) outlines the social impacts of corporate bodies in terms of voluntary CSR activities in Ghana. We noted the following initiatives: Ghana Cocoa Board, a government-controlled institution, provides scholarships to support the education of students,[21] Wienco, an agriculture company, specialized in the import and distribution of agro-inputs, has over the years supported weather forecast programmes in partnership with several media entities across the country and has extended its coverage of impact to all Ghanaians;[22] Access Bank Ghana Plc, a commercial bank, through its Access W Initiative, has connected, inspired and empowered several women entrepreneurs.[23] In 2010, it launched the Employee Volunteer Programme which has provided avenues for staff to use their time, energy, and resources to support various social projects through volunteerism.[24] These are a sample of the exemplary impactful initiatives churned out by corporate bodies to support the economic landscape of the country.

It is true that these CSR platforms are ingeniously up-scaling the social arrangements of community life, but the undefined discretion is worrying for the trajectory of Africa's development. We are at a stage of global alliance where sustainable development has shaped our thinking of the future we want; we are therefore more deliberate about what development ought to be. The bare truth is that these voluntary, sometimes one-off CSR projects, are short termed, unsustainable, and do not leave a lasting impression on the people.

Our reasoning is simple. It will be impossible to invoke the Right to Development at this stage of their philanthropy when it is not specified by law that corporations must avail themselves to a series of consultations with the people. Even if it could be inferred from a moral point of view that there is a need to seek community consent to make the people feel appreciated, there is absolutely no guarantee that the project or initiative will be useful to the community's needs.

The community consultation process, where companies are minded to adopt it, is not smooth sailing as it is confronted with many social, cultural, and logistical barriers. It has been observed by a researcher that:

> Most of the time, the meetings do not capture most of the people in the community and thus community participation has not been fairly represented. Secondly, due to the previous encounters with the company, some being violent, the people are sometimes intimidated to voice their opinions about certain actions or inactions of the company which affects them. The people sometimes fail to attend such meetings due to the outcomes of previous meetings, which has as it were been, fruitless. What is the point in attending meetings if 'nothing' seems to come out of such meetings? It is simply a waste of my precious time, lamented one of the respondents who is a farmer. Another issue also is that sometimes the chiefs or traditional leaders of these communities become a mouth piece of the company instead of the people. They are unable to speak for their people, probably because the company has made their personal situations better and they would not want to offend them by speaking against them. Thus, they either become lame ducks or advocates for the companies instead of a mouth piece for the people they lead.
>
> *(Nyamadi, 2009)*

The second side to the requirement to consult the community whilst business is running exists in law so far as the company is a going concern. At Common Law the company (a person at law) has a duty not to commit nuisance to adjoining premises of land.[25] That duty is unmoved by the grant of a licence to the company by the authorities. The law does not explicitly provide for regulations on community engagement on sustainable ways to respond to potential threats of the acts or omissions of companies. Nonetheless, where it is self-evident in the nature of the operations of the Company, that their actions will make life unbearable for the stakeholders of the development, it is imperative that all stakeholders be consulted. This is especially so in the environmental domain.

b. Environmental Stewardship

The right to a satisfactory and wholesome environment conducive to community life and business is guaranteed to all citizens.[26] The government, as duty-bearers of this right, enforces its human rights obligations through corporations by subjecting them to environmental regulations. Reminded by the likely adverse effects of business operations on the environment by the natural order of things, corporations assume the responsibility of preserving the environment and are required by law to pursue remedies to reconstitute debilitating parts of the environment. It is an established rule of international law therefore that a government that permits third parties to commit egregious human rights violations against its citizens commits an internationally wrongful act.[27] Governmental vigilance on the actions and omissions of third-party business entities is a component of environmental stewardship under CSR (Idemudia, Kwakyewah, & Muthuri, 2020).

The Ghanaian regulatory framework is fortified with laws that protect the environment and charge third-party corporations to comply with environmental standards. These laws are designed to address the negative impacts of business activities that are inextricably connected to our environmental well-being. Article 36(9) of the 1992 Constitution of Ghana provides that the State shall take appropriate measures needed to protect and safeguard the national environment for posterity; and shall seek cooperation with other states and bodies for purposes of protecting the wider international environment for mankind. Pursuant to this constitutional mandate, Ghana has established the Environmental Protection Agency (EPA). The function of this Agency is to ensure that, overall, the environment is kept safe.

The EPA is a statutory body set up to advise on the formulation of policies on all aspects of the environment and is specifically responsible for ensuring the conduct of Environmental Impact Assessments (EIA), especially when strong public concerns are raised over an intended project. Its potential impacts are extensive and far-reaching (Niber et al., 2015). The major functions of the EPA include ensuring compliance with any laid down *environmental impact assessment procedures* in the initiation and execution of development projects, including compliance in respect of existing projects; and imposing and collecting environmental protection levies.[28]

Case law typifies the mandate of the EPA in controlling the mining activities of mining companies to prevent environmental degradation. The case of *Center for Public Interest Law & Center for Environmental Law vs. Environmental Protection Agency, Minerals Commission and Bonte Gold Mines*[29] is instructive on this mandate. Here, the plaintiffs sued the defendants to compel them to perform their statutory obligations in respect of damage to the environment caused by the mining activities of the third defendant. The 3rd defendant company was a subsidiary company of a Canadian company called Akrokeri Ashanti Gold Mine Inc. registered in Ghana and operating as a mining company along the Bonte River at Bonteso in Ashanti Region until it went into liquidation. The plaintiff argued that it was alerted by a publication and by matters raised during a parliamentary debate about the numerous pond and land degradation caused by the 3rd defendant and wondered if the Minister had remedied the situation. The Minister in response mentioned that it had recognized the shunning of the 3rd defendant company's responsibility for reclamation works. According to the Minister, he had directed the company to submit a Comprehensive Costed Reclamation Plan and to carry out rehabilitation work on the abandoned sites. Workers were therefore sent to the site for investigations. Shortly, the company went into liquidation and disappeared from the country. The extent of the degradation was such that what used to be farmlands ceased to be useable as such. There were uncovered ponds posing dangers to children. River channels were blocked by sediment and a lot of local business activities dependent on the company had ground to a halt.

The plaintiffs sought, *inter alia*, an order for a mandatory injunction directed at the company to remedy the environmental degradation and to compel the 1st and 2nd defendants to take steps necessary for the rehabilitation of the environment caused by the 3rd defendant's mining operations. On the issue of the capacity of the plaintiff to sue, Brown J. noted that the Court has always jealously guarded suits pursued in the public interest and will rarely assist in attempts to exclude such cases on the basis of lack of capacity. In the mind of the court, there was no doubt that the right to a safe environment and the duties imposed statutorily on the defendants is for the benefit of all Ghanaians. The court also found that not only did the Company start operations but continued to do so for eight years without compliance with these strict mandatory provisions under the EPA Act. The EPA, although empowered to ensure compliance, had failed to do so. The court came to the conclusion that there was no dispute that the company breached its statutory obligation to reclaim and rehabilitate the mining area and upon the termination of its operations. The 3rd defendant company had failed to submit the Costed Reclamation Plan and had posted only 38,000 USD out of 1.2 USD. The money was to be used to compensate the victims for its mining operations. The sluggish disposition assumed by the EPA was a renegation of its statutory responsibilities.

The Minerals Commission, in this case, was also held to be jointly and severally liable with the other defendants for the adverse environmental degradation which affected the lives of the people and their property. The Commission had a role to monitor the implementation of government policies on minerals; as such they too had a role to ensure compliance or else revoke the licence.

As regards environmental pollution, in environmental law, the polluter pays principle is enacted to make the party responsible for producing pollution responsible for paying for the damage done to the natural environment. This will include environmental costs, such as the cost of pollution or any other harm caused to the ecology, and not just those that are immediately tangible costs.[30] In 2011, the cabinet of Ghana approved the polluter pays principle as part of efforts to generate additional revenue for environmental management, according to the then Vice President, John Mahama. The principle as accepted in Ghana will provide an opportunity for waste generators to contribute to sustainable financing of waste management services.[31]

The application for an Environmental Permit under the Environment Regulations 1999 (L.I. 1652) features a procedure for community consultation to address the likely human rights environmental impacts. Regulation 10(1) of the law is to the effect that an applicant shall submit an environmental impact statement in respect of the proposed undertaking which shall be outlined in a scoping report to the Agency. Regulation 11 states that a scoping report shall set out the scope or extent of the environmental impact assessment to be carried out by the applicant, and shall include; a draft term of reference, which shall indicate the essential issues to be addressed in the environmental impact statement (human rights issues, resettlement issues, social issues, etc.).[32] According to Regulation 12(k), the draft's terms of reference *must include a consultation with members of the public likely to be affected by the operations of the undertaking.* This ensures that any reservations or objections on the scoping report are made by the people.

It is observed that the CSR regime in environmental stewardship does not permit voluntariness or discretion in the application of the environmental principles. It is unreservedly clear that the negative impact of corporate business on the environment cannot be shelved under a voluntary corporate decision to preserve the environment. The regulation and interaction with the environment are stoutly backed by the law. This outlook is celebratory for the human rights aspect of Corporate Social Responsibility as it confers an entrenched duty on the users of the environment, including corporate bodies, to protect and conserve the resources of the environment.

c. Sustainable Development

Corporations are required by the law to conduct their activities in a way that takes into due consideration, the needs of the present and future generations. This principle is enunciated in the concept of Sustainable Development which has been enthroned as a fundamental human right. The concept is one of the core values of CSR that corporations are mandated to adhere to in accordance with the law.

The Sustainable Development Goals of the United Nations[33] also provide a useful guideline for framing policies aimed at sustainable development. As a member of the United Nations, Ghana has vowed to pursue the sustainable development agenda through the 17 Sustainable Development Goals.

> In December 2017, the then Minister for Planning, Professor Gyan-Baffour, stated that a Technical Committee set up by the government for the implementation of the Sustainable Development Goals (SDGs) had already developed indicators for measuring Ghana's SDG performance. This, he pointed out, has been ratified by the respective Ministries, Departments and Agencies. He also mentioned the fact that the government has aligned

> the SDGs and its targets with Ghana's national development priorities and aspirations.[34]

Out of these 17 SDGs, Goal 8 of the SDGs is most relevant to this discussion. The purpose of Goal 8 is to promote sustained, inclusive, and sustainable economic growth, full and productive employment, and decent work for all. Inclusive economic growth is marked by development on a larger and wider spectrum. It is said to be growth which takes place in the sectors in which the poor work and live. Further, growth is inclusive if it uses the factors of production that the poor possess, which is unskilled labour, and reduces the prices of consumption items that the poor consume.

The laws in Ghana applicable to corporate governance are not distinctively expressive of the concept of sustainable development. However, there are some laws which embody the principles of sustainable development. These principles encapsulate inclusiveness and sustained growth. Notable of them is the local content and local participation rules in the natural resources industry, which are tailored to motivate the inclusion of Ghanaians in sectors dominated by non-Ghanaians.

Local content refers to the 'quantum/percentage of locally produced materials, personnel, financing, goods and services rendered to the … industry and which can be measured in monetary terms' (Petroleum Commission, 2020). In 2017, the Energy Commission (Local Content and Local Participation) (Electricity Supply Industry (ESI)) Regulations, 2017 (L.I. 2354) was passed by the Parliament of Ghana into law.

> The objective of the regulations is to achieve a minimum of fifty-one percent (51%) equity local participation in Ghana with an initial 15% equity participation in local content and also to develop capacity in the manufacturing industry for electrical cables, solar cells, conductors, accessories, etc.
>
> *(Energy Commission, 2020)*

By regulation 3(b) of L.I. 2354, a service provider in activities of electricity supply is obliged by law to ensure that local content and local participation form a part of their activities. Regulation 7(1) of L.I. 2354 provides that the interest of a citizen of Ghana acquired under a contract or subcontract is not transferable to a non-Ghanaian citizen, whilst Regulation 7(2) of L.I. restricts the equity shareholding from being offloaded to a non-Ghanaian.

In the petroleum industry, local content requirements are imposed on holders of petroleum licenses to safeguard the interests of Ghanaian citizens in the sustainable development plan. Local Content is governed by the Petroleum (Exploration and Production) Act, 2016 (Act 919) and the Petroleum (Local Content and Local Participation) Regulations, 2013 (L.I. 2204). Under the law, a licensee, contractor, or sub-contractor is obligated to prepare and implement a local content plan as prescribed and that local content plan shall be submitted to the Commission for approval.[35] The law insists that Contractors shall ensure that Ghanaian citizens who have the requisite expertise are employed.[36] Further, a person carrying out petroleum activities shall in consultation with the Energy Commission prepare and implement plans and programmes to train citizens in all aspects of petroleum activities in accordance with the Regulations and the terms of the licence, petroleum agreement or petroleum subcontract.[37] Provision is made for the mandatory acquisition of materials from Ghanaian companies which are of the same or similar quality as foreign materials, equipment, and consumer goods.[38] The law encourages and facilitates the formation of joint ventures, partnerships, and licensing agreements between indigenous companies and foreign companies. It also creates a local content fund to be used in part to provide funding for indigenous companies in the industry.[39] The fund is exempt from tax.[40]

The laws of Ghana also contain rules for protecting Forestry Resources, which include timber and wildlife, as a measure for sustainable development. For Forestry Resources in Ghana, complete ownership is restricted. The restriction is geared towards the sustainable development of Forestry Resources. For instance, in spite of vesting Stool lands in the Stools, Article 267(3) of the 1992 Constitution states that:

> There shall be no disposition or development of any stool land unless the Regional Lands Commission of the region in which the land is situated has certified that the disposition or development is consistent with the development plan drawn up or approved by the planning authority for the area concerned.

The logical import of this law in terms of forestry resources is precise. Forestry resources on tool land cannot be disposed for exploitation without the consent of the Regional Lands Commission.

The Forestry Commission Act, 1999 (Act 571)[41] makes the Forestry Commission responsible for the regulation of the utilization of forest and wildlife resources, the conservation and management of those resources, and the coordination of policies related to them, which is a manifestation of sustainable development. The understanding of the administration of Forestry Resources by the Forestry Commission is that where the land is rich in forest resources, it is controlled and managed by the State for the benefit of actual landowners and their successive generations.

The CSR principles on sustainable development imprinted in this forestry legal regime relates to the recognition of rights of the indigenes of the local communities, having regard to their long-standing rights in the forestry resources managed by the State. The fact that the president is the trustee of forest resources on behalf of the landowners does not deride the claim of locals to their fundamental entitlements on the land. In reality, the property rights of locals who own forests are merely partially suspended and not terminated by the State. It therefore means that the law makes provision for the enjoyment of their rights, directly or indirectly.

When it comes to direct indigenous rights in relation to forest resources, the people of the community have the right to enter the land and lumber trees or timber for their own use, provided it is not inconsistent with the rights of a company or partnership operating under a Timber Utilisation Contract (TUC) or timber salvage permit. Sections 7(2) and 18(1)(a) of the Timber Resource Management Act, 1997 (Act 547) authorises the Minister to award a Timber Utilization Permit to fell trees for community development. This provision, without reserve, recognizes the inherent rights that the people of the community have, vis-a-vis the forest use rights granted by a corporate body. The corporate body therefore has a role in safeguarding these inherent rights.

The forestry laws of Ghana create rules for compensation for Stool landowners and community people. Regulation 11(d)(i) of the Timber Management Regulation (L.I. 1649) provides that an applicant for timber rights shall submit with the application an undertaking to provide specific social amenities for the benefit of the local communities that live in the proposed contract area. The law in this regard compels the performance of CSR responsibilities that have previously been treated as sheer acts of benevolence. This law, unlike its counterparts, unswervingly regulates the philanthropic aspect of CSR and this is worth commending.

In every legal regime, representation showcases that a group of people have rights which ought to be discussed and respected. In terms of indigenous rights, this is replicated under our laws and is a testament to sustainable development. Section 5(1)(d) of the Timber Resource Management Act provides that the Timber Rights Evaluation Committee shall be composed of the Administrator of Stool Lands, among others. The representation of the Administrator of Stool Lands depicts that the Stool (community) has an indirect say in who should be granted rights in respect of forest resources. They having a say is proof of recognition of rights. In conclusion to this matter, Section 14 of the same Act regulates payment in respect of Stool lands and disburses money to the Stool in exchange for the use of their resources.

The laws of Ghana impose a duty on corporate bodies to undertake mandatory CSR in the Forestry subsector by providing social amenities, which ordinarily cover elements of the SDGs. The implementation of the rest of the SDG goals, however, is a responsibility borne by the Ghanaian government. Nonetheless, corporate bodies motivated enough to improve the lives of the Ghanaian people, voluntarily undertake to assist in the development of the country by aligning their objectives with the SDGs. Asanko Gold, a mining company, in its Corporate Social Responsibility report of 2017, outlines its progress in achieving the SDGs in ways that are very revealing in this regard (Asanko Gold, 2017):

For SDG 1 – **End poverty in all its forms**: Asanko contributed to the prosperity of their local communities and host country through the provision of employment opportunities, supporting local businesses and in-country supply chains with the purchase of goods and services, community investments, and statutory payments to the government.[42]

SDG 2 – **End hunger, achieve food security, and improved nutrition and promote sustainable agriculture**: Asanko supported the development of community-based food projects and invests in skills training to build capacity among subsistence farmers and the local food sector.[43]

SDG 3 – **Ensure healthy lives and promote well-being for all at all ages**: Asanko supported improved health and well-being amongst their workforce and local communities.[44]

SDG 4 – **Ensure inclusive and equitable quality education and promote lifelong learning**: Asanko supported high-quality local educational standards through a set of measures including a literacy program, inter-schools' competitions and the provision of mobile library services.[45]

SDG 5 – **Achieve gender equality and empower all women and girls**: Asanko Gold has a zero-discrimination policy towards recruitment and has implemented female-friendly policies to ensure we attract women to Asanko, including a policy to provide new mothers with nursing assistance at the mine.[46] They also encourage the economic empowerment of women in our local communities.[47]

SDG 6 – **Ensure access to water and sanitation for all**: Asanko is committed to responsible water management and improving access to clean water: In 2017, they drilled four community boreholes and invested 25,000 USD.[48]

SDG 7 – **Promote inclusive and sustainable economic growth, employment, and decent work for all**: Asanko contributed to sustainable economic growth in their local communities and host country through employment, support for the local supply chain of goods and services, community investment, and payments to governments.[49]

Mandatory CSR

It may seem at first blush that the majority of stakeholders in CSR have gone beyond whether CSR is voluntary or mandatory. They have taken for granted the fact that there are no obvious and clear set of CSR principles binding on a company or partnership to contribute to community enhancement in conformity with its intended business goals. We have, as a continent and nation, consciously and unconsciously built CSR on a series of projects, schemes, donations, investments, and programmes.

We have established in this chapter that the CSR the average Ghanaian knows and accepts is that which promotes community development at the mercy of corporate bodies as and when they desire, due to the silence of the lawmaker and the inattention of the executive in making and executing a firm and executable policy and set of laws on Corporate Social Responsibility. However, the situation is more extensive than we think. There are laws which enforce CSR without directly stating so, and this makes CSR in Ghanaian law inappreciable and underwhelming and accounts for the theory that CSR only means voluntarily giving to the community. Even though this chapter has appropriately explained the mandatory and voluntary schemes of CSR by key references to laws and isolated existing policies, the fact still remains that there is no CSR institution in Ghana and we have to infer and read meanings into laws for it: this can be very exhausting for human rights implementation.

The undeveloped CSR institution in Ghana has caused corporate bodies to invent their own CSR objectives on their own accord. The neglect by policymakers and the legislature to concretize CSR has allowed corporations to treat CSR as a philanthropy tactic to win the support of members of the community. Corporations are therefore not inspired to align their objectives to suit social and community development as they are used to the climate of one-off voluntary exercises. However, to solidify public policy objectives and to gain real development outcomes, CSR must be well grounded in legal regulations and directives.

The unguarded attitude of CSR in Ghana and Africa is likely to lead to one or more of the following unfavourable consequences: under-exploitation of community resources; inconsistent CSR initiatives; lack of coordination of CSR projects; lack of community satisfaction; and misuse and misapplication of CSR funds. In strengthening Africa's sustainable development objectives, public policy design should be deliberate and informed, and this definitely includes the structuring of Corporate Social Responsibility. The narrative will only change if we finally commit to regularize CSR. It is important that there is a policy and flowing from it are clear-cut rules as regards its execution and maintenance; the law must reflect what society wants.

Some enthusiasts of CSR policy advocate for a compulsory scheme for CSR on all business vehicles and all corporate activities, on the score of the accelerated progress in the attainment of economic rights in Africa. Others are not so much concerned about the strong-handed approach to regulating CSR but are rather interested in instructions to limit unchecked discretion in areas where CSR regulation is missing. Both factions agree that there should be some form of regulation. The common enemy here is uncontrollable discretion.

Leaning onto the mandatory faction, for a mandatory CSR framework, it is envisioned that Corporate Social Responsibility will impose on all corporate bodies the following rules:

1. Prior community engagement and validation reports as preliminary steps towards the grant of licenses to operate;
2. Community engagement at all intervals during the course of business where there is an intention to extend the scope of work;
3. Mandatory Sustainable Development initiatives, especially towards the environment and the ending of poverty;
4. Mandatory flagship programmes for scholarships to study in Ghanaian schools and universities;

5. Mandatory mentorship and career guidance projects for the youth;
6. Mandatory quotas to Ghanaian citizens in the work force;
7. Mandatory allocation of quotas of all entry-level positions to graduates who have recently completed their service to the nation;
8. Mandatory Ghanaian equity participation in every enterprise;
9. Initiatives to cater to the health needs of the communities; and
10. Gender equity and the prioritization of the needs of the vulnerable and disadvantaged in all programming.

These common themes could be the foundation for a fruitful CSR. However, the concern is that these measures may disincentivize prospective investors and probably catalyze voluntary liquidation of companies that have mixed feelings about the financial terrain in Ghana and the profitability of their enterprises.

An alternative plan will be a design that will scale down discretion, but maintain the voluntary ambitions of corporate bodies eager to implement economically up-lifting projects in sectors where voluntariness is permissible. Thus, rather than leaving everything to the discretion of corporations, the government could insist on a degree of control in the following areas:

1. The people who ought to be beneficiaries of the projects;
2. The frequency of the projects; and
3. The assessment of financial costs of the projects.

Yet still, it is suspected that even these discretionary control measures may not be amusing to corporations because there is the introduction of some executive bird watching. We are doomed if we do not harmonize CSR regulations and we are doomed if we do.

At the international level, there are three key multilateral initiatives aimed at encouraging corporations to make a positive contribution to economic and social progress and to minimize and resolve the difficulties to which their operations may give rise. These initiatives are the *Organisation for Economic Co-operation and Development (OECD) Guidelines for Multinational Enterprises* (OECD, 2011), *the International Labour Organisation (ILO) Tripartite Declaration on Principles Concerning Multinational Enterprises and Social Policy* (ILO, 2017), *and the United Nations Global Compact* (UN Global Compact). The international legal system prescribes for States areas of freedom of actions as well as controls over state actions. Hence the question of CSR can be derived not only in the context of the municipal law of a country like Ghana but also within the context of international law. In the case of CSR, international laws and standards are particularly important because of the international, transnational and global character of the most important corporations (Atuguba & Dowuona-Hammond, 2006).

For international companies with a localized subsidiary in Ghana, these companies ordinarily originate from countries which are members of the

Organisation for Economic Co-operation and Development (OECD). Adhering to the OECD guidelines for multinational enterprises (OECD, 2018, p. 14–18), these foreign-owned companies are generally required to 'Contribute to economic, social and environmental progress with a view to achieving sustainable development' and specifically to:

> Establish and maintain a system of environmental management appropriate to the enterprise, including: (a) collection and evaluation of adequate and timely information regarding the environmental, health, and safety impacts of their activities; (b) establishment of measurable objectives and, where appropriate, targets for improved environmental performance, including periodically reviewing the continuing relevance of these objectives; and (c) regular monitoring and verification of progress toward environmental, health, and safety objectives or targets. Thus, the foreign-owned firms operating in Ghana may be largely driven by the OECD guidelines to engage in CSR.
>
> *(Oppong, 2016)*

As all Mandatory CSR battles a Voluntary CSR, and Voluntary CSR grapples with Discretionary CSR, the dilemma is how to connect the dots and strings through these ideas and find a CSR policy that is suitable for Africa's development trajectory. At least, we have the blueprint of the OECD to roll out a policy for CSR in Ghana.

Conclusion

To beef up the sustainability quotient of Africa's development, and to avoid deficiency pitfalls, public policy design should be deliberate and informed. CSR measures in particular have had encouraging results on rural-community growth, but the argument is that there are no clear guidelines for the supervision of CSR in Africa.

It could be inferred from the posturing of governments such as Ghana's that they intend the nature of CSR to be entirely hinged on the whims of corporate machines, after all, it is a moral commitment. This is a false impression. CSR has laws, but the laws in countries such as Ghana do not showcase CSR in the best way possible; they do not acknowledge CSR definitively. This means, apart from the open voluntariness that comes with some CSR initiatives, there is a lack of orderliness and precision in its governance.

Whether we stand with enthusiasts of CSR policy who advocate for a compulsory scheme for CSR on all business vehicles, or the other school of thought not so much concerned about the strong-handed approach to regulating CSR, but rather instructions to limit the exercise of wide, unchecked discretion, Africa needs a Corporate Social Responsibility Policy which would coagulate a framework to better shape her economies.

We need a head start in investigating the propriety of all mandatory CSR requirements and the uncertainties consequent on it, against the option of making CSR voluntary, with controlled discretion. This is because, CSR is embroidered in the promotion of economic and social human rights, especially in Africa, and its gains could be unmatched.

Notes

1 AN ACT to amend and consolidate the law relating to companies; to establish the Office of the Registrar of Companies; and to provide for related matters.
2 Act 992 by Section 384(1) repeals Act 179 but insists in section 384(2) that, 'despite the repeal of the Companies Act, 1963 (Act 179), the Regulations, by-laws, notices, orders, directions, appointments or any other act lawfully made or done under the repealed enactment and in force immediately before the commencement of this Act, shall be considered to have been made or done under this Act and shall continue to have effect until reviewed, cancelled or terminated.'
3 Income Tax Act, 2015 (Act 896) as amended.
4 Value Added Tax Act, 2013 (Act 870) as amended.
5 Revenue Administration Act, 2016 (Act 915) as amended.
6 Labour Act, 2003 (Act 651).
7 Factories, Offices and Shops Act, 1970 (Act 328).
8 Minerals and Mining Act, 2006 (Act 703).
9 Banks and Specialized Deposit Taking Institutions Act, 2016 (Act 930).
10 Insurance Act 2006 (Act 724). Note that as at December 2020, there was an Insurance Bill before parliament. When it eventually becomes law, it shall replace Act 724.
11 National Communications Authority Act, 2008 (Act 769); Electronic Communications Act of Ghana, 2008 (Act 775) as amended; Electronic Transactions Act, 2008 (Act 772); National Information Technology Agency, 2008 (Act 771); Communications Service Tax Act, 2008 (Act 754) as amended.
12 Renewable Energy Act, 2011 (Act 832).
13 Atuguba, R., Dowuona-Hammond, C. (2006), *supra*, note 1 at page 112.
14 (2004) AHRLR 19 (ACHPR 2003).
15 Communication 267/03.
16 Local Government Act, 1993 (Act 462), sections 1 & 3.
17 High Court, Accra (1994) (Unreported).
18 (No 2) [1977] Ch 106.
19 Article 18(2) of the 1992 Constitution.
20 [1999–2000] 1GLR 474–477.
21 (Avance Ghana, 2019, p. 10).
22 ibid.
23 id., page 11.
24 ibid.
25 *See Mantania v. National Provincial Bank Ltd: CA 1936.*
26 Article 24 of the African Charter on Human and Peoples' Rights.
27 *Velasquez Rodriguez* v. Honduras. Resolution No. 22/86, Case 7920, April 18, 1986, OEA/Ser.L/V/II.68 Doc. 8 rev. 1, 26 September 1986.
28 Section 2 of the EPA Act, 1994 (Act 490).
29 Unreported, HC Suit No. A (EN) 2005, 27 March 2009.
30 Principle 16 of the Rio Declaration on Environment and Development of 1992.
31 Cabinet approves Polluter Pays Principle. Available at: https://www.ghanabusinessnews.com/2011/12/08/cabinet-approves-polluter-pays-principle *last visited*: (2nd August, 2020).
32 Regulation 12 of LI 1652.

33 On 25th September 2015, the United Nations adopted the post-2015 development agenda outlining 17 Sustainable Development Goals to be achieved by 2030.
34 Ghana's Progress Report on SDGs to be submitted to UN General Assembly: https://www.ghanaweb.com/GhanaHomePage/business/Ghana-s-progress-report-on-SDGs-to-be-submitted-to-UN-General-Assembly-607009 *last visited:* (August 2, 2018).
35 Section 63 of Act 919.
36 Section 60(1) of Act 919.
37 Section 60(2).
38 Section 61(1) of Act 919.
39 Section 64 & 65 of Act 919.
40 ibid.
41 AN ACT to re-establish the Forestry Commission in order to bring under the Commission the main public bodies and agencies implementing the functions of protection, development, management and regulation of forests and wildlife resources and to provide for related matters.
42 (Asanko Gold, 201, p. 8).
43 ibid.
44 ibid.
45 id., p. 9.
46 ibid.
47 ibid.
48 ibid.
49 ibid.

References

Adjaye & Ors v. Attorney-General & Ors Suit No.C144/94, 30th March 1994.

African Commission v. Kenya (Endorois case), Communication 276 / 2003 - Centre for Minority Rights Development (Kenya) and Minority Rights Group International on behalf of Endorois Welfare Council v Kenya.

Ansu-Mensah, P., Marfo, E. O., Awuah, L. S. et al. (2021). Corporate social responsibility and stakeholder engagement in Ghana's mining sector: A case study of Newmont Ahafo mines. International Journal of Corporate Social Responsibility, 6, 1. Retrieved from https://link.springer.com/content/pdf/10.1186/s40991-020-00054-2.pdf (Accessed 27 March 2021).

Asanko Gold (2017) *Corporate social responsibility report*, p. 8. Retrieved from https://s24.q4cdn.com/325379252/files/doc_downloads/sustainability/Asanko-2018-CSR-Report.pdf (Accessed 5 March 2021).

Asare v. Ashanti Goldfields and Co [1999-2000] 1 GLR 474-477.

Atuguba, R., & Dowuona-Hammond, C. (2006). *Corporate social responsibility in Ghana.* Final Report submitted to Friedrich Ebert Foundation.

Avance Media (2019). *A comprehensive profiling of the 2019 Top 50 social impact companies in Ghana.* Retrieved from https://avancemedia.org/wp-content/uploads/2019/04/2019-Top-50-Social-Impact-Companies-in-Ghana-Report-Avance-Media-1.pdf (Accessed 28 February 2021).

Cabinet approves Polluter PaysPrinciple. https://www.ghanabusinessnews.com/2011/12/08/cabinet-approves-polluter-pays-principle (Accessed 2 August, 2020).

Democratic Republic of Congo v Burundi & Ors (2004) AHRLR 19 (ACHPR 2003).

Energy Commission (2020). Energy Commission setup by the Energy Commission Act 1997, Act 541. http://energycom.gov.gh/regulation/local-content-and-local-participation-regulations (Accessed 4 March 2021).

Ghana's Progress Report on SDGs to be submitted to UN General Assembly. https://www.ghanaweb.com/GhanaHomePage/business/Ghana-s-progress-report-on-SDGs-to-be-submitted-to-UN-General-Assembly-607009 (Accessed 2 August, 2018).

Idemudia, U. (2007). Community perceptions and expectations: Reinventing the wheels of corporate social responsibility practices in the Nigerian oil industry. *Business and Society Review*, 112(3), 369–405.

Idemudia, U., Kwakyewah, C., & Muthuri, J. (2020). Mining, the environment, and human rights in Ghana: An area of limited statehood perspective. *Business Strategy and the Environment*, 29(7), 2919–2926.

ILO (2017). Tripartite Declaration of Principles concerning Multinational Enterprises and Social Policy, 5th Edition, March 2017, pages 4–16. https://www.ilo.org/wcmsp5/groups/public/---ed_emp/---emp_ent/---multi/documents/publication/wcms_094386.pdf (Accessed 31 December 2021).

Matania v National Provincial Bank [1936] 2 All ER 633.

Mensah Nyamadi, V. (2009). *The role of corporate social responsibility on sustainable development: A case study of the mining community in the Obuasi Municipality* (Master's Thesis). http://uir.unisa.ac.za/bitstream/handle/10500/26993/thesis_nyamadi_vm.pdf?sequence=1&isAllowed=y (Accessed 27 March 2021).

Niber, A., Owusu-Koranteng, H., Owusu-Koranteng, D., & Greenspan, E. M. (2015). The right to decide: Free prior informed consent in Ghana. p. VII, https://s3.amazonaws.com/oxfam-us/www/static/media/files/FPIC_in_Ghana_FINAL.pdf (Accessed 27 March 2021).

OECD (2011). OECD Guidelines for Multinational Enterprises, 2011 Edition, pages 7–60. http://www.oecd.org/daf/inv/mne/48004323.pdf (Accessed 5 March 2021).

OECD (2018). OECD Guidelines for Multinational Enterprises: a Glass Half Full, pages 14–18. https://mneguidelines.oecd.org/OECD-Guidelines-for-MNEs-A-Glass-Half-Full.htm (Accessed 24 January 2022).

Office of the High Commissioner for Human Rights (OHCHR *Fact Sheet No. 37*, page 3)

Oppong, S. (2016). Corporate social responsibility in the Ghanaian context. *Key Initiatives in Corporate Social Responsibility, CSR, Sustainability, Ethics & Governance*. doi:10.1007/978-3-319-21641-6_2.

Petroleum Commission (2020). Petroleum (Local Content and Local Participation) Regulations, 2013 (L.I 2204). https://www.petrocom.gov.gh/local-content/ (Accessed 4 March 2021).

Tito v. Waddell (No 2) [1977] Ch 106.

The ten principles of the UN global impact. https://www.unglobalcompact.org/what-is-gc/mission/principles (Accessed 5 March 2021).

Velasquez Rodriguez v. Honduras. Resolution No. 22/86, Case 7920, April 18, 1986, OEA/Ser.L/V/II.68 Doc. 8 rev. 1, 26 September 1986.

Yeneabat, D. (2015). The right to development under the RTD declaration, African charter on human and people's right and FDRE Constitution: A comparative study. *International Journal of Political Science and Development*, 3(11), 441–453. https://www.academicresearchjournals.org/IJPSD/Abstract/2015/December/Yeneabat.htm (Accessed 27 March 2021).

3

CORPORATE SOCIAL RESPONSIBILITY AND CONFLICTS IN AFRICA

François Lenfant

Introduction

In the past decades, significant scholarly attention has been paid to the role of business in conflict countries, especially in the African context (e.g. Boele, Fabig, & Wheeler, 2001; Wheeler, Fabig, & Boele, 2002). Business was seen as fueling conflict by supporting corrupt governments, funding rebel groups (directly or indirectly), exacerbating community tensions, or polluting the environment and destroying livelihoods (Berdal & Malone, 2000). More recently, the Business for Peace literature has emerged as a multidisciplinary body of knowledge emphasizing the positive role business can play in peace and conflict matters. One of the main tenets of the Business for Peace literature is that by promoting (economic) development, business fosters a climate of peace (Fort and Schipani, 2004; Oetzel, Westermann-Behaylo, Koerber, Fort, & Rivera, 2009). Economic development processes that are fair, sustainable, and inclusive are more likely to promote peace than economic development that exacerbates inequalities and fuels inter-ethnic tensions (Collier, 2008; Stewart, 2000). More generally, sustainable development, embodied by the UN-led Sustainable Development Goals (SDGs) to which business is increasingly expected to contribute, is not merely an economic matter but deals with governance, redistribution, power, and capability issues (Sachs, 2005; Sen, 1999).

The scope of this chapter is to assess where, when, and how international business can contribute to peace in general and to SDG 16 in particular, in the context of (post)-conflict African countries, taking the extractive industry in the Democratic Republic of Congo (DRC) as one example. SDG 16 strives for 'the promotion of peaceful and inclusive societies for sustainable development, the provision of access to justice for all, and building effective, accountable institutions at all levels'. By looking at whether and how business contributes

DOI: 10.4324/9781003038078-4

to achieving SDG 16, this chapter will add to the CSR for development and the Business for Peace literature while explicating whether business contributes to conflict prevention and/or resolution when involved in institution building (Idemudia, 2017).

The 'Business for Peace' literature (Fort & Schipani, 2004; Wengler & Mockly, 2003) covers the contributions of business to promote peace and has been explored from different disciplines, from political science (Bennett, 2002; Haufler, 2004; Wolf, Deitelhoff, & Engert, 2007), to management (e.g. Fort & Schipani, 2004; Nelson, 2000). This body of knowledge has also been studied from different lenses, from companies' reactions to conflict while operating in conflict zones, placing emphasis on 'do no harm policies' or implementing codes of conduct, to companies' generic contribution to a peaceful environment regardless of the (conflict) context. Nevertheless, there is little evidence of business's actual contribution to peace as the 'scholarship on business and peace is decidedly a theoretical enterprise' (Katsos & Forrer, 2014, p. 154). In addition, the 'Business for Peace' literature does not systematically make a distinction between business contribution to positive peace and business contribution to conflict reduction, conflict prevention, or conflict resolution. Positive peace, coined by Galtung (1996), addresses structural causes of violence while negative peace merely refers to the absence of violence. Critics of Business for Peace argued that business is more prone to contribute to negative peace (i.e. stability or absence of violence) rather than to positive peace. This chapter contends that in order to fully contribute to sustainable development and positive peace in conflict areas (both are intrinsically correlated), business ought to take the institutional and governance context more systematically into account and help fill non-market institutional gaps. CSR in (post) conflict countries in Central Africa is not merely about contributing to economic growth, or funding health or education-related projects. It is about contributing, mostly indirectly and collaboratively with other non-state actors, to the emergence of accountable, fair, and inclusive institutions, at all levels of societies.

From CSR in Developing Countries to CSR (and Development) in Africa

In the past decades, the CSR scholarship has evolved from philanthropy to corporate citizenship, corporate political activity, and, more recently, to helping achieve the sustainable Development Goals (Kolk, 2016). The literature has recently paid attention to the manifestation of CSR in different contexts (e.g. Amaeshi, Adi, Ogbechie, & Amao, 2006). Debates around the significance of CSR outside of Western or Northern countries have been the topic of numerous studies. For some, CSR is a disguised Northern strategy serving the interests or reflecting the systems of a company's home country (Idemudia & Ite, 2006; van Tulder & Kolk, 2001). Similarly, West (2006) argues that African values are incompatible with an Anglo-Saxon corporate governance model as

Western type of structures underlying capitalist private companies can be at odds with traditional communitarian African values. Authors have stressed that CSR in Africa requires a value shift 'because deontological (that is, Kantian) ethics emphasize autonomy (that is, the individual), they are largely at odds with sub-Saharan African value systems that typically emphasize the group (heteronomy) rather than the self' (Pratt, 1991, p. 537).

Despite a growing literature on the scope and diverse manifestations of CSR in developing countries, including a political role for business (Reinecke & Ansari, 2016), a recent study argues that CSR primarily consists of philanthropy, charities, and donations to communities (Delbard, 2020). In the context of Africa, Visser (2006) reviewed Carrol's pyramid and suggested that CSR should pay attention to economic development instead of being focused on philanthropy and charity. Taking South Africa as an example, the importance of local charity is evidenced by the large number of funds set up by mining companies, which symbolizes the tradition of mining companies' culture of giving (Kapelus, 2002). Scholars have criticized the failure of CSR to address fundamental issues such as youth unemployment and wealth redistribution, precisely because they are highly political issues (Irwin, 2003). Nevertheless, governance aspects linked to the apartheid regime and its interaction with foreign firms were on the agenda from the 1960's through the 1980's (Malone & Goodin, 1997). Ethical issues surrounding foreign businesses' reaction vis-a-vis the apartheid regime and its discriminatory nature, disinvesting or not, the role of home countries, the role and responsibilities of international companies in bringing about change, were at the core of the debates on CSR. When the apartheid ended, the focus of CSR in South Africa shifted to unemployment and affirmative action through Black Empowerment and HIV-Aids (Kapelus, 2002; Hammann, 2003). The example of South Africa illustrates the potential (and difficulties) of including governance and broader political matters into CSR. On the one hand, scholars argue that CSR in South Africa had been transformed after the apartheid, i.e. its definition had broadened and it was aligned with the South African government transformative agenda, mostly in the employment sphere, through the Black Empowerment movement (Irwin, 2003). On the other hand, other scholars contend that CSR in South Africa was (and still is) overly concerned with charity and philanthropy (Kapelus, 2002; Delbard, 2020).

The important role of the state in creating an enabling environment for CSR to thrive in Africa has also been documented (Idemudia & Ite, 2006; Ite, 2004) and is a growing area of interest for the political CSR literature (Scherer, Palazzo, & Seidl, 2013). Regarding CSR in Nigeria, another African country where CSR has been extensively studied, the literature has focused on the extractive industry, and especially the role of Shell (Eweje, 2007; Idemudia & Ite, 2006; Idemudia, 2009; Ite, 2004, 2005, 2007; Wheeler et al., 2002). Shell's CSR efforts failed to contribute to development because their vision of sustainable development was not based on a Human Rights framework (Wheeler et al., 2002) and because Shell grappled with the historical and environmental tensions in the Niger Delta where institutions have a tradition of failing to deliver on their promises and to promote development (Ite, 2007). The role of government is, again, critical as Ite (2004, p. 9) points out that 'if the macro-economy is under-performing due to government institutional failure, there is a likelihood that the contributions of business to poverty alleviation may fail to achieve the desired outcomes.'

Linked to the literature on the role of the state and CSR in Africa, an emergent scholarship has paid attention to CSR in institutional voids. It contends that in such contexts, the role played by governance is not sufficiently included (Campbell, 2006). Many countries in Africa are hampered by weak institutions, or institutional voids, (Ahen & Amankwah Amoah, 2018) and crucial components of good governance such as voice and accountability, rule of law, and control of corruption are missing (Kaufmann, Kraay, & Mastruzzi, 2008). One strand of scholarship has looked at channels through which companies engage in the public arena, namely through Corporate Political Activities revealing patterns of influencing politicians for private gains, based on a logic of duality and reciprocity (Liedong, Aghanya, & Rajwani, 2020). Other scholars have also questioned the political dimension of CSR because of the lack of checks and balances and accountability mechanisms which makes companies de facto governors over communities (Ahen & Amankwah Amoha, 2018), a process facilitated by governments' lack of capabilities, or interest, in providing services to their population, as is the case in the DRC. It must be stated that most studies looking at CSR as a channel to help fill institutional gaps, typically consider failing market institutions, and not necessarily governmental, public institutions, although both are interrelated. Overall, there is a tendency in the CSR literature to oversimplify the 'institutional gap' issue by failing to consider the variety of institutional forms, often hybrid, in each of the 54 African countries (Hammann et al., 2020). Although attempts have been made to include themes such as conflict and institutional gaps in the CSR agenda (Deitelhoff & Wolf, 2010; Jamali & Mirshak, 2010), the precise nature (i.e. activity type), and scope of business responsibility (i.e. firm, community, country) in complex environments marked by poor governance in Africa remains largely unclear. In the same line of thought, how CSR relates to state building formation, to public institution building, or to enhancing the rule of law has been underexposed in the literature.

Limitations of CSR in Africa: The Resource Curse

Critiques of CSR contribution to development refer to the inherent subordination of development to the business agenda (Idahosa, 2002; Frynas, 2005), unequal power relations between companies and stakeholders (Idahosa, 2002), failure to include a social justice narrative or to tackle root causes of problems (Hammann & Kapelus, 2004), or to address powerlessness and voicelessness issues (Idahosa, 2002; Idemudia, 2009). Others argue that CSR undermines government capacity (Kapelus, 2002), suffers from a technical/managerial approach, is isolated from larger development plans (Idemudia & Ite, 2006; Ite, 2004), or is a new form of clientelism (Rajak, 2008). Authors also allude to the bolt-on nature of CSR activities instead of being built-in, and to a company focus on positive duties to the detriment of negative injunction duties (Idemudia, 2009; Ite, 2007). CSR falls short of delivering on its developmental promise because it is reproducing skewed patterns of dependency and power abuses (Rajak, 2008). Furthermore, companies do not show much concern for governance-related issues while governance reforms at national (macro) level are intertwined with corporate governance at micro level, which should lead to the institutionalization of ethics in organizations (Rossouw, 2005). Campbell (2003, p. 1) also argues that 'the quality of governance of a country is a key determinant for the development outcomes of extractive industries activities.' Business, especially in the extractive sector in Africa, has often benefited from governance failures (Reed, 2002; Watts, 2005; Idemudia, 2008).

At the heart of the conversation on CSR constraints in Africa, lies the resource curse given the abundance of natural resources in the continent (e.g. Collier & Hoeffler, 2004; Gilberthorpe & Papyrakis, 2015). Within that body of literature, the resource curse is associated with conflict, poor governance, and regulatory gaps, which induces rent-seeking behaviour, uneven redistribution of revenues, and patron–client relationships (Collier & Hoeffler, 2004; James, 2015). Conversely, studies have also emphasized the crucial role that sound institutions play in avoiding the resource curse (Kolstad, 2009; Sarmidi, Law, & Jafari, 2014). Well-enforced property laws, low corruption levels, and a good functioning justice system can prevent rent-seeking behaviour (Gilberthorpe & Papyrakis, 2015). Typically, in countries suffering from the resource curse, revenues derived from minerals decrease state reliance on tax levied from citizens which reduces public accountability (Ross, 2001). In a context of government's inability to turn revenues derived from resources into the provision of public services, resource abundance is likely to trigger grievances and violence (Mehlum, Moene, & Torvik, 2006). When operating in resource-rich countries, business is often caught in the crossfire of conflict, and can become negatively involved by 'financing conflict parties, trading conflict relevant goods and exploiting regulatory gaps' (Wolf et al., 2007, p. 295). Abundant literature highlighted how corrupt government leaders attracted foreign investments and colluded with companies to the detriment of their population (Frynas & Wood, 2001, on Angola; Reno, 1998, on Nigeria; Soares de Oliveira, 2007, on Gabon and Equatorial Guinea; Keen, 2003, on Sierra Leone). In the DRC, Montague (2002) has documented the role played by a few foreign mining companies negotiating future lucrative deals with the Kabila-led AFDL rebel group in 1996 before the latter gained power over the DRC.

Context of the DRC

The DRC has been ravaged by conflicts in the past decades. Despite formal peace agreements in 2006 and 2008, bouts of violence have continued to occur regularly, especially in the Eastern provinces. The DRC is a clear example of a fragile country trapped in a vicious cycle of conflict, poverty, and poor governance. The DRC is marked by partly missing institutions at 'market' level (product, labour, and capital) and at the level of contract enforcement and regulation (or lack thereof) within an overall climate of dysfunctional governance structures (Kolk & Lenfant, 2015). The institutional context is characterized by a complex mix of 'formal' and 'informal', of 'legal' and 'illegal' spheres, in which customary, state as well as 'practical' norms may be applied. Taxes are, for example, levied by the state; by the traditional authorities (the Mwami), often in kind; and by rebel groups (through illegal toll). More generally, the Congolese state lacks the capacity to control its territory. The army as an institution fails to protect the population, and is often the source of insecurity. The DRC's enormous wealth of natural resources has benefited a few powerful individuals and continues to feed numerous armed factions rather than contributing to the development of the population. Access to crucial resources such as land and minerals continue to provide the backdrop against which conflicts are played out. The conflict history reveals a pattern of foreign meddling in eastern DRC through proxy forces, i.e. a plethora of rebel groups that coerce local population groups to exploit local mines. This ongoing war economy, despite a multitude of mechanisms to trace minerals and try to prevent such practices, undermines the stability of the entire sub region (Lemarchand, 2009; Vlassenroot & Raymaekers, 2004).

CSR in the Extractive Industry in Africa: The Role of CSR Standards in 'Curbing' the Resource Curse

The last decades have witnessed the emergence of many Corporate Responsibility standards and initiatives in the extractive sector that are aimed at improving business conduct in conflict and low governance areas. The goal of such standards is to cut potential sources of income of warring parties given that many conflicts are motivated by gaining control over regions with abundant natural resources or are sustained by payments made from these resources. Some standards are global in nature (Kimberley Process Certification Scheme, KPCS) while others are regional/national. For instance, the International Conference of the Great Lakes Region Mineral Tracking and Certification Scheme, (ICGLR) covers the Great Lakes region while ITRI Tin Supply Chain Initiative, (iTSCI) started in the DRC and now covers four countries in the Great Lake region. Standards are often product related (Gold Free Standard deals with gold, KPCS deals with diamonds, iTSCI deals with 3T, tin, tantalum, and tungsten). All standards refer to the OECD Due Diligence Guidance for Responsible Supply Chains of Minerals from Conflict-Affected and High-Risk Areas (OECD guidance), which is the most authoritative guideline related to conflict commodities. The OECD guidance encourages companies to (a) establish strong management systems, (b) identify risks in their value chain (c) design and implement a strategy to respond to those risks (d) carry out independent audits; and (e) reporting on their supply chain Due Diligence. By adhering to the guidance, it is assumed that companies will most likely respect human rights and avoid contributing to conflict.

Corporate responsibility standards associated with conflict commodities typically have a traceability and certification component based on risks assessment and/or chain of custody, with third-party audit throughout the value chain. Some of these private corporate responsibility standards address the lack of regulatory framework, which is a pattern in Central African resource-rich countries, such as the DRC, by encouraging proper corporate behaviour beyond law adherence. Rules and regulations stipulated within these CSR standards, which cover many issues such as environmental protection, community relocation, or due diligence practices in value chains, substitute or complement (often failing) public legal frameworks. In that light, it is striking to observe the interaction between CSR private standards and the public domain, such as laws and institutions, which illustrates the blurring boundaries between private and public governance already observed in the literature (Crane, 2010). While most standards are voluntary, some have been integrated into national legislation (ICGLR) or have a sanction regime (KPCS). In the case of the ICGLR, some elements of the standard (such as the Regional Certification Manual) have been taken into the national legislation of the DRC. The ICGLR, which started as a voluntary scheme, requires that economic actors involved in the chain of custody in the Great Lakes region exercise due diligence to ascertain that the mineral chain is free from support for non-state armed groups that illegally control mine sites or otherwise control transportation routes. The scheme provides for mine inspections, certification mechanisms, and for independent audits. Consequently, the DRC Mining Ministry published a list of green and red mining sites in North and South Kivu. Minerals from sites flagged red are not conflict free and cannot be traded.

Recent studies have shown that such standards have contributed to improving transparency and accountability from suppliers in various mineral value chains, yet they have failed to deliver on their promise of making value chains in the DRC conflict free (Pole Institute, 2019). The reason accounting for this failure is their inability to tackle the underlying issues that have hampered the mining sector to flourish and become an engine for growth and development: The lack of strong and accountable governance institutions. Such standards are based on a due diligence approach, inspired by technocratic, and technological solutions (such as blockchain, which facilitates the monitoring of the minerals from the mine to Northern markets), whereby the risks to be assessed are primarily the risk to the company as opposed to the risk of a company fueling conflict. Such methods, designed in northern, developed countries, are not suitable in the messy context of predatory state authorities, as present in the DRC. Cases of sealed bags of minerals being smuggled into bordering countries (such as Rwanda), or certification labels being tampered with and sold in markets have been reported and illustrate the ineffectiveness of such schemes. As long as corruption permeates many levels of society and a climate of lawlessness prevails, business adherence to such schemes will not reduce conflict or contribute to positive peace or development.

In the same line of thought, recent studies have demonstrated that certification systems meant to label a mine 'conflict free' are fraught with intractable issues. For instance, a recent report (Pole Institute, 2019) has demonstrated the limits of a methodology consisting of ranking mines green, orange, or red based on an audit following the guidelines as stipulated by existing standards. In many cases, mines 'declared green' were still under the formal control of armed groups. Armed groups had physically disengaged from the 'green' mines during the audit by not being present directly in the mine site, yet came back shortly thereafter. In addition, the report pointed at some perverse side effects of these standards. Indeed, armed groups have an incentive in keeping the mines child-labour and 'conflict' free (or creating the illusion that mines are conflict and child labour free) precisely to maintain the 'green' label that allows them to export to markets and thus generate revenues. This shows the limitations of certification/labelling systems in complex areas where low governance, the absence of rule of law, and a history of exploitative practices (from colonial powers to the Mobutu-led state, to rebel groups[1]) make it extremely challenging, if not impossible, for business to reduce conflict in the absence of legitimate accountable institutions (such as fair justice, transparent customs officers, free press with a strong monitoring role, to name a few).

More broadly, scholars point at a culture of compliance whereby the whole certification process is reduced to a 'tick the box exercise' at a micro level, (i.e. firm risk level) to the detriment of tackling the issue at stake at the macro level (i.e. conflict level, linked to absent or non-functioning state institutions) (Rasche, 2010; de Bakker, Rasche, & Ponte, 2019). In the same line of thought, Rasche (2010, p. 285) suggests that 'there can be no predefined checklist according to which an auditor can "simply", and without much reflection, verify whether a facility complies with the standard.' Confirming the point made above, a Global Witness representative engaged at an OECD-led conference on conflict minerals suggested that 'all these initiatives, based on paper work and bureaucratic check box exercises, create the illusion that the companies have done everything they could to prevent damages, but do not fundamentally alter anything on the ground'. Rephrasing Rasche (2010, p. 287), 'at best, standards can give corporations an idea about where reflections need to start and which issues are at stake. At worst, standards promote a "going-by-the-book" and "tick-the-boxes" attitude towards corporate responsibility, which has a marginal, if any, effect on real-life practices'. Despite the multistakeholder nature of many CSR standards and the laudable attempts to tackle complex conflict-related issues found in value chains in Central Africa, such standards do not deliver on their promise because of their technical nature, their failure to take the fragile context into account, and their inability to enact structural changes and to transform institutional gaps.

CSR and SDG 16 in Low Governance Areas: What Then?

Before diving into the interaction between CSR and SDG 16, it may be wise to briefly touch upon the Business for Peace literature in order to identify possible linkages. The Business for Peace literature has identified five channels through which companies can foster a peaceful environment, namely promoting economic development, engaging in track-two diplomacy, adopting principles of external valuation, contributing to a sense of community, and conducting conflict risk assessments (Forrer & Katsos, 2015, Oetzel et al., 2009). The first channel, promoting economic development, deals with companies' core business of producing economic gains. When promoting an economic development model that is inclusive, provides fair wages and meaningful employment, transfers skills and capabilities, and creates spillover effects on local businesses, business is more likely to contribute to sustainable development and peace (Fort & Schipani, 2004). The second channel is track two diplomacy, which refers to informal conflict resolution efforts undertaken by non-state actors, which can offer a space for dialogue between warrying parties. Such cases are not common (Oetzel, Getz, & Ladek, 2007) although companies acting as brokers between two parties have been documented, such as Heineken in Burundi (Lenfant, 2016). The third channel concerns the adoption of principles of external valuation, which is similar to standards. Doing so, companies set standards for governments to follow and enable the creation of institutions supporting the rule of law, which will foster trust among trading parties and, thus, reduce conflict likelihood (Forrer & Katsos, 2015). As previously mentioned, this channel has not been highly effective in the minerals value chain in the DRC, but still holds potential in other industries (such as the sporting industry), and relatively stable contexts. The fourth channel is the contribution of business to a sense of community (Fort & Schipani, 2004). It assumes that companies foster a sense of 'togetherness' among employees by offering contact and providing a venue to voice their concerns. Finally, companies can undertake conflict risk assessments (Anderson, 2008). Given the complexities of investing in conflict-affected regions, companies' operations can unintentionally exacerbate existing tensions through their procurement or human resources policies (e.g. by unwillingly hiring staff from or doing business with certain groups or communities). The main issue with the five channels identified by the Business for Peace literature is that they are rather generic and do not unpack in high level of detail what fair wages are (channel 1), when to engage in track two diplomacy, and how (channel 2), or explicate in details how will the adoption of external valuation lead to the creation of accountable institutions. As previously mentioned, given the number of (latent) conflicts in the African context, especially in the DRC, which are often fueled or made possible by the absence of accountable institutions, specifying *how* business can contribute to the emergence of accountable institutions (i.e. justice, good governance, legitimate local, regional and national authorities, free press, sense of citizenship to name a few) becomes crucial.

Table 3.1 enumerates all the targets related to SDG 16 and illustrates the different areas in which business can contribute to its realization. One linkage between business contribution to SDG 16 and the Business for Peace literature is business intervention modality. Business can intervene directly (refrain from paying bribery, or publicly condemn a corrupt officer, in case of corruption) or indirectly (adhere to an anti-corruption standard) as well as unilaterally or collaboratively. Collaborative interventions are considered more effective in low governance areas given the complex sets of issues with which business is confronted, and because companies can benefit from the skills of other actors, such as non-governmental organizations (NGOs) (Oetzel et al., 2007). Furthermore, when involving NGOs, communities and governments in partnerships, companies are 'facilitating the development of institutional capacity and ensuring the sustainability of their CSR initiatives' (Idemudia, 2007, p. 400). Besides the intervention modality, the literature has also made a distinction between business activities at the company level (workplace/core business), at community level (mostly through project funding), and at society level (mostly through lobby and advocacy) (Nelson, 2000; Oetzel et al., 2009).

When looking at the possible contribution of CSR to the realization of SDG 16 targets, one can observe the following patterns. Most contributions are indirect and collaborative, which confirms the findings of previous research (Kolk & Lenfant, 2012). The SDG targets where business contribution is considered high and is both direct and indirect include reducing corruption (target 5), fighting child labour (target 2), and fighting discrimination (target 12). Regarding the fight against discrimination, promoting and enforcing non-discriminatory practices and policies are activities that can directly be executed at the workplace. Inclusive of employment practices, based on merit, which benefit the youth from villages surrounding companies' operations have the potential of sowing the seeds of good governance, and breaking century-old patron–client relationships.

Kolk and Lenfant (2018) have shown the challenges that mining companies experienced when deciding on the allocation of jobs because of their relationship with and the power allocated to (corrupt) local chiefs who distributed jobs based on patron–client relationships. By hiding behind the authority of a (illegitimate) local chief when redistributing developmental benefits (such as employment or community development projects), and not speaking out against those abuses, companies fuel tensions and create conflicts. The case of BANRO, a Canadian company that has won awards for its social performance, presents similar characteristics. BANRO based its dislocation plan on an institutional framework (the DRC mining code) that was not favourable to communities, instead of using other more legitimate frameworks from the World Bank or the United Nations. Furthermore, the process was highly procedural and technical in that BANRO sent engineers with rather sophisticated tools to measure the size of the fields and/or the size of the cultures. Compensation scales, counting methods, as well as the overall process were designed (in a technocratic manner) by the company with the support of corrupt local authorities, which fuelled resentment among

TABLE 3.1 Interaction Business Role in Promoting SDG 16 According to the B4P Literature

SDG 16 target (# 12)	*Role*	*Channel – activity type*
1. Reduce violence	**Limited/** indirect	**Workplace**: developing policies against all forms of violence; publicly condemning violence (leading by example – *unilateral*) **Community**: funding community projects/ awareness raising (*collaborative*) **Society**: lobby, campaign government (*unilateral and collaborative*)
2. Protect children	**High** indirect and direct	**Workplace**: adhere to CSR codes and legislation; develop policies against all forms of child abuse; demand standard adherence from suppliers in the value chain (leading by example – *unilateral*) **Community**: project funding (i.e. alternative livelihoods to mining, awareness raising) (*collaborative*) **Society**: lobby, campaign government (*collaborative and unilateral*)
3. Promote rule of law and justice	**Limited** indirect	**Workplace**: adhering to the law, support emergence of accountable institutions (leading by example: unilateral) **Community:** awareness-raising project (*collaborative* with knowledgeable NGOs) **Society**: lobby, campaign government (*collaborative*)
4. Combat organize crime and illicit financial arms and flows	Limited indirect	**Workplace:** commitment to not be involved in criminal activities or in funding arm flows; adherence to codes/legislation (leading by example: *unilateral*) **Community**: awareness project funding (*collaborative*) **Society**: lobby, campaign government (*collaborative*)
5. Reduce corruption and bribery	High indirect and direct	**Workplace**: commitment to combat corruption activities; adherence to codes/legislation (leading by example: *unilateral*); enforcing codes and good practice through the value chain **Community**: awareness project funding, encourage citizen-led coalition to demand the end of corruption practices at all levels of society to and the proper utilization of tax payer's money into public goods; (*collaborative*) **Society**: lobby, campaign government, speak out against abuses (*unilateral* and *collaborative*)

(*Continued*)

TABLE 3.1 (Continued)

SDG 16 target (# 12)	*Role*	*Channel – activity type*
6. Develop effective, accountable and transparent institutions	Limited indirect	**Workplace**: awareness raising (lead by example: *unilateral*) **Community**: awareness project funding, fund citizen-led coalition (*collaborative*) **Society**: lobby, campaign government (*collaborative and unilateral*)
7. Ensure responsive, inclusive and represent decision-making	Limited indirect	**Workplace**: awareness raising (leading by example: *unilateral*) **Community**: awareness project funding (*collaborative*) **Society**: lobby, campaign government (*collaborative and unilateral*)
8. Strengthen participation in global governance	Very limited indirect	**Society**: lobby at UN, together with other business, NGOs (*collaborative and unilateral*)
9. Provide universal legal identity	Limited indirect	**Workplace**: awareness raising (leading by example: *unilateral*) **Community**: awareness project funding (*collaborative*) **Society**: lobby, campaign government (*collaborative and unilateral*)
10. Ensure public access to info and protect fundamental freedoms	Medium indirect	**Workplace**: awareness raising (leading by example: *unilateral*) **Community**: awareness raising/engaging citizen-led coalitions/fund press (*collaborative*) **Society**: lobby, campaign government, speak out against abuses (*collaborative and unilateral*)
11. Strengthen national institutions to prevent violence/ combat crime	Limited indirect	**Workplace**: awareness raising (leading by example: *unilateral*) **Community**: awareness raising/engaging citizen led coalitions (*collaborative*) **Society:** lobby, campaign government, speak out against abuses (*collaborative and unilateral*)
12. Promote and enforce non-discriminatory laws and policies	High direct and indirect	**Workplace**: develop policies, condemn discrimination; publish reports on non-discriminatory practices; adherence to codes/ legislation; enforcing codes and good practice through value chain (lead by examples: *unilateral*) **Community**: awareness project funding, encourage citizen led coalition to demand the end of discrimination practices (*collaborative*) **Society**: lobby, campaign government, speak out against abuses (*unilateral and collaborative*)

the local population. In a context of the absence of state authority to cater to its citizens, marked by conflicts between local chiefs over land, power, and identity, BANRO found itself embroiled in a web of complex relationships characterized by illegitimate leadership and community manipulation. This case study highlights the challenges for companies operating in low-governance areas, extending earlier research suggesting that what companies do in low governance, (post) conflict areas in Africa is less important than how and with whom they do it (Kolk & Lenfant, 2018).

Concerning protecting children, companies can take a public stance (lobby) against child labour, commit not to employ children (core business/workplace), not only sign but also fully comply with standards and codes, or fund projects to deter child labour in mining sites (given the prevalence of child labour in the mining sector in the DRC). For that matter, PACT, a US-based NGO, and Apple, are engaged in a program aimed at making six mining sites in the DRC child labour free through funding alternative livelihood opportunities and vocational skills projects as well as sensitizing the broader mining communities (through theatre and films) of the importance for children to remain in school. Such projects are instrumental in inducing behavioural changes at individual and community levels. However, when implemented in isolation, without taking the broader context into account, such projects run the risk of creating frustration in the absence of a well-functioning job market, or when employment is provided within a patronage system. In that light, when combining efforts with other actors (non-state and governmental) and adopting multiple strategies (lobby, project funding, leading by example) at various levels (workplace, community, and society) business efforts are likely to have more impact.

Regarding combating corruption, the role business can play can take many forms, one, obviously being the adoption of an irreproachable ethical behaviour by not giving in the temptation to bribe, the others, subtler and politically savvy, consist in engaging the government on its behaviour, funding zero-tolerance campaigns, and encouraging the workforce, as well as surrounding communities, to speak out against corruption. In the context of the DRC, many NGO reports indicate that companies' practices are not always corruption free, as corruption permeates all spheres of society (Pole Institute, 2019). Other activities range from demanding code adherence and impeccable behaviour throughout the value chain, to funding citizen-led coalitions to pressure governmental authorities to adequately use tax payer's money to fund public goods. These findings somewhat resonate with a study of multinationals operating in Africa which showed that most strategies companies deployed to address corruption were self-regulation, and corporate policy and processes (Luiz & Stewart, 2014), although the 'public' dimension of speaking out, or lobbying, against corruption practices was not prominent. The same study concluded that despite the prevalence of corruption, firms can institutionalize ethical foundations rather than profit from weak institutional arrangements that perpetuate corruption (Luiz & Stewart, 2014).

Finally, given the importance of taxation in (post) conflict countries in Africa, especially in countries suffering from the resource curse, companies should not only behave like 'good citizens' and avoid tax evasion but should be clear about how much is paid to which government entity and on which basis tax calculations were made (volumes, sales, perimeter of the mine, etc.). Simply 'paying taxes as a legal requirement' is not sufficient. Companies ought to unpack exactly, and show in detail, the amounts paid to central governments, regional governments and local authorities. In the same line of thought, companies should encourage local village and civil society leaders to push for transparency from the authorities and demand accountability about the allocation of tax revenues received from the mining industry.

Business contribution to all other SDG 16 targets is limited, although some business-led activities may be powerful. Concerning the reduction of violence (target 1), the unilateral contribution of business is quite minimal: it can indirectly lead by example through developing policies against all forms of violence in the workplace and publicly condemning violence perpetrated by all types of actors, including governments. However, direct interventions are also possible. In Burundi, the case of Heineken opening the doors of its brewery to ethnic minorities being harassed and threatened to be killed is another (rare) example of business directly preventing violence (Homé, 2006). More generally, this entails a public role that companies ought to embrace to increase their credibility as actors genuinely committed to improving the institutional setting in which sustainable development can take place, by lobbying governments or promoting the voice of citizens to be heard. Similarly, ensuring public access to info and protecting fundamental freedoms (target 10) is also essentially a matter of lobbying. Business can use its political clout towards government, but also through strengthening national institutions and stimulating the emergence of a vibrant civil society. Finally, it must be stressed that business involvement, even in an indirect and collaborative manner, in the promotion of the rule of law and justice, or in the development of effective, accountable, and transparent institutions also depends on the company's capacities and legitimacy. Companies with an impeccable track record, a history of positive engagement with local communities, and a politically oriented CSR considering the complex context are more likely to have an impact. In that light, companies' contribution to sustainable development requires specific sets of skills and human resources (infused with empathy and sensitivity), and not merely technical, financial, or engineering expertise.

Conclusion and Discussion

This chapter reviewed the contribution of CSR to SDG 16 in low governance areas in Africa, such as in the DRC. Taking CSR standards in the extractive industry as an example, this chapter has shown the potential, yet limitations, of business initiatives to support the emergence of accountable, fair, and just institutions in fragile contexts marked by institutional gaps. This chapter has also added to the Business for Peace literature by specifying, in some level of detail, how business can contribute to the realization of SDG 16. This chapter has also demonstrated that CSR standards in the extractive sector fall short of delivering on their sustainable development and conflict reduction promises because they are based on a technical, 'check the box' exercise, and ignore the messy and complex institutional context of the Democratic Republic of Congo, a country marked by the absence of functioning state authorities.

This modest contribution exemplifies the challenges of contributing to SDG 16 and promoting accountable institutions in a messy, complex environment marked by historical injustice and predatory state authorities. Doing so, this chapter warns for oversimplification of the potential role of business to interfere in areas of low governance in Africa. Scholarship on CSR in Africa tends to overlook the diversity of the continent, economically, politically, and institutionally (Hammann et al., 2020). While CSR in Africa scholarship systematically refers to business challenges being linked to institutional voids, the voids are mostly defined in terms of their opposition to Western institutions (Bothello, Nason, & Schnyder, 2019). In addition, this chapter confirms that business modest contribution to SDG 16 and to positive peace manifests itself through co-creating conditions that can enable the emergence of accountable institutions, be it a fair justice system, ethical leadership, or absence of corruption.

More broadly, this chapter highlighted the evolving role of companies vis-à-vis poorly functioning government and state institutions, which called for the attribution of a political role to business (Reinecke & Ansari, 2016). CSR activities in weak institutional settings cannot be oblivious to governance issues such as corruption, as these reinforce poor governance and further undermine state capacities (Dobers & Halme, 2009). When operating in contexts of dysfunctioning governments that fail to provide public goods for their citizens, companies may face pressure to assume (some) governmental functions which may lead to undermining government authority (Ite, 2005). In the same line of thought, scholars question whether companies are 'knowledgeable and capable … of resolving endemic postcolonial developmental problems, or of navigating local social, ethnic, and political fault lines' (Ford, 2015, p. 456). This chapter has demonstrated that the developmental role of business in highly complex institutional environments is not to 'resolve endemic postcolonial problems' but to take this historical context into account and help build accountable and solid public institutions, which will, in turn, facilitate the promotion of sustainable development.

When there are 'no legitimate' and functioning government capacities present, such as in the DRC, companies cannot be expected to support (or even work with) corrupt, human rights-violating authorities. This chapter contends that business is not to sit on the chair of government, yet has the possibility, under certain conditions (i.e. when it is well embedded in communities, has an excellent track record in the country and has a far-reaching network), to foster the emergence of public institutions at various levels, community, regional, and national. Business intervention in such public matters is best suited when it is done in a collaborative and indirect manner, through lobby, or citizen network funding. Despite the fact that most business interventions are located outside of their core business and entail lobby and advocacy work for the public good (i.e. not for its own private gains), it becomes clear that business contribution to SDG 16 is primarily and essentially a matter of leading by example and of contributing to the emergence of accountable institutions, by inducing behavioural change, speaking out publicly, and funding/supporting civil society.

In the same line of thought, this chapter has demonstrated that corporate political activity (CPA), as a manifestation of CSR, has to be approached beyond a company-centric approach. In that light, CPA entails using firm clout to influence the institutional context by contributing to the emergence of accountable and fair institutions, not with the sole purpose to enhance firm performance (or take advantage of institutional gaps) although, in the long run, an accountable institutional context will benefit all firms (which could raise 'free riders' issues). Referring back to the Business for Peace literature, companies' potential contribution to peace has been studied from a utilitarian perspective (it is in their interest) but also from a deontological perspective, (it is the moral thing to do) as well as a teleological perspective (peace is a common good inherent to all human activities, including business) (Oetzel et al., 2009). It is time for the teleological and deontological perspectives to become dominant as to prove the Business for Peace theory right in conflict and low governance areas, such as in the DRC.

Note

1 The DRC is the only country in the history of the world that was the private property of a king (King Leopold 2), which opened the doors to many abuses and human rights violations whose impact is still felt today.

References

Ahen, F., & Amankwah-Amoah, J. (2018). Institutional voids and the philanthropization of CSR practices: Insights from developing economies. *Sustainability, 10*(7), 2400.

Amaeshi, K. M., Adi, B. C., Ogbechie, C., & Amao, O. O. (2006). Corporate Social Responsibility in Nigeria: Western mimicry or indigenous influences? *Journal of Corporate Citizenship, 24*, 83–99.

Anderson, M. (2008). False promises and premises: The challenge of peace building for corporations. In O. F. Williams (Ed.), *Peace through commerce: Responsible corporate citizenship and the ideals of the United Nations global compact* (pp. 119–132). Notre Dame, IN: University of Notre Dame Press.

Bennett, J. (2002). Multinational corporations, social responsibility and conflict. *Journal of International Affairs, 55*(2), 393–410.

Berdal, M., & Malone, D. M. (Eds.). (2000). *Greed and grievance: Economic agendas in civil wars*. Boulder, CO: Lynne Rienner Publishers.

Boele, R., Fabig, H., & Wheeler, D. (2001). Shell, Nigeria and the Ogoni. A study in unsustainable development: The story of Shell, Nigeria and the Ogoni people. Environment, economy, relationships: Conflict and prospects for resolution. *Sustainable Development, 9*(2), 74–86.

Bothello, J., Nason, R. S., & Schnyder, G. (2019). Institutional voids and organization studies: Towards an epistemological rupture. *Organization Studies*. 40(10) 1499–1512 doi:10.1177/0170840618819037.

Campbell, B. (2003). Factoring in governance is not enough. Mining codes in Africa, policy reform and corporate responsibility. *Minerals and Energy - Raw Materials Report, 18*(3), 2–13.

Campbell, B. (2006). Good Governance, security and mining in Africa. *Minerals and Energy – Raw Materials Report, 21*(1), 31–44.

Collier, P. (2008). *The Bottom billion*. Oxford: Oxford University Press.

Collier, P., & Hoeffler, A. (2004). Greed and grievance in civil war. *Oxford Economic Papers, 56*(4), 563–595.

Crane, A. (2010). From governance to governance: On blurring boundaries. *Journal of Business Ethics, 94*(S1), 17–19.

De Bakker, F. G. A., Rasche, A., & Ponte, S. (2019). Multi-stakeholder initiatives on sustainability: A cross-disciplinary review and research agenda for business ethics. *Business Ethics Quarterly, 29 (3), 343–383.*

Deitelhoff, N., & Wolf, K. D. (Eds.) (2010). *Corporate security responsibility? Corporate governance contributions to peace and security in zones of conflict*. New York: Palgrave Macmillan.

Delbard, O. (2020). *The Corporate social responsibility agenda: The case for sustainable and responsible Business*. NJ: World Scientific Publishing.

Dobers, P., & Halme, M. (2009). Corporate social responsibility and developing countries. *Corporate Social Responsibility and Environmental Management, 16*(5), 237–249.

Eweje, G. (2007). Multinational oil companies' CSR initiatives in Nigeria. The skepticism of stakeholders in host communities. *Managerial Law, 49*(5/6), 218–235.

Ford, J. (2015). Perspectives on the evolving "business and peace" debate. *Academy of Management Perspective, 29*(4), 451–460.

Forrer, J. J., & Katsos, J. (2015). Business and peace in the buffer state. *Academy of Management Perspective, 29*(4), 438–450.

Fort, T. L., & Schipani, C. A. (2004). *The role of business in fostering peaceful societies*. Cambridge: Cambridge University Press.

Frynas, J. G. (2005). The false development promise of corporate social responsibility: Evidence from multinational oil companies. *International Affairs, 81*(3), 581–598.

Frynas, J. G., & Wood, G. (2001). Oil and war in Angola. *Review of African Political Economy, 28*(90), 586–606.

Galtung, J. (1996). *Peace by peaceful means: Peace and conflict, development and civilization*. London: Sage.

Gilberthorpe, E., & Papyrakis, E. (2015). The extractive industries and development: The resource curse at the micro, meso and macro levels. *Extractive Industries and Society, 2*(2), 381–390.

Hammann, R. (2003). Mining companies' role in sustainable development: The why and how of corporate social responsibility from a business perspective. *Development Southern Africa, 20*(2), 237–254.

Hammann, R., & Kapelus, P. (2004). Corporate social responsibility in mining in Southern Africa: Fair accountability or just greenwash. *Development, 47*(3), 85–92.

Hammann, R., Luiz, J., Ramaboa, K., Khan, F., Dhlamini, X., & Nilsson, W. (2020). Neither colony nor enclave: Calling for dialogical contextualism in management and organization studies. *Organization Theory, 1*(1), 1–21.
Haufler, V. (2004). International diplomacy and the privatization of conflict resolution. *International Studies Perspectives, 5*(2), 158–163.
Home, J. L. (2006). *Le businessman et le conflit des grands lacs.* Paris: L'Harmattan.
Idahosa, P. (2002). Business ethics and development in conflict (zones): The case of Talisman Oil. *Journal of Business Ethics, 39*(3), 227–246.
Idemudia, U. (2007). Community perceptions and expectations: Reinventing the wheels of corporate social responsibility practices in the Nigerian oil industry. *Business and Society Review, 112*(3), 369–405.
Idemudia, U. (2008). Conceptualising the CSR and development debate: Bridging existing analytical gaps. *Journal of Corporate Citizenship, 29*, 1–20.
Idemudia, U. (2009). Oil extraction and poverty reduction in the Niger Delta: A critical examination of partnership initiatives. *Journal of Business Ethics, 90*(S1), 91–116.
Idemudia, U. (2017). Shell–NGO Partnership and peace in Nigeria: Critical Insights and implications. *Organization and Environment*, 31(4), 384–405.
Idemudia, U., & Ite, U. E. (2006). Corporate-community relations in Nigeria's oil industry: Challenges and imperatives. *Corporate Social Responsibility and Environmental Management, 13*(4), 194–206.
Irwin, R. (2003). Corporate social investment and branding in the new South Africa. *Brand Management, 10*(4–5), 303–311.
Ite, U. E. (2004). Multinationals and corporate social responsibility in developing countries: A case study of Shell in Nigeria. *Corporate Social Responsibility and Environmental Management, 11*(1), 1–11.
Ite, U. E. (2005). Poverty reduction in resource-rich developing countries: What have multinational corporations got to do with it? *Journal of International Development, 17*(7), 913–929.
Ite, U. E. (2007). Changing times and strategies: Shell's contribution to sustainable community development in the Niger Delta, Nigeria. *Sustainable Development, 15*(1), 1–14.
Jamali, D., & Mirshak, R. (2010). Business-conflict linkages: Revisiting MNCs, CSR, and conflict. *Journal of Business Ethics, 93*(3), 443–464.
James, A. (2015). The resource curse: A statistical mirage. *Journal of Development Economics, 114*, 55–63.
Kapelus, P. (2002). Mining, corporate social responsibility and the "community": The case of Rio Tinto, Richards Bay Minerals and the Mbonambi. *Journal of Business Ethics, 39*(3), 275–296.
Katsos, J. E., & Forrer, J. (2014). Business practices and peace in post-conflict zones: Lessons from Cyprus. *Business Ethics: a European Review, 23*(2), 154–168.
Kaufmann, D., Kraay, A., & Mastruzzi, M. (2008). *Governance matters VII: Aggregate and individual governance indicators for 1996–2007.* World Bank Policy Research Working Paper no. 4654.
Keen, D. (2003). Greedy elites, dwindling resources, alienated youths: The anatomy of protracted violence in Sierra Leone. *International Politics and Society, 2*, 321–360.
Kolk, A. (2016). The social responsibility of international business: From ethics and the environment to CSR and sustainable development. *Journal of World Business, 51*(1), 23–34.
Kolk, A., & Lenfant, F. (2012). Business-NGO collaboration in a conflict setting: Partnership activities in the Democratic Republic of Congo. *Business and Society, 51*(3), 478–511.

Kolk, A., & Lenfant, F. (2015). Cross-sector collaboration, institutional gaps and fragility: The role of social innovation partnerships in a conflict-affected region. *Journal of Public Policy and Marketing, 34*(2), 287–303.
Kolk, A. & Lenfant, F. (2018). Responsible business under adverse conditions: Dilemmas regarding company contributions to local development. *Business Strategy and Development, 1*, 8–16.
Kolstad, I. (2009). The resource curse: Which institutions matter? *Applied Economics Letter, 16*(4), 439–442.
Lemarchand, R. (2009). *The dynamics of violence in Central Africa*. Philadelphia: University of Pennsylvania Press.
Lenfant, F. (2016). *On business, conflict and peace: Interaction and collaboration in Central Africa*. Amsterdam: University of Amsterdam.
Liedong, T. A., Aghanya, D., & Rajwani, T. (2020). Corporate political strategies in weak institutional environments: A break from conventions. *Journal of Business Ethics, 161*(4), 855–876.
Luiz, J. M., & Stewart, C. (2014). Corruption, South African Multinational Enterprises and institutions in Africa. *Journal of Business Ethics, 124*(3), 383–398.
Malone, D., & Goodin, S. (1997). An analysis of U.S. disinvestment from South Africa: Unity, rights, and justice. *Journal of Business Ethics, 16*(16), 1687–1703.
Mehlum, H., Moene, K., & Torvik, R. (2006). Cursed by resources or institutions? *World Economy, 29*(8), 1117–1131.
Montague, D. (2002). Stolen goods: Coltan and conflict in the DRC. *SAIS Review, 22*(1), 103–118.
Nelson, J. (2000). *The business of peace*. London: Prince of Wales Business Forum.
Oetzel, J., Getz, K. A., & Ladek, S. (2007). The role of multinational enterprises in responding to violent conflict: A conceptual model and framework for research. *American Business Law Journal, 44*(2), 331–358.
Oetzel, J., Westermann-Behaylo, M., Koerber, C., Fort, T. L., & Rivera, J. (2009). Business and peace: Sketching the terrain. *Journal of Business Ethics, 89*(S4), 351–373.
Pole Institute (2019). *Dynamiques politiques et économiques autour de l'exploitation du cobalt*. Goma : Pole Institute.
Pratt, C. B. (1991). Multinational corporate social policy process for ethical responsibility in Sub-Saharan Africa. *Journal of Business Ethics, 10*, 527–541.
Rajak, D. (2008). Uplift and empower: The market, morality and corporate responsibility on South Africa's platinum belt. *Research in Economic Anthropology, 28*, 297–324.
Rasche, A. (2010). The limits of corporate responsibility standards. *Business Ethics: A European Review, 19*(3), 280–291.
Reed, D. (2002). Resource extraction industries in developing countries. *Journal of Business Ethics, 39*(3), 199–226.
Reinecke, J., & Ansari, S. (2016). Taming wicked problems: The role of framing in the construction of corporate social responsibility. *Journal of Management Studies, 53*(3), 299–329.
Ross, M. (2001). Does oil hinder democracy? *World Policy, 53*(3), 325–361.
Rossouw, G. J. (2005). Business ethics and corporate governance in Africa. *Business and Society, 44*(1), 94–106.
Sachs, J. (2005). *The end of poverty*. New York: Penguin Books.
Sarmidi, T., Law, S. H., & Jafari, Y. (2014). Resource curse: New evidence on the role of institutions. *International Economic Journal, 28*(1), 191–206.
Scherer, A. G., Palazzo, G., & Seidl, D. (2013). Managing legitimacy in complex and heterogeneous environments: Sustainable development in a globalized world. *Journal of Management Studies, 50*(2), 259–284.

Sen, A. (1999). *Development as freedom*. New York: Anchor books.

Soares de Oliveira, R. (2007). *Oil and politics in the Gulf of Guinea*. New York: Columbia University Press.

Stewart, F. (2000). Crisis prevention: Tackling horizontal inequalities. *Oxford Development Studies, 28*(3).

Van Tulder, R., & Kolk, A. (2001). Multinationality and corporate ethics: Codes of conduct in the sporting goods industry. *Journal of International Business Studies, 32*(2), 267–283.

Visser, W. (2006). Revisiting Carroll's CSR pyramid. An African perspective. In E. R. Pedersen & M. Huniche (Eds.), *Corporate citizenship in developing countries* (pp. 29–56). Copenhagen: Copenhagen Business School Press.

Vlassenroot, K., & Raeymaekers, T. (Eds.). (2004). *Conflict and social transformation in eastern DR Congo*. Ghent, Belgium: Academia Press.

Watts, M. (2005). Righteous oil? Human rights, the oil complex and corporate social responsibility. *Annual Review of Environment and Resources, 30*(1), 373–407.

Wengler, A., & Mockly, D. (2003). *Conflict prevention: The untapped potential of the business sector*. Boulder, CO: Lynne Rienner.

West, A. (2006). Theorising South Africa's corporate governance. *Journal of Business Ethics, 68*(4), 433–448.

Wheeler, D., Fabig, H., & Boele, R. (2002). Paradoxes and dilemmas for stakeholder responsive firms in the extractive sector: Lessons from the case of Shell and the Ogoni. *Journal of Business Ethics, 39*(3), 297–318.

Wolf, K. D., Deitelhoff, D., & Engert, S. (2007). Corporate security responsibility: Towards a conceptual framework for a comparative research agenda. *Cooperation and Conflict, 42*(3), 294–320.

4

CORPORATE SOCIAL RESPONSIBILITY AND COMMUNITY DEVELOPMENT IN AFRICA

Issues and Prospects

Uwafiokun Idemudia, Francis Xavier Dery Tuokuu, Marcellinus Essah, and Emmanuel Graham

Introduction

Historically, development theory and practice have placed different emphasis on the roles that both government and the private sector play in growth and development (Garforth, Phillips, & Bhatia-Panthaki, 2007). However, the global restructuring of state-society relationships driven largely by neoliberal logic has not only allowed for the taming of the 'state', which paradoxically accentuated its inadequacies, but it has also facilitated, for better or for worse, the emergence of business, especially Transnational Corporations (TNCs) as a major factor in development practice (Idemudia, 2017). Hence, Knorriga and Helmsing (2008) have argued that there is a need for critical development scholars to move *beyond the enemy perception* of the private sectors, as only limited attention has so far been given to the changes within the private sector, and how these changes might have influenced the interaction between the state, civil society, and the market. According to them, the call to move 'beyond the enemy perception' does not mean we should overlook the critical issues of power or inequality or fall into the trap of assuming that business can solve all our developmental problems if only other actors 'would get out of the way'. Rather, what is required is the need to unpack the changing roles of business in development and consider their implications for development theory and practice. This is particularly important given that there appears to be a growing consensus that the pursuit of sustainable development can no longer be a matter of choosing between the state and the market; instead, it is now a matter of creating the appropriate mix of government and private sector action to maximize social welfare (Thomas, 2000; Garforth et al., 2007).

Consequently, some scholars have also argued that the achievement of the United Nations Sustainable Development Goals in rural communities in Africa

DOI: 10.4324/9781003038078-5

is more likely if there are constructive inputs from government, business, and civil society (see Idemudia, 2014; Pogge & Sengupta, 2014). The assumption here is that the challenges of community development can best be understood as a wicked problem, which makes it impossible for a single organization to be in charge of its substantive resolution (Schmitt, 2010). As such, the push for sustainable community development today is now partly informed by the need to identify the appropriate balance between the roles of different actors and then to explore how they can best be combined to maximize business contribution to sustainable development (Ward, 2004).

However, while the role of government and civil society in development is well established and often not in dispute, the idea that the private sector is an important factor in development has remained controversial and a subject of intense disagreements (see Idemudia, 2008, 2014). Blowfield (2012) attributes this to the distrust of business and the reluctance to make business accountable for development outcomes. For example, critics of the role of the private sector in development have argued that business involvement in development allows business to appropriate the meaning of ethics, redefine the meaning of development and allow market rationality to dominate development thinking and practice such that business logic now dominates a wider sphere of our life to the detriment of the poor and marginalized (see Jones, 1996; Smith, 2003; Blowfield & Frynas, 2005; Blowfield, 2005; Jenkins, 2005; Newell, 2005). Similarly, others have also argued that business contribution to development is structurally constrained by the logic of capitalist production and profitability such that business at best can only be 'development tools' rather than a development agent (Frynas, 2005; Idemudia, 2008; Idemudia et al., 2019).

According to Blowfield (2012), business as a development tool implies that business is an unintentional actor in development whose contributions to development are largely a function of its wealth-generating role in society and thus have no responsibility for development outcomes. Here, businesses see contributions to community development largely in terms of short-term compensation and benefits to local communities (Esteves & Barclay, 2011). In contrast, business as a development agent implies the willingness of a business to deploy its resources for activities with expected development benefits and to take responsibility for the outcomes of such developmental efforts. Blowfield (2012) notes that whereas the approach of business as a development tool is essentially driven by managerial calculations of related cost, returns, and competition (i.e. business case logic), business as a development agent is also motivated by stakeholder concerns, pressures, and demands (i.e. societal case logic).

Focusing on this analytical distinction between business as a development tool and business as a development agent, we contend that if CSR is to become a more effective vehicle for promoting sustainable community development in rural communities in Africa, business would have to become more of a development agent and less of a development tool by shifting their CSR policies and practices geared towards community development (CD) from an emphasis on an imposed/directed community development framework to an emphasis on enabling self-help community development projects. Crucially, therefore, is the need to rethink CSR practices through the lens of community development rather than framing community development through the lens of CSR (see Banks et al., 2016). Put differently, for CSR to contribute to community development in Africa, it must shift from being a band-aid pragmatic initiative towards a commitment to becoming genuinely sustainable over time (Porritt, 2005). The implication is that commitment to sustainability is more likely to foster CD when firms approach their CD-related CSR efforts via what has been labelled 'open strategizing'. Open strategizing is a type of strategizing that requires that, instead of firms trying to dictate what people should or should not do, they should try to follow a process of logic, create conditions that facilitate effective stakeholder interactions, enable institutional arrangements for coping with difficult issues, and act as a facilitator, coach, and most importantly a team player (Schmitt, 2010). It is this possibility of pursuing CD objectives as a development agent and adopting an open strategizing approach that would likely make CSR contribution to CD in Africa meaningful.

Framing Community Development

While there is no universally accepted definition of community development, how it is conceptualized shapes and influences the different efforts meant to contribute to community development (Denise & Harris, 1990). It is therefore important to clarify its usage and deployment in the present analysis. Community development is defined here as the process by which the efforts of the people themselves are linked with those of other agents and actors to improve the socio-economic and cultural conditions of the community, such that the people become more competent to fully contribute to national progress, live with, and gain some control over local conditions and the changing world (Ajayi, 1995; Ajayi & Otuya, 2006). At the heart of this definition are the following issues:

1. Improvement of socio-economic and cultural conditions in a host community
2. Capacity building and self-help in host communities, and
3. Community empowerment in host communities

The choice of this conception of community development is because it avoids the limitations of being conceptually vague and it is appropriate for the kind of micro-level analysis to be undertaken here (Bhattacharyya, 2004). Besides, the essence of community development is to build 'solidarity and agency' by privileging the principles of self-help, felt needs, and participation (Bhattacharyya, 2004). According to Bhattacharyya (2004), self-help builds and utilizes the agency of community members, allows for the mobilization of communities' cultural and material resources, and prevents dependency. Similarly, felt needs imply that community development projects should respond to the needs of community members as they see them rather than being imposed by the developer. As such, the translation of the principles of self-help and felt needs into practice based on active participation can lead to the building of community agency and solidarity both of which constitute the cornerstone for successful community development.

The implication is that it is important to recognize that it is not everything that supposedly contributes to community improvement that necessarily amounts to being community development (Bhattacharyya, 2004). Nonetheless, Owen and Westoby (2012) have noted that a critical first step in community development requires the building of good local-level relationships via effective interpersonal communication that sits at the heart of community-building activities. This is because community development is a facilitating process by which local human, physical, and economic resources are combined to mobilize common pool resources to empower communities. However, for contributions to community development to be sustainable and meaningful, they must also protect, preserve, and conserve the lives and resources of the rural inhabitants (Ukponson & Onu, 2004). The implication is that the environmental dimension of CD cannot be ignored or relegated to the background in favour of its social dimension if community development is to be sustainable.

Nonetheless, Matarrita-Cascante and Brennan (2012) have suggested that community development functions with various elements (stakeholders and resources) that go through various procedures to improve the community. Based on the different strategies that have been developed to improve living conditions in rural communities, Matarrita-Cascante and Brennan (2012) identified three forms of community development models. The first community development model is the imposed type of community development (Imposed CD). Here, the predominant view is that the community is a place where interactions are largely understood in terms of transactions meant to ensure people's survival by contributing to some sort of progress in the community. As such, the private sector seeks to improve the living conditions of a community through contributions to physical infrastructures and support for economic development activities. The goal is to provide the community with assets that make life possible and easier. For example, the construction of roads, schools, and support for microcredit schemes by oil companies operating in the Niger Delta area of Nigeria (Idemudia, 2009, 2007). Hence, the Imposed CD model tends to focus on 'hard' as opposed to 'soft' aspects of community development.

However, the process of implementing the Imposed CD model reflects a development in community process as the community developer does not seek inputs from or involve community members in the design, implementation, and monitoring of community development projects. Instead, the community developer would rely on their judgement and expertise. Consequently, this approach to community development can often lead to a mismatch in corporate and community priorities and result in numerous abandoned community development projects, incidences of corporate-community conflicts, and the enshrinement of community dependence as opposed to community empowerment.

The second CD model is the directed model, which is at the mid-point between Imposed and the self-help models. In this type of community development, the tendency is to view the community as a place where the exchange of goods and services essential for survival takes place. In some limited cases, communities can become a place to establish meaningful relationships and associations. However, like the Imposed form of community development, contributions to the community are mainly to facilitate survival, and projects are often geared towards infrastructural improvements to the community. As such, while there are some elements of community participation in the process of community development, these involvements are often directed and guided towards programs or projects that have been previously designed by the CSR team of the company. Hence, community participation is essentially limited to providing feedback to an already determined community development agenda. In some cases, such feedback is used to modify the corporate lead community development initiatives. This kind of a tokenistic form of participation can often lead to internal fragmentation of local communities and fail to lay a solid foundation for building community solidarity and agency. For example, Shell's consultation of the local elite in the implementation of community development projects in the Niger Delta often lead to accusations of local chiefs of corruption and conflicts that undermine local traditional institutions, and in other instances, has sparked incidences of intra and inter-community conflicts (Idemudia, 2011).

The third is the self-help CD model. In this case, the community is viewed as a place where people and other stakeholders associate with each other to foster community solidarity and strengthen community agency. In this model, emphasis is on relationship building and establishing positive stakeholder relations as a basis for identifying and addressing community development problems. The self-help CD model is different from the Imposed CD approach that tends to only seek to deal with CD problems that are meaningful from a corporate perspective (i.e. problems amenable to business case logic and good for public relations). Indeed, the self-help model is informed by and evolves from community priorities and active stakeholder interactions. As such, a key strength of the self-help CD model is that community members are the leading voices and actors in the efforts to set out a community development agenda and to identify solutions that are relevant to their well-being. Given the central role of the community in decision-making, the self-help model provides an excellent opportunity for community learning, knowledge acquisition, and solidarity building. It also promotes capacity building, affirmative successes, and local empowerment, all of which are underpinned by positive stakeholder relationships. These elements (i.e. capacity building, and empowerment) of community development that are essential for human development have previously been classified as 'soft issues' by Botes and van Resenburg (2000). The focus on soft issues of CD does not mean that this model ignores the 'hard' aspects of CD; rather the goal is often to establish mechanisms that strengthen community members' capacity and agency over their development as a way to ensure sustainable progress within their locality.

Business-Community Relations: CSR Strategies for Community Development

A corporation's motivation for CSR could either be because of a strong moral commitment to its stakeholders or because it has a strong pragmatic interest to do so (Ackerman, 1973; Kaplues, 2002; Gutierrez, 2004). This informs how and why business can be either a development tool or a development agent. Whichever of these motivations underpin a corporate action, it is bound to have significant ramifications for the success or failure of CSR initiatives for CD. For example, research has shown that the key to community relations' success is genuine involvement as opposed to traditional approaches like making charitable contributions or being a good employer (Davis & Blomstrom, 1975; Humphrey, 2000). Furthermore, while altruistic motivations alone such as charitable donation might not withstand economic downturns, actions motivated by pragmatic interest only would distance important social partners (Kapelus, 2002; Gutierrez, 2004). Hence, a sustainable venture is likely to occur when both motivations are at play. Nonetheless, it is generally possible to talk of a corporation as operating closer to one end of the extremes than the other. Hence, in retrospect, it is fairly easy to determine whether a corporate action benefited shareholders, society, both, or neither (Kapelus, 2002). Dalton and Cosier (1982) argued that no approach a company takes is completely immune to criticism of social irresponsibility. They pointed out the importance of risk, consequence, and temptation in terms of how these can affect the choice of corporate strategy. They argued that when faced with high temptation with low risk and consequences, businesses are likely to pursue self-serving business practices. They assert that this was relevant in both developed and developing countries. However, it is not difficult to see that this is particularly more relevant to African countries where minimum standards are often non-existent and enforcement of regulation can be relatively poor.

Nevertheless, Zadek (2001) captured businesses' CSR response to demand for business to contribute to CD in terms of the three generations of corporate citizenship. The first generation of responses focused on how businesses can respond to clamour for it to be socially responsible without detracting from profit-making and if possible, add commercial value to the business. Zadek (2001) characterized this generation of response as being largely defensive and CSR policies as bolt-on in business strategy. The second-generation responses focused on whether CSR can underpin or at the very least be an integral part of businesses' long-term strategy for success. This generation of response was largely couched in the language of the business case for CSR. The third generation of the response focused on whether CSR can make a significant contribution to poverty, social exclusion, and environmental degradation. This generation of response informs the touting of partnership as an effective strategy to address the complex challenges that now confront society. However, contrary to Zadek's (2001) assertion that business adoption of CSR is merely a response to external pressure and enlightened leadership, Utting (2005) has argued that businesses have also actively influenced, controlled, and led contemporary mainstream CSR agenda. This is demonstrated in the consistency between the generations of business policy response to the demand for CSR and the predominant voluntary nature CSR has taken despite opposition from civil society. Hamann and Acutt (2003) have suggested that this active business engagement with CSR through its policy response has largely been a strategy of accommodation and legitimization. According to them, while to accommodate means to adapt to, or reconcile with changed circumstances, legitimization entailed justification and rationalization. This strategy of accommodation by legitimization allows businesses to respond to societal pressures in their own terms such that the changes they make to policy or practice do not fundamentally alter their preferences but are sufficient enough to insulate them from further public criticisms.

In practice, the CSR initiatives of most business enterprises in Africa cover a wide range of issues such as labour rights, employee relations, human rights, environmental performance, sustainable development, health issues, issues of corporate governance, and transparency. In addition, varied practical strategies are employed to tackle these different CSR issues. CSR practices, therefore, take any one of the following forms captured in Figure 4.1: Corporate philanthropy and social investment; volunteerism; engagement; and corporate Citizenship (CC).

Figure 4.1 suggests that, while businesses might opt to use only philanthropy and social investment as the avenue for addressing their CSR obligations within rural communities, they can also simultaneously employ stakeholder engagement

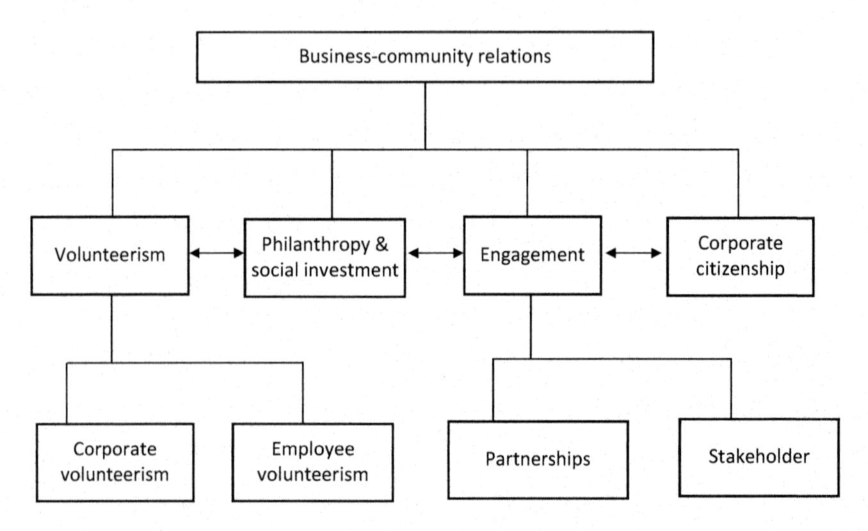

FIGURE 4.1 Business–community relations strategies.

and volunteerism. In other words, these different CSR practices are not mutually exclusive and in fact, most companies tend to engage their CSR initiatives through more than one form of CSR practices. In addition, Figure 4.1 suggests that volunteerism can be either employee or corporate-driven and stakeholder engagement can be via partnership or stakeholder dialogue.

Corporate Philanthropy (CP) is a corporate charitable contribution to address economic, environmental, and social problems as part of the corporate overall strategy for implementing CSR initiatives (BSR, 2004). Philanthropic ideals have been said to be deeply entrenched in religious beliefs. However, over the years, philanthropy has become a tool for responding to civic obligations and as such has been gradually institutionalized (Burke, Logsdon, Mitchell, Reiner, & Vogel, 1986; Gutierrez, 2004). CP has evolved from ad hoc philanthropy to social investment and then to strategic philanthropy (Porter & Kramer, 2002). These changes correspond to changing business emphasis from just a concern or a need to give, to laying more emphasis on effective grantmaking (Burke et al., 1986). Burke et al. (1986) asserted that corporate philanthropy to meet social needs generally takes one of three forms: (a) donation of funds either directly or through associated foundations, (b) contribution of goods and services, and (c) volunteerism, with a large proportion of these contributions often going to the communities in which a corporation's facilities are located. However, corporate philanthropy has also been criticized for often failing to address core social and environmental issues at the heart of business day-to-day operations. Besides, philanthropic gestures very rarely address the problems that they are supposedly expected to solve, as some of the problems are not amenable to the quick-fix nature of philanthropy.

Corporate volunteerism refers to achieving public goals through the actions of individuals who provide their services at no charge and out of free will (Imagine et al., 2002). While volunteerism has long been a part of human society, volunteer work as a part of corporate mission or strategy is just a few decades old (Thomas & Christoffer, 1999). The easy and uncomplicated nature of volunteerism, coupled with the associated low cost for the firm, has made volunteerism attractive to corporations (Davis & Blomstrom, 1975; Thomas & Christoffer, 1999). However, the extent to which corporate volunteerism can deliver for CD in rural African settings remains unclear.

Over the years, stakeholder engagement has become a common business practice. In some cases, companies have defined engagement policies as a crucial component of their business strategy and use stakeholder engagement to enter challenging markets, resolve or prevent confrontation with stakeholder activism, and improve and preserve their reputation in communities and marketplaces (BSR, 2004). Engagement policies may be conceived of as business practices that culminate in a collaborative effort to resolve shared problems. The principles that should guide engagement processes are inclusiveness, commitment, accessibility, participation, accountability, and productivity. Nevertheless, the notion of engagement potentially spans passive and active practices such as disclosure and transparency by businesses to their stakeholders, and direct involvement, consultation, or partnership with stakeholders (IISD, 2004b). Consequently, critics argue that passive engagement by businesses can serve to legitimize businesses' positions and shield them from criticism even when they fail to address their CSR obligations (i.e. engagement as a strategy of accommodation by legitimation).

Common engagement methods are consultation papers, perception surveys, stakeholder workshops, public and private meetings, liaison groups, and academic roundtables. The choice of engagement method a company employs depends on the company's unique circumstance and the nature of the target stakeholder being engaged. For example, Shell claims that holding a series of stakeholder workshops as a means of engaging different stakeholders concerning its operation in the Niger Delta allowed the company to redefine its community development strategy as well as reassess its role within its host communities (Idemudia, 2007a). However, stakeholder engagement has also been criticized for being time consuming or expensive. Moreover, if the engagement process is not properly designed or if it goes out of hand, especially in a conflict zone, it can be catastrophic for corporate reputations. Critics also note that stakeholder engagement can often open the corporation to unlimited demands from different sections of the community. Such situations can lead to conflict with those community members whose demands are not met.

Partnerships between business enterprise, government, NGOs, and communities have also become a common practice. Partnerships could take the form of a formal agreement with clear-cut objectives or take an informal structure. Partnerships normally involve two parties from the same or different sectors. However, multiple partners across and within sectors are now also common. An example is the conservation partnership between Rio Tinto and the World-Wide Fund (WWF) Australia. Partnerships are generally perceived to be good, and likely to have a positive impact on community relations (NAB&UNV, 2003). However, like every other CSR policy or strategy, partnerships have their peculiar shortcomings. For example, due to differential power distribution among partners, partnerships can effectively allow for so-called regulatory or institutional capture, co-optation, and the dilution of radical alternative agendas (Utting, 2005). Hamman (2006) has also argued that partners do not necessarily need to be equal in power. Rather, they only need to acknowledge that each partner is capable of inflicting significant costs on the other.

Corporate citizenship practice is underpinned by the assumption that corporations are citizens like people, but have greater resources at their disposal than most other citizens, and are expected to be good corporate citizens just as a private citizen would (Davis & Blomstrom, 1975; Carroll, 1998). Hence, besides being economically viable, a good corporate citizen is under obligation to obey the laws of the land, be ethical, support philanthropy, and engage in volunteerism. These obligations constitute what Carroll (1998) referred to as the four faces of corporate citizenship. Corporate citizenship is therefore not only a way of looking at the relationship between businesses and communities but also a business practice in its own right (NAB &UNV, 2003).

The Challenges of Corporate Social Responsibility and Community Development in Africa

The relationship between CSR and community development in Africa remains highly contested such that there continues to be disagreement about the scope of business responsibility for community development and the effects of CSR initiatives in terms of ability to deliver on the developmental promise. For example, in the context of Nigeria, Frynas (2005) and Akpan (2006) have argued that the CSR initiatives of oil companies have not only failed to contribute to CD, but they have also exacerbated conditions that marginalize local communities. In contrast, Eweje (2006) and Ite (2007) share an opposing view and instead argue that oil companies through their CSR initiatives have made important contributions to the CD of their host communities. Idemudia (2008) has partly attributed this disagreement in the assessment of CSR impact on community development in Africa to the fact that analysts have often failed to specify how CD is understood.

However, it is important to also recognize that despite this lack of conceptual specificity, a majority of studies have highlighted the different ways in which CSR initiatives have been ineffective in supporting or providing sustainable development benefits for rural dwellers in Africa (see Idemudia, 2009; Rajak, 2006, Egbon, Idemudia, & Amaeshi, 2018). Underpinning the inability of CSR efforts to effectively facilitate CD in Africa is the tendency to view CD from a CSR perspective as opposed to viewing CSR from a CD perspective. Put differently, CSR practices meant to contribute to CD are often geared towards meeting corporate objectives and are assessed as such as opposed to how well CSR initiatives enable the building of community solidarity and strengthening of community agency.

Consequently, business engagement with CD in Africa has largely been as a development tool rather than a development agent. This is manifested in that fact CD from a CSR lens is largely understood in terms of efforts to reduce social risk, generate a return of social investments for the firm, and minimize transaction cost. In this scenario improvements to the community are merely unintended consequences. This approach to CD, unfortunately, limits CSR impacts in rural settings. For example, David O'Reilly, chief executive of Chevron noted that while oil companies now accept their social responsibilities to host communities, the needs of host communities are so numerous that they cannot all be satisfied (cited in Onishi, 2002). This challenge is then handled by modifying the definition of the 'affected community' in ways that restrict the number of claims that arise from communities (Esteves & Barclay, 2011). The unintended consequence of this corporate decision to reduce cost is that it leads to a breakdown in corporate-community relations, the proliferation of unmet felt needs of community members, and the creation of active barriers that militate against community members' involvement in their own development. This is because communities often do not agree with the artificial boundaries that are created to limit corporate contributions to CD (Mclennan & Banks, 2018).

Furthermore, CSR has also failed to contribute to CD in Africa partly because of the nature of the dominant neoliberal logic of how business–society relationship in the continent is often understood. CSR initiatives of most businesses in Africa are largely informed by a *business and society* logic rather than a *business in society* logic (Idemudia, 2009). Consequently, by framing business as not a part of the community where they operate and instead external to it, CSR initiatives inadvertently become merely a mechanism for meeting corporate transaction needs and not for facilitating or building long-term stakeholder relationships. The outcome is that the dominant model of CD supported by CSR in Africa is the Imposed CD model. The attractive nature of the Imposed CD model stems from the fact that it allows for corporate control and minimizes community involvement in decision-making. As such, in designing CSR initiatives, priority is given more to projects that are easily captured in corporate reports for public relations purposes and not based on community felt needs. Similarly, emphasis is on reducing CSR costs rather than the pursuit of corporate social innovations. Unfortunately, these perceived managerial benefits undermine community agency, limits opportunities for community learning, and often fail to engender either a sense of solidarity between the corporation and their host communities or between members of the communities (Idemudia, 2007a). Indeed, Idemudia (2007b) has shown how this leads to the breakdown of the psychological contract between firms and their host communities, culminating in conflict. Hence, the absence of a strong positive corporate-community relationship that is partly rooted in the tendency to see local communities as the 'other' represents a major challenge for the ability of CSR practices to make impactful contributions to CD in Africa.

In addition, any effort to foster community development is likely to be time consuming, slow, and requires constant negotiations to resolve competing and conflicting stakeholder interests and views. The emphasis on stakeholder participation also means the outcome of the process of engagement is often uncertain despite the likely allocation of significant human and material resources. These conditions can often conflict with managerial logic that is based on business timelines, and cost-benefit calculations. Consequently, the design and implementation of CSR initiatives are often in conflict with the slow and deliberate processes that are required to enable meaningful stakeholder engagement that can facilitate effective community development. For example, it is not uncommon for oil companies operating the Niger Delta to privilege the timelines for the completion of their oil extraction project over the timelines needed for effective community consultation and engagement. The unintended consequence is that communities feel disrespected and alienated while CSR projects are perceived as gifts from oil companies rather than community-owned development projects. For example, Osei-Kojo and Andrews (2018) pointed to how a marketplace constructed by Chirano Mines in Ghana was used as a public toilet in the community because of a lack of community sense of ownership. This lack of community sense of ownership of CSR projects also tends to foster dependency rather than empowerment as communities treat such CD projects as gifts.

Finally, another challenge facing CSR contribution to CD in Africa is the fragmented nature of the policy environment for CSR practices. According to Fox et al. (2002), an enabling environment for CSR implies a policy environment that encourages and provides incentives for business activities that minimize environmental and social costs while at the same time maximizing economic gains for stakeholders. Alternatively, an enabling environment is one in which the obstacles to CSR policies and practices are minimized and the incentives for CSR practices are maximized (Idemudia & Ite, 2006a). Unfortunately, in most countries in Africa, an enabling environment for CSR is either lacking, or yet to be developed, or at best ineffective (Ite, 2004). Consequently, CSR practices are not only made difficult but also there is often a lack of corporate innovation to deal with unique challenges within the continent (see Muthuri et al., 2012).

As a result, Naor (1982) has argued that the environment of developing countries presents formidable challenges and, in some cases, constitutes a hostile environment to CSR policies and practices. The issue here is that given that CD issues are complex and are directly or indirectly affected by broader macro-economic conditions of a country, if the macro-economy is underperforming due to governance failure then there is very limited likelihood that CSR practices by themselves would be able to make considerable contributions to CD. This is because CSR practices do not take place in a vacuum and thus the extent to which other stakeholders meet or fail to meet their reciprocal responsibilities has a direct impact on how well CSR initiatives can contribute to CD (Idemudia, 2014). Put differently, the CSR context in Africa is one in which the cost of social irresponsibility is low for the firm because very few communities are able to enforce any kind of social licence to operate.

Rethinking CSR through Community Development Lens in Africa: The Self-Help Model as a Basis for Sustainable Community Development

CSR policies and strategies geared towards fostering CD in Africa have over time, due to a number of local and international stakeholder pressures, evolved from community assistance (i.e., Imposed CD model) to the directed community development model. For example, Shells' strategies for contributing to community development in the Niger Delta metamorphosed from an outright refusal to accept community development responsibility in the 1950s to a community assistance approach in the 1970s, and then to what the company later called a community development approach in the 1990s and recently into the new strategy of sustainable community development in the 2000s (Ite, 2007, Idemudia,

2007b). This suggests that while the impact of CSR on CD may have been limited, there is some anecdotal evidence to suggest that there has also been a gradual change in corporate CSR policies meant to facilitate community development in rural communities.

However, there is sufficient anecdotal evidence to suggest that these changes in corporate strategy are more of a strategy of accommodation and legitimation rather than a deliberate effort to transform firms into development agents. This is because these changes in policies have not necessarily meant the reframing of CSR from a community development perspective that is rooted in the lived experience of rural dwellers. In other words, despite changes to CSR strategies, CD-related CSR initiatives still do not begin with an understanding and the privileging of the lived experiences of rural dwellers and putting them as architects of their development. Consequently, there is a need for firms to actively rethink their CSR initiatives from this perspective to being development agents. This in turn would require firms to build, strengthen, and develop community development capabilities (CDC). This is because firms often lack a full understanding of the complexity of relationships that shape and inform a diverse range of social, cultural, and political dynamics in their host communities (Mclennan & Banks, 2018). Community development capabilities are a set of internal resources, knowledge, processes, procedures, communication frameworks, and relationships geared towards meeting community development objectives defined in terms of fostering community solidarity and agency. CDC would allow firms to be better able to leverage internal and external resources and relationships to effect CSR programs that can make positive contributions to CD that goes beyond mere community improvement.

First, a crucial part of CDC CD-related CSR policies and strategies should be less about problem-solving and more about problematizing CD issues. According to Freire (1973), while the problem-solving approach to CD requires an outsider to define the nature and scope of CD problems as well as offer solutions, a problematizing approach requires the people to determine for themselves and own the problem as a basis for them to exert themselves for the solution. Consequently, CSR efforts to contribute to community development in Africa would need to shift from the present tendency to prefer the directed model or imposed model to the self-help model, if they are to be better positioned to make an impactful contribution to rural communities. This is because a self-help model approach to CD is agency generating and can stimulate solidarity building within the communities and strengthen the psychological contract between communities and businesses. A self-help model of community development provides rural community members with the opportunities to develop their capacities, share knowledge, mobilize internal resources more effectively, pursue a common goal, and build self-reliance (Matarrita-Cascante and Brennan (2012). The opportunity here is that a self-model can allow for local knowledge, experiences, and relationship to be harnessed for the development of innovative solutions for community development problems.

Given that the self-help model necessarily requires a democratic process, it also provides a space for communities to take on their shared responsibility and contribute to meeting their reciprocal responsibility in CSR-related efforts to meet CD objectives. The turn to a self-help model is likely to be effective if companies invest in building a long-term relationship with their host rural communities. This is because members of rural communities tend to view development more in terms of their relationships and connections with the companies even though they do appreciate material benefits (Idemudia, 2007c, Mclennan & Banks, 2018). A key part of developing an effective self-help model is to elevate the focus on relationship building from an expected unintended outcome of CSR efforts to an intentional CSR goal. The practical implication is that as stakeholder relationships strengthen, transaction costs and social risks will simultaneously decrease or become more manageable (Esteves & Barclay, 2011).

Second, firms would need to rethink business–society relationships in Africa in terms of *business in society* by shifting away from conventional stakeholder theory that is managerialist in orientation and reduces complexity in favour of increased conceptual clarity (Schmitt, 2010). At issue here is the recognition that firms embedded in their local context are more likely to make more sustainable contributions to their host communities than those that are not (see Idemudia et al., 2019). In addition, embeddedness requires open strategizing that allows firms to pursue the co-creation of solutions for CD as opposed to unilateral efforts. Consequently, firms need to develop effective listening abilities and foster mutual learning opportunities that can be time consuming in the short term but generate sustainable solutions in the long term. The implication is that 'open strategizing' requires both active stakeholder engagement and the formation of partnership as critical ingredients for addressing CD problems. However, all of this is only possible if firms are willing to accept that while they cannot always respond to all the wishes and concerns of communities, it is also not desirable for them to simply get their way.

Emerging Issues and Conclusion

Although research on CSR impact on CD in Africa is only just emerging, there is sufficient evidence to suggest that there are still significant gaps between corporate claims that they contribute to CD and community experiences on the ground. However, today, very few firms operating in Africa would deny that they do not have any social responsibility obligations to their host communities. This is reflected in the numerous CSR policies, practices, and projects undertaken by firms on the African continent (Muthuri et al., 2012). Yet, the disjuncture between corporate rhetoric and community lived experiences suggest that there might be opportunities to rethink CSR practices in a manner that might allow such private sector development efforts to become more meaningful and relevant to local communities. We have suggested that such an opportunity lies in rethinking CSR from a community development lens rather than seeing CD from a CSR lens. Underpinning this shift is the need for an approach to business–society relationships in Africa that are rooted in business in society, which enables firms to become development agents and not just development tools. To be development agents, firms in Africa must adapt to their local context by developing and strengthening what we see as community development capabilities. It is the development of these capabilities and the pursuit of a self-help model of CD (that foregrounds questions of power and inequality) that would make CSR an effective vehicle for CD and potentially allow firms to secure their long-term social licences in the communities where they operate.

References

Ackerman, R. W. (1973). How companies respond to social demand. *Harvard Business Review*, July-August, 51 (4), 88–98.

Ajayi, A. R. (1995). Community self-help projects' implementation procedures: A case study of Ekiti South-West Local Government Area of Ondo State. *Agrosearch*, *1*(1), 47–55.

Ajayi, R., & Otuya, N. (2006). Women's participation in self-help community development projects in Ndokwa agricultural zone of Delta State, Nigeria. *Community Development Journal*, *41*(2), 189–209.

Akpan, W. (2006). Between responsibility and rhetoric: Some consequences of CSR in Nigeria's oil province. *Development Southern Africa*, *23*(2), 223–240.

Banks, G., Scheyvens, R., McLennan, S., & Bebbington, A. J. (2016). Conceptualising corporate community development. *Third World Quart*, *37*, 1–19. doi:10.1080/01436597.2015.1111135

Bates, F. L., & Bacon, L. (1972). The community as a social system. *Social Forces*, *50*(3). Oxford Academic: 371–379. doi:10.1093/sf/50.3.371.

Bhattacharyya, J. (1995). Solidarity and agency: Rethinking community development. *Human Organization*, *54*(1), 60–69. doi:10.17730/humo.54.1.m459ln688536005w.

Bhattacharyya, J. (2004). Theorizing community development. *Community Development Society. Journal*, *34*(2), 5–34. doi:10.1080/15575330409490110.

Blowfield, M. (2005). Corporate social responsibility reinventing the meaning of development. *International Affairs*, *81*(3), 515–524.

Blowfield, M. (2012). Business and development: Making sense of business as a development agent. *Corporate Governance: International Journal of Business in Society*, *12*(4), 414–426.

Blowfield, M., & Frynas, J. G. (2005). Setting new agenda: Critical perspectives on corporate social responsibility in the developing world. *International Affairs*, *80*(3), 499–513.

Botes, L., & Van Rensburg, D. (2000). Community participation in development: Nine plagues and twelve commandments. *Community Development Journal*, *35*(1), 41–58.

Burke, L., Logsdon, M. J., Mitchell, W., Reiner, M., & Vogel, D. (1986). Corporate community involvement in the San Francisco Bay Area. *California Management Review*, *28*(3), 122–141.

Business for Social Responsibility (BSR) (2004). Philanthropy investment in CED. *BSR issue briefs*. Retrieved from http://www.bsr.org/print/printThisPage.cfm (accessed 19 July 2004).

Carroll, A. B. (1998). The four faces of corporate citizenship. *Business and Society Review, 100/101*(1), 1–7.

Dalton, D. R., & Cosier, R. A. (1982). The four faces of social responsibility. *Business Horizon, 25*(3), 19–27.

Davis, K., & Blomstrom, R. L. (1975). *Business and society: Environment and Responsibility* (3rd ed.). New York: McGraw-Hill.

Denise, P. S., & Harris, I. (1990). *Experiential education for community development* (1st ed.). New York: Praeger.

Egbon, O., Idemudia, U., & Amaeshi, K. (2018). Shell Nigeria's Global Memorandum of Understanding and corporate-community accountability relations. *Accounting, Auditing and Accountability Journal, 31*(1), 51–74.

Esteves, A. M., & Barclay, M. A. (2011). New approaches to evaluating the performance of corporate–community partnerships: A case study from the minerals sector. *Journal of Business Ethics, 103*(2), 189–202.

Eweje, G. (2006). The role of MNEs in Community Development Initiatives in Developing Countries: Corporate social responsibility at work in Nigeria and southern Africa. *Business and Society, 45*(2), 93–129.

Fox, T. (2004). Corporate social responsibility and development: In quest of an agenda. *Development, 47*, 26–36.

Fox, T., Ward, H., & Howard, B. (2002). *Public Sector Roles in Strengthening Corporate Social Responsibility: A Baseline Study*. Washington: The World Bank.

Freire, P. (1973). *Education for critical consciousness*. New York: Seabury Press.

Frynas, J. G. (2005). The false developmental promise of corporate social responsibility: Evidence from multinational oil companies. *International Affairs, 81*(3), 581–598.

Garforth, C., Phillips, C., & Bhatia-Panthaki, S. (2007). The private sector, poverty reduction and international development. *Journal of International Development, 19*(6), 723–734.

Gutierrez, R. (2004). Corporate social responsibility in Latin America: An overview of its characteristics and effects on local communities. In INDES-Japan Program Workshop on Corporate Social Responsibility in the Promotion of Social Development: Experiences from Latin.

Hamann, R. (2006). Can business make decisive contributions to development? Towards a research agenda on corporate citizenship and beyond. *Development Southern Africa, 23*(2), 175–195

Hamann, R., & Acutt, N. (2003). How should civil society (and Government) respond to 'corporate social responsibility'? A critique of business motivations and the potential for partnerships. *Development Southern Africa, 20*(2), 255–270.

Humphreys, D. (2000). A business perspective on community relations in mining. *Resources Policy, 26*(3), 127–131.

Idemudia, U. (2007a). *Corporate social responsibility and community development in the Niger Delta, Nigeria: A critical analysis* (Doctoral dissertation), University of Lancaster.

Idemudia, U. (2007b). Community perceptions and expectations: Reinventing the wheels of corporate social responsibility practices in the Nigerian oil industry. *Business and Society Review, 112*(3), 369–405.

Idemudia, U. (2008). Conceptualising the CSR and development debate: Bridging existing analytical gaps. *Journal of Corporate Citizenship, 29*, 1–20.

Idemudia, U. (2009). Assessing corporate-community involvement strategies in the Nigerian oil industry: An empirical analysis. *Resources Policy, 34*, 133–41.

Idemudia, U. (2011). Corporate social responsibility and developing countries: Moving the critical CSR research agenda in Africa forward. *Progress in Development Studies, 11*(1), 1–18.

Idemudia, U. (2014). Corporate-community engagement strategies in the Niger delta: Some critical reflections. *The Extractive Industries and Society, 1*(2), 154–162.

Idemudia, U. (2014a). Corporate social responsibility and development in Africa: Issues and possibilities. *Geography Compass, 8*(7), 421–435.

Idemudia, U. (2014b). Oil companies and sustainable community development in the Niger Delta, Nigeria: The issue of reciprocal responsibility and its implications for corporate citizenship theory and practice. *Sustainable Development, 22*(3), 177–187. doi:10.1002/sd.538.

Idemudia, U. (2017). Business and peace in the Niger Delta: What we know and what we need to know. *African Security Review, 26*(1), 41–61.

Idemudia, U., & Amaeshi, K. (Eds.). (2019). *Africapitalism: Sustainable business and development in Africa*. London: Routledge.

Idemudia, U., & Osayande, N. (2018). Assessing the effect of corporate social responsibility on community development in the Niger Delta: A corporate perspective. *Community Development Journal, 53*(1), 155–172.

Imagine (2002). Defining corporate community involvement and investment: A draft definition for discussion. Canadian Centre for Philanthropy. Retrieved from http://www.rotman.utoronto.ca/chaoticinterface/definitions%20of%20community%20involvement-%20Chris%20Pinney.pdf (accessed 18 July 2004).

International Institute for Sustainable Development (2004). Issue briefing note: Stakeholder engagement, ISO and corporate social responsibility. Retrieved from http://www.iied.org/docs/cred/ISO_Stakeholders.pdf (accessed 17 July 2004).

Ismail, M. (2009). Corporate social responsibility and its role in community development. *Journal of International Social Research, 2*(9), 11.

Ite, U. (2004). Multinationals and corporate social responsibility in developing countries: A case study of Nigeria. *Corporate Social Responsibility and Environmental Management, 11*(1), 1–11.

Ite, U. E. (2007). Changing times and strategies: Shell's contribution to sustainable community development in the Niger Delta, Nigeria. *Sustainable Development, 15*(1), 1–14.

Jenkins, R. (2005). Globalisation, corporate social responsibility and poverty. *International Affairs, 81*(3), 525–540.

Jones, T. M. (1996). Missing the forest for the trees: A critique of the social responsibility concept discourse. *Business and Society, 35*(1), 7–41.

Kapelus, P. (2002). Mining, corporate social responsibility and the 'community': The case of Rio Tinto, Richards Bay minerals and the Mbonambi. *Journal of Business Ethics, 39*(3), 275–296.

Knorringa, P., & Helmsing, A. H. J. (2008). Beyond an enemy perception: Unpacking and engaging the private sector. *Development and Change, 39*(6), 1053–1062.

Matarrita-Cascante, D., & Brennan, M. A. (2012). Conceptualizing community development in the twenty-first century. *Community Development, 43*(3), 293–305. doi:10.1080/15575330.2011.593267.

McLennan, S., & Banks, G. (2018). Reversing the lens: Why corporate social responsibility is not community development. *Corporate Social Responsibility and Environmental Management, 26*(1), 117–126. doi:10.1002/csr.1664.

Muthuri, J. N., Moon, J., & Idemudia, U. (2012). Corporate innovation and sustainable community development in developing countries. *Business and Society, 51*(3), 355–381.

New Academy of Business (NAB), & United Nations Volunteers (UNV) (2003). *Enhancing business-community relations: The role of volunteers in promoting global corporate citizenship: A global report*. Retrieved from http://www.new-academy.ac.uk/research/businesscommunity/unvpages/ (accessed 1 August 2004).

Newell, P. (2005). Citizenship, accountability and community: The limits of CSR agenda. *International Affairs*, *81*(3), 541–557.

Noar, J. (1982). A new approach to multinational social responsibility. *Journal of Business Ethics*, *1*(3), 219–225.

Onishi, N. (2002). As oil riches flow, poor village cries out. *New York Times*. Retrieved from http://www.earthrights.net/nigeria/news/richesflow.html (accessed 3 September 2004).

Osei-Kojo, A., & Andrews, N. (2018). A developmental paradox? The "dark forces" against corporate social responsibility in Ghana's extractive industry. Environment, Development and Sustainability, 22, 1051–1071. doi:10.1007/s10668-018-0233-9.

Owen, J. R., & Westoby, P. (2012). The structure of dialogic practice within developmental work. *Community Development*, *43*(3), 306–319.

Pogge, T., & Sengupta, M. (2014). Rethinking the post-2015 development agenda: Eight ways to end poverty now. *Global Justice: Theory, Practice, Rhetoric*, 7, 3–11.

Porter, E. M., & Kramer, R. M. (2002). The competitive advantage of corporate philanthropy. *Harvard Business Review*, *80*(12), 57–68.

Rajak, D. (2006). The gift of CSR: Power and the pursuit of responsibility in the mining industry. In W. Visser, M. McIntosh, & C. Middleton (Eds.), *Corporate citizenship in Africa. Lessons from the past; paths to the future* (pp. 190–200). Sheffield: Greenleaf Publishing.

Schmitt, R. (2010). Dealing with wicked issues: Open strategizing and the Camisea case. *Journal of Business Ethics*, *96*(1), 11–19.

Smith, C. N. (2003). Corporate social responsibility: Whether or how? *California Management Review*, *45*(4), 52–76.

Thomas, A. (2000). Development as practice in a liberal capitalist world. *Journal of International Development*, *12*(6), 773–787.

Thomas, S., & Christoffer, B. (1999). Corporate volunteerism: Essential tools for excellence in corporate community involvement. Boston College Centre for Corporate Community Relations, Carroll School of Management. Retrieved from www.bc.edu/centers/ccc/media/volunteerism.pdf (accessed 18 August 2004).

Ukpongson, M., & Onu, D. (2004). Development efforts of oil companies as perceived by rural households in selected oil producing communities of Rivers State, Nigeria. *Journal of Agriculture and Social Research*, *4*(1), 60–71.

Utting, P. (2005). Corporate responsibility and the movement of business. *Development in Practice*, *15*(3&4), 375–388.

Ward, H. (2004). *Public sector roles in strengthening corporate social responsibility: Taking stock*. Washington, DC: World Bank.

Zadek, S. (2001). *Third generation corporate citizenship: Public policy and business in society, A Foreign Policy Centre/accountability report*. London: Foreign Policy Centre.

5

CORPORATE SOCIAL RESPONSIBILITY (CSR) AND TAXATION IN AFRICA

The Battle for the Ethics of Tax and Responsible Governance

Adaeze Okoye

Introduction

Taxation is a fundamental norm of the relationship between business and society. At the basic level, tax represents the outsourcing of responsibilities for development, public goods, and infrastructure to the government. Tax appropriately designed for developing economies and linked to development objectives and priorities, is thus essential, because modern states rely on tax systems which generate significant revenue for public services (Mirrlees, Adam, & Institute for Fiscal Studies (Great Britain), 2011). This chapter explores the relationship between CSR and tax in an African context. It examines feasible experimentation with tax regimes to further CSR objectives but also highlights the limitations of such an approach. It examines the Mauritian example and makes potential suggestions for the African context.

In African states, despite the fairly high levels of taxation, tax revenues accruing from such taxation remain at low levels. The Africa average tax to GDP ratio is 17.2% according to OECD estimates in 2019 covering a period from 1990 to 2017 (OECD, 2019). This lags behind Latin America and Caribbean countries with an average of 22.8%. However, this average also hides internal disparities within the continent, such as the difference between Nigeria (5.7%) and Seychelles (31.5%) in 2017 (OECD, 2019). Tax ratios are derived from total tax revenue as a proportion of total GDP. This revenue would include income tax as a direct tax on corporations and individuals and indirect taxes such as consumption taxes (e.g. VAT) (Ganghof, 2008). Historical and political contexts are intertwined with tax agendas. Littlewood (2019, p. 55) captures this when he states that:

> in most societies, at most points in their history, the political process has been largely devoted to determining how that question is to be

DOI: 10.4324/9781003038078-6

> answered – and differences of opinion over taxation have often produced constitutional crises, rebellions, revolutions and wars. Tax history, therefore, is not just the history of taxation, but political and economic history, cut at a particular angle.

Within Africa, some connection to current levels of total tax revenues and tax structures can be found in historical perspectives too. Mkandawire (2010, p. 1663) suggests that

> colonisation has left institutional arrangements and practices that have proved remarkably resilient over the years. One such arrangement has been the structure and level of taxation. The colonial status of African economies has significant implications for taxation in Africa today – half a century after 1960, the modal year of independence.

To evidence, the legacy of tax institutional design elements retained in postcolonial states, Mkandawire refers to Amin's classification of African economies under colonialism. There are three categories: Africa of colonial trade economies, Africa of concessionary companies, and Africa of labour reserve. The first category roughly coincides with West African states, the second category, with Central Africa (Congo basin) and the third category, with the East and Southern African states (Amin, 1972). Amin exempts Ethiopia, Somalia, Madagascar, Reunion, and Mauritius as well as Cape Verde Island from the strict three micro-regions classifications although they display elements of each in a mixed fashion (Amin, 1972).

Mkandawire discovers that the tax design aspect of colonial history has an impact on two levels. First, levels and structures of tax and second, on the three key features of the political economy which are: '(1) state capacity; (2) levels of formalisation and informalization of the economy; and (3) levels of inequality.' (p. 1651). He suggests that 'exigencies of the labour reserve economies were bound to render the revenue imperative quite high and lead to larger bureaucracies to implement state policies, administer law and order, and actually collect revenue' (2010, p. 1653). Yet, in labour reserve economies, there were high levels of inequality and differential taxation often across racial lines: income taxation versus poll tax (citing the case of South Africa) (Mkandawire, 2010). Therefore, levels of informalization appear higher in colonial trade (cash crop) economies. This would result in '"exit options"' that can undermine the state's tax efforts' (Mkandawire, 2010). This could explain to a certain degree the contrast between a tax to GDP ratio of 28.4% for South Africa in 2017 and 5.7% for Nigeria in 2017 (OECD, 2019, see Table 5.1). While historical perspectives could give an overview of inherited tax systems, there is a renewed emphasis on improving the domestic capacity and tax regimes of modern African states.

This is captured in the UN Sustainable Development Goal 17 which requires strengthening of global partnerships especially target 17.1:

> Strengthen domestic resource mobilization, including through international support to developing countries, to improve domestic capacity for tax and other revenue collection' And 17.7: 'encourage and promote effective public, public-private, and civil society partnerships, building on the experience and resourcing strategies of partnerships'.

With the UN SDG goal 17 target, the partnerships between public sector institutions and private sector frameworks in the handling of social goals should involve consideration of traditional tools such as tax to set new goals aligned to CSR objectives. This is an approach that is explored in this chapter, where tax design could permit forms of business taxation which would represent both the extra cost of the negative externalities of companies' impact on society as well as the progressive cost of the contribution of the business to societal objectives under the CSR umbrella.

Companies are required to address their contribution to development under CSR strategies and this nurtures questions about the role of tax (Jenkins & Newell, 2013). The question is: what role (if any) can the adoption of CSR and its approach towards taxation in Africa bring to the mix? The sub-questions will include: whether, and if, taxation examined through the prism of social responsibility will result in a different attitude, not only towards corporate responsibility for taxation but also towards ensuring that the taxation is used for public interest purposes, which would include social development objectives. To analyze these questions, the chapter will focus on connections between CSR and tax in the first section. The next section will then examine tax ethics debates within CSR. The third section will examine the role of corporate tax specifically and briefly review corporate tax statistics publicly available for African countries. It will look at the example of Mauritius and its integration of CSR into the tax framework. Finally, the chapter considers whether the relationship between CSR and corporate tax could allow corporations to leverage their power to ensure that tax revenues are directed, more accountably towards development.

CSR and Tax

CSR is an essentially contested concept with meanings that can be regarded as unclear and difficult to pinpoint. Basic tax compliance as a business legal norm exists even within the most traditional accounts of CSR, such as that given by Friedman (1970). Friedman re-states this traditional legal account of tax and then uses it in his arguments, to negate additional voluntary responsibility of CSR action at business expense:

> This process raises political questions on two levels: principle and consequences. On the level of political principle, the imposition of taxes and the expenditure of tax proceeds are governmental functions. We have established elaborate constitutional, parliamentary and judicial provisions

> to control these functions, to assure that taxes are imposed so far as possible in accordance with the preferences and desires of the public— after all, "taxation without representation" was one of the battle cries of the American Revolution. We have a system of checks and balances to separate the legislative function of imposing taxes and enacting expenditures from the executive function of collecting taxes and administering expenditure programs and from the judicial function of mediating disputes and interpreting the law.
>
> *(1970)*

In this account then, additional CSR action is viewed as a political action, where the businessman assumes purposes to spend shareholders' monies guided by lofty ideals like: 'to restrain inflation, improve the environment, fight poverty and so on and on' (Friedman, 1970). There are echoes of these questions of tax ethics, how tax is conceived, the role of private property ownership such as companies and its perceived impact on tax regimes.

However, at the core of CSR is an analysis of the changing relationship between business and society (Okoye, 2009). Although its origins are as a 'western concept', its application and use, is increasingly prevalent in the global south (Amaeshi, Adi, Ogbechie, & Amao, 2006). It is a useful and flexible concept, which captures aspects of the relationship between society and business in context. It covers issues of the environment, human rights, economics, and social issues that fall within and beyond the direct remit of law. Therefore, this would include financial issues such as tax avoidance and tax payments. In 2011, the European Commission redefined CSR to recognize this contextual and multidimensional aspect. It defined CSR as 'the responsibility of enterprises for their impact on society' suggesting that companies could be more socially responsible by 'integrating social, environmental, ethical, consumer and human rights concerns into their business strategy and operations' as well as follow the law (EC, 2011).

Contextual definitions of CSR within Africa cannot escape the focus on the development objective (Okoye, 2012). However, the need for more empirical evidence of adequate link between current CSR practice and the achievement of those development objectives has also been highlighted (Idemudia, 2014). There are also varied influences on CSR in Africa, which include the regulatory, social, and cultural pillars (Muthuri, 2012). Tax as a regulatory influence can also have significant social implications in the delivery of capital relevant for the development of infrastructure and services.

To gain a picture of African perspectives of CSR, an instructive example is the speech of the Mauritius prime minister at the launch of the AU African Economic Platform (AEP), where he points out that: 'in Mauritius, we have encouraged the private sector to take on social responsibilities. Amongst the various projects that corporate social responsibility has led to in this country, is a project of low-cost housing for the most vulnerable' (AEP, 2017). This to an extent, still represents a form of legislating corporate philanthropy (Pillay, 2015), but it can be shaped to form a partnership towards stated developmental goals. This is similar to findings in Kenya and Zambia which cite the need to strengthen private sector contribution to sustainable development through tackling capacity constraints, strengthening the business case, and localizing the CSR agenda (Kivuitu, Yambayamba, & Fox, 2005). The example of Mauritius will be analyzed later in the chapter.

Four Tax Aspects within CSR

Carroll (1991) identified four main types of responsibilities within the CSR pyramid. These include: economic, legal, ethical, and philanthropic responsibilities. Visser (2005) revisited this pyramid in the African context and prioritized aspects of it. He reordered priorities as follows: economic, philanthropic, legal, and ethical responsibilities. The economic responsibilities as most fundamental cover investments, job creations, and payment of taxes, the philanthropic includes involvement in community projects although he points out that this emphasis may be linked to an immaturity of CSR in context. Next, the legal responsibilities include obeying the law but this has a lower priority given to that there is less pressure for social responsibility via laws in the African context. Finally, from his re-ordering, the least priority is given to ethical responsibilities because of the representativeness of corruption in some African states. However, this is a flexible classification as tax will feature in all four categories as it is part of the legal, economic, ethical and even philanthropic responsibilities. Therefore, the suggestion is that the use of tax in the CSR context should involve a re-ordering of the Carrol pyramid to consider legal, ethical, economic, and discretionary.

This is because tax is firstly a legal compulsion. Tax is a financial contribution to government revenue but it is also an aspect of regulatory and legal compliance. Governments are unable to function without adequate tax revenue and taxation comes with the force of law (Mirlees et al., 2011). Taxation as a legal responsibility is the fundamental justification for societal benefits and the basis for protection of private interests. This also involves the negation of double taxation of shareholder interests such as reductions in dividend taxation (Wilkinson & Fancher, 2004).

It is also important to accept that taxation does not stand separate from the property (tangible and intangible) ownership system. It is a part of this system and entangled within its present construct (Murphy & Nagel, 2002). This can be seen clearly in the design of company law and minimization of risk through limited liability. This is a design that has been copied in most countries (Kraakman et al., 2017) including many African states. One of the curious features of companies (as the most popular business organization forms) is that:

> A parent company may spawn a number of subsidiary companies, all controlled directly or indirectly by the shareholders of the parent company.

> If one of the subsidiary companies, to change the metaphor, turns out to be the runt of the litter and declines into insolvency to the dismay of its creditors, the parent company and the other subsidiary companies may prosper to the joy of the shareholders without any liability for the debts of the insolvent subsidiary.
>
> *(1979, Re Southard & Co. Ltd, Templeman LJ)*

This analogy would apply to the taxation of corporate groups, as each company within the group is treated as a separate taxable unit and this is further complicated by territorial incorporation laws, which apply tax rates and systems within each territorial state. Thus, the legal basis of tax within CSR is fundamental and it opens up the potential of CSR laws as an allocative device (Okoye, 2019). However, it is also insufficient because the legal interpretation of tax requirements has varied results and minimum legal compulsion leaves gaps through which tax avoidance thrives. Tax avoidance in this sense is neither legal nor illegal. Rather it is simply the absence of binding legal rules to cover the situation, or gaps found and exploited to reduce revenues remitted to the state.

This is important, in view of limitations in the state capacity of many African states to independently ascertain and control corporate taxation (BMZ, 2017) and the need for transparency of payments at each level of governance, intra-country (Kolk & Lenfant, 2018). With regard to companies, there is significant discussion around the use of multinational companies and territorial principles to minimize tax bills and in the case of developing countries to ensure capital flight from Africa (Ndikumana, 2014). Other questions of tax planning within the law such as: the nature of transfer pricing within the associated corporate group, debt shifting, and even registration of intangible IP assets in tax havens (Jansky & Palansky, 2019), indicate the insufficiency of a strictly legal approach. Yet the legal remains the starting point, as it will be ironical to have a company do good gestures without paying the basic rate of tax.

Tax should be also be seen as part of the ethical responsibilities within CSR. Furthermore, tax can be treated as an ethical issue due to its links with the sustainability of society and social services. This is what pushed the centrality of tax to CSR and highlights functions that can be used in new ways. The functions of tax include: (a) to raise funds for the government to provide public goods and services, (b) for equity and justice – thus it has a redistributive function, and (c) for regulatory purposes which can incentivize good action in the private sector and penalize wrongful action (Avi-Yonah, 2006). Tax is context-specific and the context should alter tax design especially for states in the global south. In this context, states are no longer capable of solely carrying out all public functions, companies are accused of avoiding significant amounts of taxes thus violating even the basic legal norm, and companies have voluntarily assumed social responsibilities through community projects and activities. The potential for varying approaches to tax has resulted in distinctions made between tax ethics within tax compliance (Alm & Torgier, 2011) as well as questions of aggressive tax avoidance within tax planning (EC, 2017; UNCTAD, 2016). These questions surrounding tax avoidance are taking place in both the global south and the global north as indicated by the issues raised in the case of Ireland, Apple and the European Commission (Vestager, 2020). Therefore, there is also renewed interest in the role of tax avoidance in CSR (Sika, 2010; Hasseldine & Morris, 2013) and the potential of responsible taxation as an emerging norm in the corporate social responsibility (CSR) mix (McCluskey, 2015).

African states are also facing severe development challenges and governance challenges. Despite the economic growth witnessed since the early 2000s, African states are yet to transform their economies and level of social development (Economic Commission for Africa, 2016). Although historical perspective emphasizes that these tax structures were designed to suit colonial objectives in this context, this inadvertently implies the importance of social governance and ethical objectives. Therefore, where objectives change, then tax designs can and should adapt to the new objectives. The new objectives for Africa, are envisioned in the African Union Agenda 2063 documents and the UN Sustainable Development Goals. This involves an Africa, 'that is a prosperous continent where the citizens have a high standard of living, are well educated with a skilled labour force, transformed economies, productive agriculture and healthy ecosystems, with well-preserved environment and a continent resilient to climate change' (Agenda 2063 framework document, 2015). This is the stated 50-year plan for year 2063, so it is imperative that there is a link between these aspirations and domestic capacity for tax revenue generation and collection (SDG 17) including increased and tangible corporate contribution to tax revenues and a just society. This highlights the issue of ethical attitudes towards tax and minimization of incentives for creative accounting. Therefore, it is important that questions of social justice and social contract within tax are prioritized, as this will impact tax design and structures as well as influence capabilities and power, in such as a way that companies could elect following declared ethical principles to direct CSR tax towards identified development objectives. This is seen in its infancy, in the approach taken by Mauritius.

Tax will also feature as part of the economic responsibilities within CSR. This aspect will cover issues of the financial contribution of companies and the integration of costs for the negative externalities of the companies. It could also include economic incentives within taxation systems that allow for company investment and shareholder interest but also recognize CSR impact on stakeholders. A traditional example is the manner in which high-risk investment nature within oil and gas projects often results in tax reliefs for a period of time (Adomaitis & Solsvik, 2020).

Finally, the question of additional voluntary donations towards projects of a philanthropic or discretionary nature would become another aspect of tax within CSR. Thus, governmental direction of CSR voluntary giving could be incorporated into a scheme of financial incentives which may feature as part of a CSR tax or levy within corporate taxation. This also gives the opportunity for mutually beneficial arrangements between society and business. This could also rectify the legitimacy problem for directors, identified by Friedman, because the CSR giving will not be solely arbitrary choices of a benevolent manager or director. Rather it would be a tax useful and societally beneficial action, which sees multi-stakeholder action towards central development priority goals. Philanthropic action, especially when carried out, at the expense of meaningful tax compliance, is not always responsible or beneficial. It is perhaps more important that the company not only pays tax in a basic compliance manner but that it then adopts the best practice standard of compliance, even in circumstances where there are loopholes. There is also some evidence that CSR philanthropic initiatives may not be effectively aligned to wider developmental goals (Frynas, 2005, Jenkins & Newell, 2013) and that companies do not measure the long-term impact of the initiatives on communities involved (Idemudia & Osayande, 2018). This is what raises the question of CSR driving a responsible tax arrangement. This could include trade-offs in tax design where there are rewards (reliefs, rebates) for additional philanthropic projects taken on, in the direction of developmental goals.

There is flexibility and fluidity within the CSR pyramid which means that this will operate in a multifaceted way and intertwined such that, it is very difficult to distinguish the legal from the ethical, or the philanthropic from the economic, as this should all be part of a holistic framework that pushes for taxation to be approached from a socially responsible basis. This would mean a consideration of the ethical, economic, and philanthropic in addition to the legal. However, this approach still leaves the question of 'why' unanswered, i.e. what is the purpose of looking at tax through CSR lens especially in our context? This is why the next section will examine tax ethics or rationale within CSR.

Tax Ethics Debates within CSR

Tax is the priority of the ruling government, and therefore the interest of the governments has often driven the tax design. However, this is only legitimate because governments are viewed in their representative capacity as vehicles for collective societal decision-making and voice. This is not always the case and African states have had their fair share of self-interested governments. This can be seen in the early examples given in the chapter introduction about colonial governments in Africa and the self-interested tax designs that still linger in the structures of African states (Mkandawire, 2010). However, CSR partly emanates from the acceptance that the goals which society and responsible governance seek can only be achieved through multi-stakeholder partnerships between public and private sectors. This could also have the potential to balance the self-interested governments and businesses and re-focus attention towards societies' sustainable development objectives. This is made as an explicit objective under the UN Sustainable Development Goal (SDG 17). Yet, when multinational companies tax records are examined, there are significant estimates on base erosion and profit shifting (BEPS), which results in significant losses of tax revenues in especially low-income countries (Cobham & Jansky, 2016). Crivelli, De Mooij, and Keen (2016) estimate global revenue losses at around US $650 billion annually, of which around one-third relate to developing countries. The intensity as a share of gross domestic product (GDP) is somewhat higher in the latter compared with Organization for Economic Co-operation and Development (OECD) economies. Cobham and Gibson (2016) combine this finding with data on the relatively greater reliance on corporate tax revenue in developing countries to show that the estimated losses are around 2–3% of total tax revenue in OECD countries, but 6–13% in developing countries (2018, p. 207). Cobham and Jansky also confirm the findings but re-estimate the specific amount to US$500 billion annually (2018). Therefore, the moral questions and ethical justifications for tax design and adequate tax compliance become vital to the relationship between such companies and society. On the general level, there are three main debates, which can be derived from the earlier definition of tax functions. These include regulatory compulsion, redistributive justice, and the social contract. The latter two functions represent key ethical debates within tax and inform the willingness or reluctance to pay appropriate tax globally and within African countries. They would also underline justifications for any proposed adjustments or changes along CSR lines.

Redistributive Justice

Equity and fairness should drive tax design and structures and inform the responsiveness to tax regimes. These responses could be described as the behavioural aspects of tax and are fundamental to tax efficiency (Porcano, 1984). The behaviours and motivations of taxpayers play a major role in the efficacy of the tax system but also underlie some of the reasoning behind tax design. Equity can reflect equal treatment (horizontal equity) and appropriate differential treatment (vertical equity) (Porcano, 1984). Fairness demands application of the same rules in a similar manner across defined categories and groups. A universal application of the same rules within similar categories in a consistent and fair manner, yet it also raises the question of capabilities, which pushes for an evaluation of social arrangements in a manner where there are freedoms which enhance functioning and capabilities of individuals (Sen, 1999). Conversely, the relevant institutions involved in this enabling process can be gauged through their capacities and capabilities too.

Huber, in her comparative work, demonstrates the presence of three maxims of distributive justice in Swiss tax law. They are: the ability to pay, the uniformity maxim (including horizontal and vertical equity), and the universality maxim (2019). This analysis also points to a context (Swiss) specific delineation of Justice. Hongler (2019) also suggests that 'the idea of what a just domestic tax system should look like might also change over time, as the underlying idea of political institutions, such as the state, might change' (p. 10). This subjectivity and fluidity are similar to the wider conception by Murphy and Nagler, who determine that:

> taxes must be evaluated as part of the overall system of property rights that they help create. Justice or injustice in taxation can only mean justice or injustice in the system of property rights and entitlements that result from a particular tax regime.
>
> *(2002, p. 8)*

Sugin suggests that this is an indication that 'no tax system, by itself, is capable of carrying out a conception of economic justice, and fairness in government cannot be determined by isolating elements of any tax system' (2004, p. 1193). Nevertheless, this means that tax systems should be viewed from a more holistic approach, such as that found within CSR and that there is a mutual benefit to engineering the tax system to suit rights holders at all levels of society.

Justice debates, therefore, oscillate between the focus on who should contribute and how much each legal person should contribute; and questions of who should benefit, what it should be used for, and how much, and the state as coordinator, should determine this agenda. This unsettled nature also appeals to the nature of CSR especially where there is similar flexibility and bargaining often present in CSR. The particular concept of Justice, which bears resonance in Africa can be found in the communitarian spirit represented in philosophy emerging from the Ubuntu concept (Letseka, 2015). It is a communitarian philosophy that sees human value in the collective of society. This is typified by the African proverb: 'It takes a village to raise a child' (Mugumbate & Nyanguru, 2013 p. 95). This concept of justice focuses on the benefits of the collective and interdependence. This also bears some semblance to social contract principles to be discussed in the next section.

Social Contract

Another ethical philosophy which supports the notion of tax from a CSR perspective is the social contract. McEwen captures this business perspective when she states that, 'tax is a social contract with society and it goes without saying, it is businesses' duty to pay their fair share' (2018). Perspectives on the social contract as a basis for society date back to Hobbes, Rousseau, and Locke (Laskar, 2013). There are also elements of social contract principles in the Ubuntu African Philosophy (Letseka, 2015). Rousseau, for example, represents a relevant perception of social contract because he undertakes the contracting from an initial position of liberty in society for each legal person but subjects that liberty to the sovereign, which in this case, is the general will of all society and not just the narrow perspective of government. Rousseau vitally indicates the role the social contract plays in equality, when he states that:

> I shall end this book with a remark that ought to serve as the basis of the whole social system: and this is, that, instead of annihilating the natural equality between mankind, the fundamental contract substitutes, on the contrary, a moral and legal equality, to make up for that natural and physical difference which prevails amongst individuals, who, though unequal in personal strength and mental abilities, become thus all equal by convention and right.
>
> *(1795, p. 30)*

In more contemporary literature on Justice, Rawls Theories of Justice and Sen's idea of Justice also echo elements of social contract principles. Rawls (1971) refers to an original start position which is hypothetical, where justice can be perceived as fairness at a starting point where people make rational choices at the point of social contract. He suggests more specifically that the social contract may be 'rather, the guiding idea … that the principles of justice for the basic structure of society are the object of the original agreement' (1971, p. 11).

Sen differs from Rawls because he focuses not on a hypothetical social contract situation but on a transcendental approach, which is focused on a rational 'and reasoned choice of policies, strategies and institutions' (2009, p. 15). This takes place in the context that has the potential of the plurality of competing principles and policies, which may have a legitimate claim on assessment of justice Sen (2009). Sen argues that there may be no reasoned agreement on an ideal just society and that practical reasoning involves an actual choice: 'a framework for comparison of justice choosing among the feasible alternatives' (2009, p. 9). Furthermore, the emphasis is on consequential outcomes, that is, 'actual realizations and accomplishments', not just the institutions and rules (Sen, 2009, p. 10). This is a realistic approach, which may be better suited to social contracting within the tax sphere because of the competing legitimate interests. Elements of this could be balanced with Rousseau's view of bargaining and reciprocity within social contract to ensure a situation whereby tax within CSR could become the way for projects taken on by the private sector could be realigned with development objectives and matched with the planned use of government revenues from tax. Therefore, the issues become:

1. Redistribution and negotiations about the means of achieving the tax revenues
2. How action taken in other aspects of CSR, could be tax deductible

Picciotto (2020) casts some doubt on the ability of the social contract concept to truly apply to transnational corporations in the international tax regime, which straddle more than one domestic jurisdiction and thus cannot be viewed as entirely within a government or sovereign jurisdiction. In the absence of agreed international rules, he doubts the feasibility of the lasting contract through effective power bargaining. He examines this in the context of OECD BEPS. Nonetheless, this is an incomplete picture, because despite the moderate effect of voluntary CSR regulatory instruments, they can be viewed through the lens of soft law, which affects regulatory parties and interest groups in disruptive ways (Newman & Posner, 2018). This can be partially seen in the way that publicity, public pressure, and transparency have forced a change in direction and agenda for businesses on many levels. This would include environmental pressure following climate change evidence, social pressure for the recognition of the business impact on human rights and the resulting push for environmental, and modern slavery and human rights due diligence laws cross-nationally. None of these examples represent perfect solutions but they do demonstrate the disruptive effect that soft law within CSR can have when it is used to focus minds on an issue.

The next section takes on the particular example of corporate taxation across African countries and looks specifically at the example emerging from Mauritius, which has integrated a form of CSR within the tax regime as an attempt to leverage that social contract between corporations in society. This is in the form of contributions, which would directly count towards the tax bill. Also, this can be used as an incentive for companies to directly or indirectly contribute and collaborate in the development projects that tax revenues should have been aimed at. This also slightly differs from the challenging sectoral tax incentives such as those found in the mining sector of many developing countries (Readhead, 2018). A CSR tax represents one way of actualizing the social contract in the domestic context, although there is still scope for more experimentation.

The Potential Role of Corporate Tax

The corporate person is a legal creation embodied with legal personality and typically, limited liability. Corporate tax is therefore taxation of income derived from incorporated business profits (Mirlees, 2011). There is considerable academic debate about the relevance of corporate tax to the tax revenue mix, because of the artificial nature of the corporate entity (Huber, 2019). However, it remains a major source of income for developing countries, with some estimates placing it at 25% of total revenues (Avi-Yonah, 2016). There are also more reasons for its strategic use. Avi-Yonah (2016) points to three crucial ones for developing countries and they include: the importance of corporate actors to the global economy, the ease of collection when compared with difficulties faced in the collection of individual income tax, and its role in averting potential 'backstops for progressivity of individual tax' (p. 139–142). The first reason recognizes that corporate tax can allow a developing country to craft incentives and disincentives, which influence the behaviour of large corporate actors in the domestic economy. It may also allow businesses to influence how the development objectives within social responsibility are co-created. Cobham and Gibson (2016) point out that 'corporate tax avoidance remains the top public concern when it comes to business behaviour' (p. 10) And 'African countries both north and south of the Sahara are consistently the most exposed to corporate tax dodging in terms of proportion to GDP/tax revenues' (p. 16) This is seen as the reason for the OECD BEPS project, which involves 137-member-states (as at December 2019) in the OECD/G20 Inclusive Framework on BEPS (OECD, 2020). Many African countries are participating in this initiative which aims to close gaps that allow for abuses within the international tax regime.

However, challenges remain with capacity issues and implementation strategies that would favour African interests (Oguttu, 2017). Also, there are still unsettled issues that involve reconciling the often-contradictory state interests. There have been suggestions of unitary taxation for multinational corporations (Ezenagu, 2019). Though this is unlikely to fully succeed as it works against the interests of home states versus those of host states, nevertheless there has been a 2020 statement by the OECD/G20 Inclusive Framework on BEPS on the Two-Pillar Approach to Address the Tax Challenges Arising from the Digitalisation of the Economy which appears to have reached a fragile accord on a unified approach. Picciotto describes key elements as:

> Pillar One would be the 'new taxing right', now with a wide scope definition of 'consumer-facing' business, but which would still exclude non-digital business-to-business services. Pillar Two would be a new 'global anti-base erosion tax' to ensure that all TNCs would pay a minimum effective tax rate on their global profits.
>
> *(Picciotto, 2020)*

Nevertheless, the focus in this section is on the corporate tax at the domestic level across Africa. The average rate of corporate tax in Africa lies around 28% (Donald, 2018). The range is from 15% to 35% with disparities between African states such as Mauritius at 15% and Zambia at 35% (Donald, 2018). From a statistical correlation between revenues and economic growth, Donald (2018) observes that government revenues do not increase exponentially with higher rates of corporate tax. EY 2020 also published the worldwide corporate tax guide which lists detailed corporate tax regulations in over 160 jurisdictions including most African countries. It demonstrates this disparity within Africa and confirms the tax range and disparity but it also highlights an original approach taken by Mauritius within its corporate tax framework towards CSR.

The Mauritius Approach

This innovative approach used in Mauritius directly refers to CSR within the tax system. The general corporate income tax rate in Mauritius is 15%, however, with regard to CSR within the tax system, there is:

> A requirement to establish a Corporate Social Responsibility (CSR) fund applies to companies. Companies must set up a CSR fund equal to 2% of chargeable income for the preceding year. Companies use this fund to implement a CSR program in accordance with their own CSR framework.

> For this purpose, the CSR program must have as its object the alleviation of poverty, the relief of sickness or disability, the advancement of education of vulnerable persons or the promotion of any other public object beneficial to the Mauritian community.
>
> *(EY, 2020, p. 1076)*

The initial change which brought CSR into the tax legislative framework occurred in 2009 when the Income Tax Act (ITA) 1995 was amended by the Finance (Miscellaneous Provisions) Act 2009 (Pillay, 2015, p. 245). There were subsequent amendments which include the Finance Act 2011 and 2012 (Pillay, 2015).

The 2020 EY guide also notes that following further legal amendments contained in the Finance (Miscellaneous Provisions) Act 2016 (FMPA 2016) and the Finance (Miscellaneous Provisions) Act 2017, the current position is that:

> at least 50% of any CSR fund set up during the period from 1 January 2017 to 31 December 2018 must be paid to the National Social Inclusion Foundation (CSR Foundation) through the (Mauritius Revenue Authority) MRA. Effective from 1 January 2019, the contribution to the CSR Foundation will be 75%. The balance must be applied to the entity's own CSR framework for CSR funds set up by 31 December 2018.
>
> *(p. 1077)*

Subsequently, companies are allowed to contribute to a non-governmental organization implementing a CSR program in the designated priority areas which coincide with developmental objectives.

The 2021 MRA CSR guide specifies that

> Remaining % of the CSR Fund – the remaining 50%/ 25% of the CSR Fund shall be used by the company – i. in respect of a CSR Fund set up before 1 January 2019, to implement a CSR Programme in accordance with its own CSR Framework; ii. in respect of a CSR Fund set up on or after 1 January 2019, to implement a CSR Programme or finance a non-governmental organisation implementing a CSR Programme in the priority areas of intervention.
>
> *(p. 5)*

These priority areas include: education, health, social housing, family protection, peace and nation-building, poverty alleviation, and disability support among others (MRA, 2021). This represents a clear bargaining, negotiation, and choice framework that integrates valid development objectives within CSR and the tax framework as there is also a prohibitions list that includes contributions to government departments and parastatal body as well as any activity targeting shareholders, senior staff or their family (MRA, 2021). The Mauritius Revenue Authority latest guide on corporate social responsibility in February

2021 specifies that 'Where, in respect of a year of assessment, the Director-General has reason to believe that money has not been spent in respect of a CSR Fund ..., he may raise an assessment under section 129 of the ITA' (p. 11).

This framework for CSR and tax is built on a tax legal framework, the ITA. It also codifies the ethical values within the act by emphasizing redistribution and social contract with the Mauritian community. For example, Section 2 of the ITA defines CSR as 'a programme having as main objective to alleviate poverty, to relieve sickness or disability, to advance education of vulnerable persons or to promote any other public object beneficial to the Mauritian community'. The economic aspects are also clearly delineated by the benchmark of '2% of chargeable income for the preceding year'. This gives an economic calculable value to the CSR fund. Finally, there is still scope for further discretionary or philanthropic giving.

Mauritius is regarded as one of Africa's success stories with one of the highest per capita income and stable governance (Frankel, 2014). Yet it has faced accusations of being a tax haven (Oxfam, 2019). This is because of preferential regimes for offshore companies such as the global business company. It can be noted that one of the exceptions to the CSR fund, is the global business company form (MRA, 2021, p. 2). However, Mauritius has refuted this tax haven status accusation with some success, as in 2019 they were taken off the EU list of tax havens (Oxfam, 2019).

It is also a small country with the population of Mauritius being approximately 1.25 million and a mixed colonial heritage with Dutch, French, and British eras (Frankel, 2014). Therefore, there are still questions about how easy it will be to duplicate its type of experimentation for larger populations in Africa's larger countries. Nevertheless, it is an African example and the country could play a key role in indicating potential indigenous solutions for development.

In 2017, Mauritius hosted the inaugural launch of the African Economic Platform (AEP), where it suggested to the gathering of African leaders, the value of a joint African approach and engagement with the private sector and CSR (AEP, 2017). The results which emerge from such CSR and tax experimentation will provide clear, definite, and measurable objectives against a human development government agenda. This type of tax design opens up the potential that companies could leverage on their payment for and involvement in these CSR projects to request reciprocal governance accountability for direct taxation.

Potential Tentative Recommendations for a CSR and Tax Framework

The preceding example and earlier analysis on linkages between CSR and tax, therefore, suggests the potential for contextual integration of CSR frameworks into tax systems through:

1. Tax incentives for directed CSR action for example: a portion of existing tax rates or a tax reduction for action taken within a clear framework.

2. Defined priority list for contextual CSR programmes and projects linked to human development and infrastructure needs.
3. Defined list of non-governmental and civil society partners.
4. A coordinating multi-stakeholder accountable platform with designated responsibilities and transparency.
5. Defined review periods which measure progress on objectives and efficient use of tax revenues thereby gained.
6. Extensive publicity of good practice examples such as those companies which choose to go beyond the statutory minimum.

Conclusion

There is a social contract bargaining, present within the tax system which should be aimed at ensuring maximization of tax revenues, efficient use of those resources and the equity and fairness within the overall system. Corporate tax revenues are a significant portion of revenues for African countries. Focus of tax revenues in African countries should be geared towards priorities which are imminent and contextually relevant. This includes development priorities. However, the tax system could be the result of a contractual set of rational choices between society and the individual or corporate person, elements of the negotiation, will constitute both societal and self-interested purposes however tax becomes the reconciling of those purposes to the objectives of society in general through a collective bargaining. There are principles which can underpin this flexibility within the tax system and such bargaining can take place from a CSR perspective. This indicates the potential for the government (especially representative government) becoming involved in directing CSR frameworks towards developmental goals. The trade-off would be that tax takes on a truly contractual perspective, where there are incentives for projects which are carried out in line with the objectives of governance and through transparent channels. This could result in tax reductions or reliefs and the ability to work with civil society towards needs in communities and in localities, where the companies operate. This may also push the idea of companies leveraging on their already significant tax contribution to ensure that transparent governance and accountability in the use of such tax funds. Accountable use, may then also encourage companies to contribute more visibly through such a CSR framework and thereby avoid less tax. Nevertheless, this will not negate the need for legal changes to the tax framework internationally but it will create potential for better domestic use of tax revenues of corporations.

References

Adomaitis, N., & Solsvik, T. (2020). Norway parliament grants more tax relief to oil sector. *Reuters*. Retrieved from https://uk.reuters.com/article/uk-health-coronavirus-norway-oil-idUKKBN23F1NT

African Economic Platform (AEP) (2017). *Statement of hon. Pravind Kumar Jugnauth, prime minister of Mauritius at the launching of the African economic platform.* Retrieved from https://au.int/sites/default/files/speeches/32240-spaep_hon_prime_minister_speech_20_mar_2017.pdf

Alm, J., & Torgier, B. (2011). Do ethics matter? Tax compliance and morality. *Journal of Business Ethics, 101*(4), 635–651.

Amaeshi, K., Adi, B., Ogbechie, C., & Amao, O. (2006). Corporate social responsibility in Nigeria: Western mimicry or indigenous influences? *Journal of Corporate Citizenship, 24*, 83–99.

Amin, S. (1972). Underdevelopment and dependence in black Africa-Origins and contemporary forms. *Journal of Modern African Studies, 10*(4), 503–524.

Avi-Yonah, R. (2016). Hanging together: A multilateral approach to taxing multinationals. *Michigan Business and Entrepreneurial Law Review, 5*(2), 137–159. Retrieved from https://repository.law.umich.edu/mbelr/vol5/iss2/3.

Avi-Yonah, R. S. (2006). The three goals of taxation. *Tax Law Review, 60*(1), 1–28.

BMZ (2017). *No taxes—No development.* German Federal Ministry for Economic Ministry and Development. Retrieved from https://www.bmz.de/de/zentrales_downloadarchiv/themen_und_schwerpunkte/governance/170606_BMZ_factsheet_tax.pdf.

Carroll, A. B. (1991). The pyramid of corporate social responsibility: Toward the moral management of organizational stakeholders. *Business Horizons, 34*(4), 39–48.

Cobham, A., & Gibson, L. (2016). Ending the era of tax havens. Why the UK government must lead the way. Oxford. Retrieved from http://oxfamilibrary.openrepository.com/oxfam/bitstream/10546/601121/4/bp-ending-era-tax-havens-uk-140316-en.pdf

Cobham, A., & Janský, P. (2018). Global distribution of revenue loss from corporate tax avoidance: Re-estimation and country results: Global Corporate Tax Avoidance. *Journal of International Development, 30*(2), 206–232.

Combating international tax avoidance — OECD webpage. Retrieved from https://www.oecd.org/about/impact/combatinginternationaltaxavoidance.htm

Crivelli, E., De Mooij, R., & Keen, M. (2016). Base erosion, profit shifting and developing countries. *Public Finance Analysis, 72*(3), 268– 301.

Donald, N. (2018). Taxation in Africa: Comparative Analysis vs Development Index -Africa taxation at a glance. KPMG Africa Advisory. Retrieved from https://www.icpak.com/wp-content/uploads/2018/08/2.-Taxation-in-Africa-FCCA-Donald-Nsanyiwa.pdf

Economic Commission for Africa (2016). *UN ECA. The African social development index: Measuring human exclusion for structural transformation.* Retrieved from https://www.uneca.org/sites/default/files/PublicationFiles/asdi_report_technical_eng.pdf.

European Commission (2011) A renewed EU strategy 2011-14 for Corporate Social Responsibility /* COM/2011/0681 final */.

European Community (2017). *Aggressive tax planning indicators final report*, WORKING PAPER No. 71, 2017. Retrieved from https://ec.europa.eu/taxation_customs/sites/taxation/files/taxation_papers_71_atp_.pdf

EY (2020). *Worldwide corporate tax guide 2020.* Retrieved from https://www.ey.com/en_gl/tax-guides/worldwide-corporate-tax-guide-2020.

Ezenagu, A. (2019). *Unitary taxation of multinationals: implications for sustainable development.* Centre for International Governance Innovation.

Frankel, J. (2014). *Mauritius: African success story* (No. c13441). National Bureau of Economic Research. Retrieved from https://www.nber.org/books-and-chapters/african-successes-volume-iv-sustainable-growth/mauritius-african-success-story

Friedman, M. (1970). The social responsibility of business is to increase its profits. *New York Times Magazine*, 13 September 1970, pp. 122–126.

Frynas, J. (2005). The false developmental promise of corporate social responsibility: Evidence from multinational oil companies. *International Affairs*, *81*(3), 581–598.

Ganghof, S. (2008). The politics of tax structure. In I. Shapiro, P. Swenson, & D. Donno (Eds.), *Divide and deal: The politics of distribution in democracies* (pp. 72–98). New York University Press.

Hasseldine, J., & Morris, G. (2013). Corporate social responsibility and tax avoidance: A comment and reflection. *Accounting Forum*, *37*(1), 1–14.

Hongler, P. (2019). *Justice in international tax law: A normative review of the international Tax Regime (IBFD).*

Huber, G. L. (2019). Conceptual problems of corporate tax IBFD, Netherlands.

Idemudia, U. (2014). Corporate social responsibility and development in Africa: Issues and possibilities: CSR and development in Africa. *Geography Compass*, *8*(7), 421–435.

Idemudia, U., & Osayande, N. (2018). Assessing the effect of corporate social responsibility on community development in the Niger Delta: A corporate perspective. *Community Development Journal*, *53*(1), 155–172.

Janský, P., & Palanský, M. (2019). Estimating the scale of profit shifting and tax revenue losses related to foreign direct investment. *International Tax and Public Finance*, *26*(5), 1048–1103.

Jenkins, R., & Newell, P. (2013). CSR, tax and development. *Third World Quarterly*, *34*(3), 378–396.

Kivuitu, M., Yambayamba, K., & Fox, T. (2005). How can corporate social responsibility deliver in Africa? Insights from Kenya and Zambia. In *Perspectives on corporate responsibility for environment and development*. International Institute for Environment and Development. Retrieved from https://pubs.iied.org/sites/default/files/pdfs/migrate/16006IIED.pdf.

Kolk, A., & Lenfant, F. (2018). Responsible business under adverse conditions: Dilemmas regarding company contributions to local development. *Business Strategy & Development*, *1*(1), 8–16.

Kraakman, R. H. et al. (2017). *The anatomy of corporate law: A comparative and functional approach* (3rd ed.). Oxford: Oxford University Press.

Laskar, M. (2013). Summary of social contract theory by Hobbes, Locke and Rousseau (April 4, 2013). Retrieved from SSRN https://ssrn.com/abstract=2410525 or doi:10.2139/ssrn.2410525.

Letseka, M. (2015). Ubuntu and justice as fairness. *Mediterranean Journal of Social Sciences*, *5*, 544–551.

Littlewood, M. (2019). John Tiley and the thunder of history. In P. Harris & D. de Cogan (Eds.), *Studies in the history of tax law* (pp. 55–92). Oxford: Hart Publishing.

Mauritius Revenue Authority (MRA) (2021). Guide on corporate social responsibility (CSR). Retrieved from https://www.mra.mu/download/CSRGuide.pdf.

McCluskey, R. (2015). Is responsible tax behaviour the next frontier of CSR? Retrieved from https://www.ictd.ac/blog/is-responsible-tax-behaviour-the-next-frontier-of-csr/. The International Centre for Tax and Development (ICTD).

McEwen, R. (2018). Tax is a social contract. SSE. Retrieved from https://www.sse.com/news-and-views/2018/06/tax-is-a-social-contract/.

Mirrlees, J. A., Adam, S., & Institute for Fiscal Studies (Great Britain) (Eds.). (2011). *Tax by design: The Mirrlees Review*. Oxford University Press. Retrieved from https://www.ifs.org.uk/publications/5353

Mkandawire, T. (2010). On tax efforts and colonial heritage in Africa. *Journal of Development Studies*, *46*(10), 1647–1669.

Mugumbate, J., & Nyanguru, A. (2013). Exploring African philosophy: The value of ubuntu in social work. *African Journal of Social Work*, *3*(1), 82–100.

Murphy, L. B., & Nagel, T. (2002). *The myth of ownership: Taxes and justice*. Oxford: Oxford University Press.

Muthuri, J. (2012). Corporate social responsibility in Africa: Definition, issues and processes seminar Royal Holloway 28 November 2012. Retrieved from https://intranet.royalholloway.ac.uk/management/documents/pdf/events/2012-judy-muthuri-seminar.pdf

Ndikumana, L. (2014). Capital flight and tax havens: Impact on investment and growth in Africa. *Revue D'Économie du Développement*, *22*(HS02), 99–124.

Newman, A. L., & Posner, E. (2018). *Voluntary disruptions: International soft law, finance, and power*. Oxford: Oxford University Press.

Oguttu, A. W. (2017). *Tax base erosion and profit shifting in Africa – Part 2: A critique of some priority OECD actions from an African perspective (February 2017)*. ICTD Working Paper 64. Retrieved from SSRN https://ssrn.com/abstract=3120528 or doi:10.2139/ssrn.3120528.

Okoye, A. (2009). Theorising corporate social responsibility as an essentially contested concept: Is a definition necessary? *Journal of Business Ethics*, *89*(4), 613–627.

Okoye, A. (2012). Exploring the relationship between corporate social responsibility, law and development in an African context: Should government be responsible for ensuring corporate responsibility? *International Journal of Law and Management*, *54*(5), 364–378.

Okoye, A. (2019). CSR and a capabilities approach to development: CSR laws as an allocative device? In O. Osuji, F. Ngwu, & D. Jamali (Eds.), *Corporate social responsibility in developing and emerging markets: Institutions, actors and sustainable development*. Cambridge: Cambridge University Press.

Organization for Economic Co-Operation and Development (2019). Revenue Statistics in Africa 2019 Statistiques des recettes publiques en Afrique 2019: 1990–2017 1990–2017 | OECD iLibrary. Retrieved from https://www.oecd-ilibrary.org/sites/5daa24c1-en-fr/index.html?itemId=/content/publication/5daa24c1-en-fr.

Organization for Economic Co-Operation and Development (2020). *Member List OECD/G20 Inclusive Framework on BEPS*. Retrieved from https://www.oecd.org/tax/beps/inclusive-framework-on-beps-composition.pdf.

Organization for Economic Co-Operation and Development, & BEPS (2020). *Statement*. Retrieved from http://www.oecd.org/tax/beps/statement-by-the-oecd-g20-inclusive-framework-on-beps-january-2020.pdf.

Oxfam (2019). EU governments whitewash tax havens of Mauritius and Switzerland. Oxfam International. Retrieved from https://www.oxfam.org/en/press-releases/eu-governments-whitewash-tax-havens-mauritius-and-switzerland

Picciotto, S. (2020). Taxation of transnational corporations and the social contract. Retrieved from https://www.afronomicslaw.org/2020/07/17/taxation-of-transnational-corporations-and-the-social-contract/ & Retrieved from https://www.oecd.org/tax/beps/statement-by-the-oecd-g20-inclusive-framework-on-beps-january-2020.pdf.

Pillay, R. (2015). *The changing nature of corporate social responsibility: CSR and development in context -- The Case of Mauritius*. Abingdon: Routledge.

Porcano, T. (1984). Distributive justice and tax policy. *Accounting Review*, *59*(4), 619–636.

Rawls, J. (1971). *A theory of justice*. Cambridge, Massachusetts: Harvard University Press.

Readhead, A. (2018). Tax incentives in mining: Minimising risks to revenue. Retrieved from https://www.oecd.org/tax/beps/tax-incentives-in-mining-minimising-risks-to-revenue-oecd-igf.pdf.

Rousseau, J.-J. (1795). *A treatise on the social compact, or, the principles of political law.* London: D. I. Eaton.

Sen, A. (1999). *Development as freedom.* Oxford: OUP.

Sen, A. (2009). *The idea of Justice.* London: Allen Lane (Penguin).

Sikka, P. (2010). Smoke and mirrors: Corporate social responsibility and tax avoidance. *Accounting Forum, 34*(3–4), 153–168.

Sugin, L. (2004). Theories of distributive justice and limitations on taxation: What Rawls demands from tax systems (SSRN Scholarly Paper ID 555988). *Social Science Research Network.* Retrieved from https://papers.ssrn.com/abstract=555988.

Templeman, L. J. (1979). Re Southard & Co. Ltd 1 WLR 1198.

The African Union (2015). *The Africa we want agenda 2063 framework document.* Retrieved from https://www.un.org/en/africa/osaa/pdf/au/agenda2063-framework.pdf

UNCTAD (2016). *Trade mis-invoicing in primary commodities in developing countries: The cases of Chile, Côte d'Ivoire, Nigeria, South Africa and Zambia.* New York and Geneva: UNCTAD.

Vestager, M. (2020). Statement by Executive Vice-President Margrethe Vestager on the Commission's decision to appeal the General Court's judgment on the Apple tax state aid case in Ireland [Text]. European Commission - European Commission. Retrieved from https://ec.e.

Visser, W. (2005). Revisiting Carroll's CSR pyramid. In Rahbek & Huniche (Eds.), *corporate citizenship in a development perspective,* 2005. Copenhagen: Copenhagen Business School Press.

Wilkinson, B., & Fancher, M. M. (2004). Eliminating 'double taxation': The dividend imputation alternative: Certified public accountant. *CPA Journal, 74*(8), 15–16.

6

TACKLING CLIMATE CHANGE IN AFRICA THROUGH CORPORATE SOCIAL RESPONSIBILITY

Tahiru Azaaviele Liedong, Olushola Emmanuel Ajide, and Oluyomi Abayomi Osobajo

Introduction

Society and economy are threatened by climate change, which refers to a statistically significant change in the mean state or the temporal variability of the climate due to natural variation of external forcing, anthropogenic changes in the atmosphere's composition, or changes in land use. In other words, it is the increase in the atmospheric composition, known as greenhouse gas emissions, induced by human activities leading to the depletion of the ozone layer. Besides water vapour, other primary greenhouse gases include carbon dioxide (CO_2), nitrous oxide (N_2O), halocarbons or CFCs (gases containing fluorine, chlorine, and bromine), and methane (Ramanathan & Feng, 2009). By burning fossil fuels such as coal and oil, CO_2 (the most important global warming gas) is released into the atmosphere. A single CO_2 molecule can remain in the air for hundreds of years (Revelle, 1982). CO_2 and other greenhouse gases heat the globe by absorbing the sun's energy and preventing heat from escaping back into space (El Zein & Chehayeb, 2015). Thirty-six billion tonnes of CO_2 are emitted annually (Nejat et al., 2015).

While Africa's contribution to carbon emissions could be termed minor, it has been recognized as the world's most vulnerable region to climatic changes and global warming (Masipa, 2017; Tacoli, 2009). Africa is likely to be more impacted than other continents due to its economic exposure to climatic variation. Over the past few decades, it has experienced more frequent and intense climate extremes than any other region in the world (Shepard, 2018). Changes in the climate have health and physical consequences, including severe weather events (e.g. droughts, storms, floods, and heat waves) and disrupted water systems. These consequences accentuate Africa's perennial developmental problems by especially harming agriculture, one of the mainstays of the region's economy

DOI: 10.4324/9781003038078-7

(Abay, Asnake, Ayalew, Chamberlin, & Sumberg, 2021; Branca et al., 2021; Oluwatayo and Ojo, 2016). It is estimated that Africa's GDP exposure and vulnerability to changing climate patterns would likely grow from $895 billion in 2018 to about $1.4 trillion by 2023 (Dahir, 2018). However, this impact is expected to vary widely across the region, with southern Africa predicted to get hotter and drier and eastern Africa to get wetter.

Globally, the devastating effects of climate change have caused the emergence of movements and the adoption of actions, principles, and conventions to tackle the destruction of the natural environment (Hulme & Mahony, 2010). Prominent among them is the United Nations Framework Convention on Climate Change (UNFCCC).[1] Several agreements including the Montreal Protocol (aimed at protecting the stratospheric ozone layer), Kyoto Protocol (aimed at limiting greenhouse gases emissions), Cancun Agreement (aimed at addressing the long-term challenge of climate change and particularly helping developing nations deal with climate change), and the Paris Agreement have been signed and adopted to implement the principles and goals provided by the UNFCCC. The Paris Agreement, which is the most recent and most significant international climate change pact signed in 2015 to limit the average rise in global temperatures to 2°C above pre-industrial levels and keep the increase below 1.5°C, has prompted many African countries to commit towards transiting to low-carbon economies. Moreover, the UN Sustainable Development Goals (SDGs), which most African countries aspire to achieve, capture the need for urgent action to combat climate change and its impacts.

Despite efforts by the international community to tackle climate change, progress has been slow. Some works have cited poorly designed, weakly incentivized and unmonitored transnational climate change mitigation initiatives (Michaelowa & Michaelowa, 2017; Rosen, 2015) as well as the limited consideration of the role of regional and local governments in global climate change policies (Galarraga, Gonzalez-Eguino, & Markandya, 2011) as main causes of the slow progress. Others have acknowledged the lack of leadership and commitment in mitigating climate change, with countries backtracking or unwilling to accept far-reaching climate measures (Gupta, 2010). This low commitment arises from either the limited institutional capacities of national governments to implement the measures (Rabe, 2007) or the realization that full implementation of the measures could create international competitive disadvantages for domestic industries especially when other countries are not adhering to measures. For instance, President Donald Trump withdrew the United States (U.S.) from the Paris Agreement because he saw it as an obstacle to his vision of revitalizing the U.S. economy with fossil fuel production. He also viewed it to be unfair to his country's economic competition with other countries like China and India which, unlike the U.S., are free to use fossil fuels.[2]

Peering into national-level implementation of climate change policies and measures, it is important to acknowledge that climate change outcomes are a function of climate change politics between vested interest groups, including

State and non-State actors (Beeson & McDonald, 2013; Broto, 2017; Dubash, 2013; Hale, 2010; Hochstetler & Viola, 2012; Newell, Pattberg, & Schroeder, 2012). Interest groups, including businesses, non-governmental organizations, civil society organizations, and communities have stakes in climate change, and often lobby governments to ensure that their preferences are considered in final decisions. One of the interesting things about the politics of climate change is that it brings the multifaceted role of business in climate change to the fore (Wright & Nyberg, 2016). First, businesses are often defensive about maintaining the climate status-quo and are dominant in advocating short-term self-interests over long-term low-carbon policies (Carter, 2014). Second, governments are wary of imposing new regulations and taxes, two critical tools for addressing climate change, due to the power of businesses to affect the economy through job cuts, offshoring, and relocations. In this sense, businesses can limit the powers of national governments to implement climate change measures (Eberlein & Matten, 2009; Hale, 2010; Jones & Levy, 2007; Vesa, Gronow, & Ylä-Anttila, 2020). Consequently, market mechanisms for dealing with climate change may run afoul of low political will or self-interested market imperatives such as the tendency to focus on profit maximization rather than emission reduction (Gupta, 2010).

Notwithstanding the complicity of businesses in perpetuating climate change, it is worth noting that some firms are offering innovative solutions to decarbonize economies (Wright & Nyberg, 2016). Increasingly, businesses are coming under pressure to respond and contribute to combating the challenge of climate change. This has caused them to treat the environment as a business agenda (Pinkse & Kolk, 2009; Begg, Van der Woerd & Levy, 2018), often approaching ecological problems as a responsibility imposed by regulation. Other businesses approach climate change as an economic opportunity for serving new markets with 'green' goods, services, and practices (Kolk & Pinkse, 2004; Roman Pais Seles et al., 2018). As innovators, investors, experts, polluters, manufacturers, employers and lobbyists, businesses are obviously significant players in environmental issues and environmental governance (Jones & Levy, 2007). Yet, though recent climate actions in the private sector are encouraging, business response to climate change continues to lag promise and potential. As societies are beginning to hold businesses responsible and accountable for their contribution to, and impact on the environment, there is an increasing awareness and expectation for businesses to play more effective roles in curbing climate change (Wright & Nyberg, 2017; McIntyre, Ivanaj & Ivanaj, 2018).

In Africa where the climate change discourse is still gaining traction, it has become important to amplify why and how businesses can join efforts to arrest carbonization of the African economy. To this end, this chapter focuses on discussing climate change challenges in Africa and how businesses operating in Africa could address these challenges through their corporate social responsibility (CSR) activities. Using Carroll's corporate social performance model (Carroll, 1979, 1998), this chapter explores how climate change is a CSR issue along the ethical, philanthropic, economic, and legal dimensions of corporate citizenship. In doing so, it provides suggestions and highlights potential climate change actions that businesses could integrate into their CSR initiatives.

The Climate Change Challenge in Africa

In diverse ways, climate change poses a significant challenge for Africa. Its foremost impact is on agriculture, a source of livelihood for most people living in the region (Alobo Loison, 2015; Milder, Hart, Dobie, Minai, & Zaleski, 2014; Shiferaw et al., 2014; Sissoko et al., 2011). The effect of climate change on agriculture occurs through various mechanisms, such as changes in temperature and precipitation (Toulmin, 2009). Globally, mean temperatures have risen by 1°C compared to pre-industrial levels (Hawkins et al., 2017). Accordingly, higher temperatures have been recorded in Africa. For example, Collier, Conway, and Venables (2008) argue that northern and southern Africa will become much hotter (4°C or more) and drier, with precipitation falling by 10–20% or more. West and Central Africa will particularly experience large increases in the number of hot days. Temperatures are expected to rise by 2°C in southern Africa, while southwestern African countries such as South Africa, Namibia, and Botswana are expected to experience the greatest increases in temperature (Shepard, 2018). The Sahel region in West Africa is regarded as a climate change hotspot where maximum temperatures can be as high as 40°C.[3] Climate change is expected to make this region even hotter. High temperatures make farmlands drier and difficult to till, thus affecting agricultural output.

Higher temperatures are often associated with intense rainfall. Indeed, Africa records torrential rainfall due to high-temperature levels in the region. However, the rains do not fall over a long period. In other words, the wet seasons are short, often lasting three months in most African countries. Consequently, Africa is more prone to drought than any other region in the world. The Sahel region is particularly characterized by repeated dearths, i.e., low, poorly distributed, and extremely variable monthly and seasonal random rainfall (Slegers & Stroosnijder, 2008). Some researchers earlier predicted that eastern Africa, the Horn of Africa, and parts of Central Africa will experience an increase in rainfall by 15% or more (Shepard, 2018). However, others have countered these predictions with the 'East African paradox' regarding how rains may start later and end sooner, thus leading to an overall decrease in rainfall. In Central Africa, home to the world's second-largest rainforest system, decline in rainfall is fast approaching the minimum level required to sustain the forests.[4] In southern Africa, precipitation is projected to decrease by about 20% (Shepard, 2018). South Africa is especially positioned geographically within a drought belt with a typically warm temperature ranging between 0°C and 35°C with a mean rainfall of only 464 mm to a world average of 857 mm (United Nations Development Programme (UNDP), 2021).

Low rainfall, longer dry spells, and drought cause land degradation – i.e., the reduction (or loss) in land's ability to produce the expected associated economic gain, for example, ecological degradation (Kassas, 1995). Obviously, one of the areas where land degradation is most felt is agriculture. Drought makes land unsuitable for crop farming (Mbah, Ezeano, & Saror, 2016). Crops die and when they do not, harvest yields are low. Similarly, drought impacts livestock production by obliterating grazing fields (Douglas et al., 2008). Conclusively, drought causes agricultural collapse (Toulmin, 2009), as it poses challenges for food security and sustenance of the African population. Already, farmers in some African countries have noticed the ramifications of climatic changes (Kabubo-Mariara & Karanja, 2007), but they may not know how to respond because the required mitigating strategies are likely beyond their expertise.

To put the scale of this challenge into context, it is worth highlighting that hundreds of millions of people in Africa depend on rain to grow food. Put differently, Africa is largely dependent on rain-fed agriculture (Shepard, 2018), which accounts for around 97% of total cropland (Calzadilla, Zhu, Rehdanz, Tol, & Ringler, 2013). With agriculture, the main source of livelihood, especially in rural Africa, as well as a major source of export revenue for African countries (Binswanger & Townsend, 2000; Shiferaw et al., 2014; Sissoko et al., 2011), climatic impacts on agriculture will cause devastating socio-economic consequences, ranging from hunger and malnutrition to economic recessions. According to Dahir (2018), African countries' GDP exposure to changing climate patterns is likely to grow from $895 billion in 2018 to about $1.4 trillion by 2023. This projection recognizes how agriculture supports about 80% of employment in Africa, contributes about 30% of Africa's GDP and 40% of Africa's exports, and supports the livelihoods of about 90% of Africa's population (Commission for Africa, 2005; Mukasa, Woldemichael, Salami, & Simpasa, 2017).

Due to the agriculture industry's importance to Africa, it is seen to be central to poverty reduction in the region (Christiaensen & Demery, 2007). In sub-Saharan Africa, poverty in rural areas where farming is the main source of sustenance for 80% of the poor accounts for 90% of total poverty in the region (Dixon, Gulliver, & Gibbon, 2001). Hence, any negative effects of climate change on the industry could perpetuate destitution and hamper poverty alleviation efforts. This problem is accentuated by high population growth in sub-Saharan Africa (especially in the rural areas). According to the United Nations, African countries could account for half of the growth of the world's population by 2050.[5] This would increase pressure not only on agricultural production but also on natural resources such as water (Calzadilla et al., 2013). In 2006, the Food and Agricultural Organization (FAO) of the United Nations estimated Africa's population to double by 2050 and projected this would increase agricultural consumption by 2.8% annually until 2030, and by 2% between 2030 and 2050. Yet, in 2018, FAO reported that agricultural productivity is lagging in Africa.[6] To paint a clearer picture, agriculture has consequences for other facets of Africa's socio-economic development, which makes its vulnerability to climate change a concerning challenge for policymakers, development practitioners, and some businesses.

Besides impacting agriculture and poverty, climate change also poses challenges for health and sanitation. Due to drought, the availability of fresh water in Africa is projected to decrease, impacting between 75 and 250 million people by 2020 (Tacoli, 2009). A recent report estimated that approximately 400 million people in sub-Saharan Africa do not have access to drinking water (Mason et al., 2019), showing a stark worsening of the situation. Drawing attention to the dire challenge of water shortages on the continent, Climate Watch (2019) asserts that less than 40% of the Nigerian population has direct access to potable water. Hence, Nigerians are at risk of water stress attributed to the escalated inconsistency in rainfall resulting in a decrease in surface water resources and droughts in some parts of the country. Water shortages lead to water poverty. For instance, in rural Kenya, 80% of the population experiences dehydration (FAO, 2011). Water shortages can also have health effects, especially when people drink dirty water. Several diseases related to the consumption of contaminated water, such as cholera, diarrhoea, dysentery, typhoid, and polio, have been recorded in Africa (Adelodun et al., 2021; Ashbolt, 2004; Bordalo & Savva-Bordalo, 2007; Glass, Blake, Waldman, Claeson, & Pierce, 1991; Tumwine et al., 2002; Yang et al., 2020). In fact, Africa contributes a significant proportion to the total global cholera and diarrhoea cases reported to the World Health Organization (Mengel, Delrieu, Heyerdahl, & Gessner, 2014). For instance, 54% of all cholera cases recorded in 2016 occurred in Africa.[7] Between 1996 and 2018, Africa recorded about 280 cholera outbreaks across several countries.[8] These cases, besides causing the loss of human life, put pressure on the already fragile and burdened healthcare systems in African countries (de-Graft Aikins et al., 2010; Kiriga & Barry, 2008).

Furthermore, there is a growing acknowledgement that climate change poses security challenges in Africa (Gleditsch, 2012; Salehyan, 2008). Some scholars have found that rainfall deviations and temperature variations are associated with conflict in Africa (Hendrix & Salehyan, 2012; Koubi, 2019; Nordas & Gleditsch, 2007; Raleigh & Kniveton, 2012). Fighting among pastoral communities, or between pastoral communities, herders, and farmers over access to water and grazing lands are common in eastern Africa (Adano, Dietz, Witsenburg, & Zaal, 2012; van Baalen & Mobjörk, 2018). The migration of people in search of lands that can support their livelihoods (through farming or animal husbandry) increases the likelihood of ethnic and communal clashes, most of which are violent due to the competition for resources and the chances of displacement (FAO, 2011). Furthermore, drought induces conflict through its downward effect on livestock prices (Maystadt & Ecker, 2014). Africa is already grappling with conflict and its ramifications for socio-economic development (Salehyan et al., 2012). The role of climate change in exacerbating this problem is a great concern and challenge for the region (van Weezel, 2020; Witsenburg & Adano, 2009).

Climate Change and Business: Effect and Response

Climate change has been recognized as a business and management issue (Daddi, Todaro, De Giacomo, & Frey, 2018; Howard-Grenville, Buckle, Hoskins, & George, 2014), mainly as it poses challenges and presents opportunities for businesses (Roman Pais Seles et al., 2018; Winn, Kirchgeorg, Griffiths, Linnenluecke, & Günther, 2011; Wittneben & Kiyar, 2009). From an external focus, works have highlighted how climatic variations expose businesses to material, regulatory, reputational, physical, and litigation risks (Amran, Ooi, Wong, & Hashim, 2016; Nikolaou, Evangelinos, & Leal Filho, 2015). These variations cause disruptions to organizational activities and operations (Shen, Ochoa, Shah, & Zhang, 2011), increased insurance cost (Wei & Fang, 2012), and hamper effective service delivery (Allen & Craig, 2016). Preston (2013) observed that by 2050 the increased variability in climate change could cost organizations 3.9 times their current financial commitment.

Moving from an external to an internal focus, Okereke et al. (2012) organized climatic effects on organizational activity into four strata, namely capabilities, culture, structure, and processes. First, they argue that climate change demands new capabilities throughout organizations. These capabilities are required for not only diagnosing and assessing climatic risks, but for also developing appropriate responses, and may range from science to leadership (Thistlethwaite, 2011). Second, they advance that there is an imperative for organizations to change or adapt their cultures to be able to address climate change, which is not always easy. The need for fundamental changes in behaviour, values, and routine becomes complicated when employees resist change. Third, they note that organizations are faced with challenges in restructuring their operations to keep up with climate change mitigation pressures. Embarking on a 'green culture' may call for new reporting lines, chains of command, and even new units or departments. Most of these structural changes have cost implications. Finally, structural changes may require new processes which, like culture, can be challenging to institutionalize. A combination of the external and internal perspectives threatens business survival and performance, as has been recorded in the tourism industry (Brouder & Lundmark, 2011; Craig & Feng, 2018).

To counter the effects of climate change, several business responses have been proposed and reported (Galbreath, 2011). Among these responses include using climate SWOT as a quicker and cost-efficient way to strategically plan for climate change (Pesonen & Horn, 2014), implementing climate-proof operations and supply chains (Wittneben & Kiyar, 2009), developing organizational resilience to manage environmental change (Linnenluecke & Griffiths, 2010), using a new approach of climate change accounting in order to overcome some important weaknesses of previous environmental accounting methods (Evangelinos, Nikolaou, & Leal Filho, 2015), and improving processes, developing new products or seeking new markets (Kolk & Pinkse, 2004). While these responses may be proactive and voluntarily adopted to gain competitive advantage or avoid stricter regulation, they could also be reactively undertaken (Eberlein & Matten, 2009). Overall, business response to climate change spans operational and management activities (Jeswani, Wehrmeyer, & Mulugetta, 2008), and can be classified into six categories, namely emission reduction commitment, product improvement, process and supply improvement, new market and business development, organizational involvement, and external relationship development (Lee, 2012).

Synthesizing the literature, it becomes apparent that business response to climate change assumes a 'business-as-usual' approach (Andersson & Keskitalo, 2018; Wright & Nyberg, 2016), as businesses act based on climate change being an opportunity or a hindrance. In Africa, this approach is problematic. First, Africa is home to several developing countries and a large proportion of the poor population in the world. Considering that climate change is a lesser concern during economic downturns (Kahn & Kotchen, 2011) or in developing countries, business leaders in Africa are less likely to take measures for tackling environmental challenges. There may be a recognition of human-induced climate change among elites in Africa (Steynor et al., 2020; Steynor & Pasquini, 2019), but interest to address the problem or public appreciation of climate change efforts is low. Second, the innovation and capabilities required to turn climate change into a business opportunity are farfetched for most businesses in Africa. Due to the limited capacity to profit from climate change mitigation, managers are likely to overlook the issue on purely business grounds. Therefore, the way forward is for businesses in Africa to see and treat climate change as a corporate social responsibility. Though CSR can be instrumental and targeted at business profitability, this instrumentality is often tempered with elements of altruism that can go a long way to reduce climate change opportunism. Treating climate change as a CSR issue will also increase the scope of participation for all types and sizes of businesses, as it will no longer be limited to only those capable of exploiting it for economic gain.

Climate Change Mitigation as Corporate Social Responsibility

Corporate social responsibility has been attributed to organizations' ongoing desire and need to foster social, economic, and environmental change through corporate intervention (Tencati, Perrini, & Pogutz, 2004; Lakshman, Ramaswami, Alas, Kabongo, & Pandian, 2014). CSR, which covers a broad range of responsibilities expected of an organization towards society (Osobajo, Ajide, & Otitoju, 2019; Morsing & Schultz, 2006), has developed from relatively voluntary and uncoordinated practices to more explicit commitments towards stakeholder needs. The concept has been linked to other concepts like corporate citizenship, business ethics, and corporate social performance because they share common themes such as accountability, ethics, morals, and community (Schwartz & Carroll, 2008; Carroll & Shabana, 2010). Yet, there is no unanimously agreed definition of CSR due to its multifaceted nature (Clarkson, 1995). As business environments keep evolving, what makes an organization as responsible changes over time (Rivoli & Waddock, 2011). However, understanding the dimensions of social responsibility is a good starting point for businesses to appreciate the dynamic and ambiguous nature of CSR and to better translate this appreciation into practice. In this respect, this chapter builds on Carroll's (1979, 1991) four dimensions of CSR to make a connection between climate change and CSR and to highlight why and how the social interventions of businesses must address environmental protection.

The four dimensions of CSR provide a holistic understanding of the scope of corporate citizenship (Carroll, 1979, 1998). They include the economic dimension (i.e. being profitable and fulfilling economic responsibilities); the legal dimension (i.e. obeying the law and fulfilling legal responsibilities); the ethical dimension (i.e. behaving ethically and morally); and the philanthropic dimension (i.e. giving back or making contributions to society). These dimensions have received considerable attention in the CSR literature, and have stood the test of CSR scrutiny over time. Thus, they provide the theoretical framework for the ensuing discussion. These dimensions allow for a broadening of the need for businesses to be responsible and accountable for their contribution and impact on the environment, beyond the dominant coverage of how economic value propositions are influenced by climate change (Porter & Kramer, 2006) and the imperative for businesses to reconfigure operations to reduce climate change while enhancing their competitive positions (Kolk & Pinkse, 2008). In line with Porter and Reinhardt's (2007) assertion that CSR activities are starting to play a strategic role in climate change-related issues, explicating the dimensions of CSR will help to further enhance business responsibility towards the environment and present businesses operating in Africa the opportunity to redefine their activities.

Economic Dimension of CSR

The fulfilment of an organization's economic responsibility is underpinned by profit maximization (Johnson, 1971; Carroll 1979). According to Fassin (2009) and Friedman (1962), profit maximization remains the primary reason why business organizations provide offerings that meet society's needs. Generating profits allows businesses to survive, thus guaranteeing their continuity in the provision of critical and essential products and services to society. Business survival and profitability also have cascading effects on employment and tax revenue – two important lifelines to economic prosperity (Hale, 2010). As businesses expand, they recruit more people, reduce unemployment levels, and support livelihoods. With the consequent rise in living standards, people become more likely to care about climate change and the environment (Kahn & Kotchen, 2011). Profit maximization also has ripple effects for other stakeholders such as shareholders and lenders who depend on the returns from their investments to survive. As investors become wealthier, they would care more about climate change. There are also effects on entities within the supply chain whose prosperity and subsequent ability to support livelihoods and combat climate change depends on how much business they get from partners.

It is worth noting that the economic dimension has further implications for governments and their ability to mitigate climate change. A common fact known to climate change experts and scholars is that African countries lack the financial and institutional capacity to mitigate the harm done to the environment (Collier, Conway, & Venables, 2008; Kumssa & Jones, 2010). For instance, the International Energy Agency estimated that African countries must spend US$2.7 trillion on low-carbon technologies by 2030 to meet climate change targets (Adenle, Manning, & Arbiol, 2017). Though raising this amount will be difficult, the collection of taxes from businesses can help. Conventionally and progressively, the more profits businesses make, the more tax they pay. Therefore, the economic dimension of CSR can impact government interventions on climate change by availing the needed funds. Moreover, when businesses are profitable, they reduce calls and pressures for governments to use limited public funds for bailing bankruptcies or providing unemployment benefits to people laid off from work. This avails funds for financing climate change mitigation. In a nutshell, the economic dimension has a multiplier effect on the ability of individuals, organizations, and governments to fight climate change.

While the foregoing shows how the economic dimension can cater for the natural environment, the reality is quite different. There is a dominant focus on financial performance, but less on improving the quality of life and creating value through sustainable economic-related activities (Allen & Craig, 2016). Against this backdrop, some initiatives for African businesses are worth highlighting. First, businesses operating in Africa should integrate targets for carbon emissions in their investment decision planning. Second, as climate change presents individuals and the society at large in Africa with challenges in agriculture, health, and sanitation, businesses could embark on social entrepreneurship or social investments by providing 'green' products and services. This would entail product innovations that can improve the bottom line while mitigating climate change. Third, businesses in Africa can improve the quality of life of individuals, the community, and society by creating decent jobs and being conscious of the possible harm resulting from their economic decisions (Brei & Böhm, 2013). Even though fulfilling this responsibility could raise costs, it would enhance business legitimacy in society, raise living standards and help draw public attention to climate change.

Conclusively, the economic dimension aligns with Barnett (2007) and Becchetti, Ciciretti, Hasan, and Kobeissi (2012), assertion that businesses should not overly focus on meeting their shareholders' needs at the expense of the natural environment. As businesses seek economic gain, there is a need to avoid creating environmental problems (Ihlen, 2009). The challenges posed by climate change present businesses with the need to redefine economic views towards sustainable development (Allen & Craig, 2016). Hence, as businesses in Africa pursue profit maximization as economic responsibility, they must conduct their operations in a way that respects the concerns and values of the natural environment and society at large to mitigate climate change challenges.

Legal Dimension of CSR

Business organizations, as legal entities, must follow laws and regulations (Carroll & Shabana, 2010). Laws represent the basic 'rules of the game' that govern business relationships with stakeholders, including consumers, employees, the community, and natural environment (Carroll, 1998). Therefore, even as organizations fulfil the economic dimension, they must do so within legal frameworks. Proponents of the legal dimension to CSR argue that an organization's legal responsibility constitutes a contract wherein society grants a company a license to operate and in return expects the company to behave acceptably. In recent times, climate change mitigation has become an expectation in society, and governments in African countries have been enacting laws and setting priorities to address the problem. For instance, about all 16 West African countries have, at least, one national policy document on climate change (Sorgho et al., 2020). Businesses are expected to operate and function within these climate policies to guarantee greater good for all stakeholders.

However, while it is obvious that businesses operating in developed countries such as the United Kingdom are bound by stringent climate change requirements, businesses operating in Africa where regulation is either nonexistent or weakly enforced (Liedong, Peprah, Amartey, & Rajwani, 2020) have more laxity to do what they deem appropriate, which is often inadequate. As environmental dynamism is pushing ecological concerns to the fore of societal concerns (Asrar-ul-Haq, Kuchinke, & Iqbal, 2017), the need for businesses to confer a stakeholder status on the non-human natural environment has become prominent (Starik, 1995; Phillips & Reichart, 2000; Lischinsky, 2015) for legitimacy purposes (Driscoll & Starik, 2004). They can do this by following climate change regulations, at the very least. For example, businesses should aim to comply with any mandatory GHG mitigation law and regulations to harness their contribution towards climate change commitments.

Adhering to climate change regulations is a reactive behaviour. Beyond reaction, businesses in Africa can be proactive in championing climate change policies. Being proactive involves two things. The first is self-regulation, through which businesses can establish and institutionalize industry standards for mitigating climate change, such as carbon disclosures (Andrew & Cortese, 2011). Businesses can also establish internal guidelines and requirements for their own operations. Such self-regulatory proactive initiatives have been documented elsewhere (Eberlein & Matten, 2009; Jeswani et al., 2008; Kolk & Pinkse, 2004). In Africa, there have been calls for self-regulation to counter the impact of climate change (Kumssa & Jones, 2010), but action has been abysmal. The second proactive thing businesses in Africa could do is engage in institutional entrepreneurship, particularly of formal institutions. This will entail doing corporate political activity (CPA), or what is popularly called lobbying (Hillman & Hitt, 1999). Research works have recorded how firms do CPA in African countries to enhance their profitability and competitive advantage (Liedong & Frynas, 2018; Liedong, Aghanya, & Rajwani, 2020; Liedong, Rajwani, & Mellahi, 2017; Mbalyohere, Lawton, Boojihawon, & Viney, 2017; Wocke & Moodley, 2015). There is the need for the focus of CPA to shift from economic competition to the strengthening of the institutional frameworks for climate change mitigation. Just as businesses are encouraged to lobby for anti-corruption regulation in Africa (Idemudia, Liedong, Agbiboa, & Amaeshi, 2019; Liedong, 2017), so are they encouraged to lobby for climate change policies. At the least, businesses should contribute their expertise to climate change policymaking.

CPA or lobbying, despite raising some ethical concerns (Liedong, 2020), has been assessed as a social responsibility. Some scholars argue that businesses need to participate in political processes and contribute to social welfare by filling regulatory gaps and sponsoring or endorsing 'best political candidates' (Alzola, 2013; Scherer et al., 2013). Others argue that policymakers often lack information needed for policy formulation, which makes it a responsibility for businesses to fill knowledge gaps where they exist (Hamilton & Hoch, 1997). Moreover, CPA is seen as a way for businesses to represent their shareholders and stakeholders in policy processes (Leong et al., 2013), in which case lobbying is deemed a socially responsible behaviour that is not only permissible but also obligatory (Neron, 2016). The foregoing arguments provide the basis for firms to engage in pro-climate change CPA to redefine and strengthen the institutions moderating environmental protection in Africa.

Ethical Dimension of CSR

According to Carroll (1991), CSR's ethical dimension focuses on expectations, norms, standards, or behaviour expected of an organization by society but not specified in law. Ethical responsibility supports the principle of organizations being fair by protecting and respecting their stakeholders' moral rights (Kilcullen & Kooistra, 1999). Some of the proponents of this view argue that organizations should accept their moral responsibility beyond simple obedience to society's laws. For instance, McWilliams and Siegel (2001) defined CSR as a situation where the firm goes beyond compliance and engages in actions that appear to further some social good, beyond the firm's interests and that which is required by law. In this respect, there is a strong belief that acting in an environmentally friendly manner is essential for fulfilling an organization's ethical responsibility. For instance, Groves, Frater, Lee, and Stokes (2011) argue that organizations must be committed to acting socially to foster social well-being, which entails protecting the ecological balance. In the same vein, if any business operations or activities result in harm, effort must be made to provide redress or remedy (Campbell, 2007). Behaving ethically does not only help businesses to develop and maintain social legitimacy (Werther Jr & Chandler, 2010; Hopkins, 2005) but it also helps to avert climate change.

Due to their natural resource wealth, African countries have been attractive for businesses looking to expand their operations and global footprint beyond their domestic markets. These businesses need to try to protect the environment by conducting their activities without harming the environment. For instance, industries such as oil and gas and agriculture depend on resources and/or raw materials that are prone to changing weather conditions and depletion (Lash & Wellington, 2007). In the exploitation of natural resources, businesses should act in a stewardship capacity by ensuring that the resources used in production and manufacturing can be replenished for future use. The oil and agricultural industries particularly require higher levels of ethical consideration in Africa due to their potential contribution to greenhouse gases through their flaring and bush-burning activities. It is imperative for businesses operating in these industries to employ strategies that keep track of greenhouse gas emissions. Other industries such as mining should assess and remedy the desertification associated with their operations has on global warming. Overall, self-enforced initiatives underpinned by moral beliefs, not by legal obligations, are needed to stop the tide of climate change in Africa. This is particularly true because the regulatory frameworks in African countries are relatively weak to buffer significant gains in climate protection (Collier et al., 2008; Kumssa & Jones, 2010). Thus, relying on only the law will not help much.

Philanthropic Dimension of CSR

Businesses are expected to give back to society, mainly because they would not exist without society. According to Carroll (1991), CSR's philanthropic dimension entails all business programs and activities directed at meeting society's expectations in promoting goodwill and welfare. Kotler and Lee (2005, p. 3) capture this dimension as 'a commitment to improving community well-being through discretionary business practices and contributions of corporate resources'. The gift of goods and donations in funds are mediums through which organizations make philanthropic contributions. However, organizations are not perceived as unethical if they are not philanthropic (Carroll, 1991). Hence, the main difference between the ethical and philanthropic dimensions is that the latter is an act of goodwill while the former is a moral act. The philanthropic dimension to CSR is also perceived as organizations investing in their society. Just like the ethical dimension, philanthropy is not a legal requirement.

Africa, being underdeveloped, records a lot of human activity that significantly influences the earth's temperature and climate, including deforestation and fossil fuel usage. Despite these devastating activities, philanthropic CSR in the region assumes the form of equipment and financial donations to health, education, and other causes in local communities (Adeleye, Luiz, Muthuri, & Amaeshi, 2020; Amaeshi et al., 2016; Cranenburgh & Arenas, 2014; Kühn,

Stiglbauer, & Fifka, 2018), but overlooks the environment. It is important that philanthropic CSR shifts in two ways. The first is a move towards 'pro-green' donations, which could manifest in the form of providing renewable energy such as solar lamps, establishing wind energy farms, and donating gas to rural communities to reduce dependency on, or end the usage of fossil fuels. The second is a move from material donations to knowledge sharing. Businesses can alter the trajectory of climate change by 'donating' their knowledge to help enlighten rural areas on the challenges, risks, and remedies of climate change. For instance, they could offer charitable donations and aids that would foster information sharing and learning about climate change. They could also target their philanthropy at charities, non-governmental and civil society organizations whose work focuses on climate change mitigation. Further, they could donate equipment for facilitating the works of public agencies that are crucial to climate change mitigation, such as agricultural and environmental departments.

Conclusion

This chapter explored the challenges posed by climate change in Africa and discussed how businesses could tackle these challenges through their CSR activities. It explores four CSR dimensions that broaden the scope of what businesses can do to help mitigate the adverse effects of climate change. To address climate change, businesses must commit to engage in meaningful and sustainable development activities. As economic agents, they can empower individuals and nations to fight climatic variations through their economic decisions. As legal entities, they can adhere to existing regulations while lobbying to strengthen climate change regulatory regimes. Furthermore, as ethics champions and philanthropists, they can act respectively as environmental stewards and climate change resource providers. Through these diverse roles, businesses can help protect the future while also creating the conditions that support their survival, profitability, and competitive advantage.

Notes

1 https://unfccc.int/
2 https://www.bbc.co.uk/news/science-environment-54797743
3 https://eros.usgs.gov/westafrica/node/157
4 https://www.bbc.co.uk/news/world-africa-50726701
5 https://population.un.org/wpp/Publications/Files/WPP2019_Highlights.pdf
6 http://www.fao.org/3/mv737en/MV737EN.pdf
7 https://www.who.int/gho/epidemic_diseases/cholera/en/
8 https://www.who.int/csr/don/archive/disease/cholera/en/

References

Abay, K. A., Asnake, W., Ayalew, H., Chamberlin, J., & Sumberg, J. (2021). Landscapes of opportunity: Patterns of young people's engagement with the rural economy in sub-Saharan Africa. *Journal of Development Studies*, *57*(4), 594–613.

Adano, W. R., Dietz, T., Witsenburg, K., & Zaal, F. (2012). Climate change, violent conflict and local institutions in Kenya's drylands. *Journal of Peace Research, 49*(1), 65–80.

Adeleye, I., Luiz, J., Muthuri, J., & Amaeshi, K. (2020). Business ethics in Africa: The role of institutional context, social relevance, and development challenges. *Journal of Business Ethics, 161*(4), 717–729.

Adelodun, B., Ajibade, F. O., Ighalo, J. O., Odey, G., Ibrahim, R. G., Kareem, K. Y., ... Choi, K. S. (2021). Assessment of socioeconomic inequality based on virus-contaminated water usage in developing countries: A review. *Environmental Research, 192*, 110309.

Adenle, A. A., Manning, D. T., & Arbiol, J. (2017). Mitigating climate change in Africa: Barriers to financing low-carbon development. *World Development, 100*, 123–132.

Allen, M. W., & Craig, C. A. (2016). Rethinking corporate social responsibility in the age of climate change: A communication perspective. *International Journal of Corporate Social Responsibility, 1*(1), 1–11.

Alobo Loison, S. (2015). Rural livelihood diversification in sub-Saharan Africa: A literature review. *Journal of Development Studies, 51*(9), 1125–1138.

Alzola, M. (2013). Corporate dystopia: The ethics of corporate political spending. *Business & Society, 52*(3), 388–426.

Amaeshi, K., Adegbite, E., Ogbechie, C., Idemudia, U., Kan, K., Issa, M., & Anakwue, O. (2016). Corporate social responsibility in SMEs: A shift from philanthropy to institutional works? *Journal of Business Ethics, 138*(2), 385–400.

Amran, A., Ooi, S. K., Wong, C. Y., & Hashim, F. (2016). Business strategy for climate change: An ASEAN perspective. *Corporate Social Responsibility and Environmental Management, 23*(4), 213–227.

Andersson, E., & Keskitalo, E. C. H. (2018). Adaptation to climate change? Why business-as-usual remains the logical choice in Swedish forestry. *Global Environmental Change, 48*, 76–85.

Andrew, J., & Cortese, C. (2011). Accounting for climate change and the self-regulation of carbon disclosures. *Accounting Forum, 35*(3), 130–138.

Ashbolt, N. J. (2004). Microbial contamination of drinking water and disease outcomes in developing regions. *Toxicology, 198*(1), 229–238.

Asrar-ul-Haq, M., Kuchinke, K. P., & Iqbal, A. (2017). The relationship between corporate social responsibility, job satisfaction, and organisational commitment: Case of Pakistani higher education. *Journal of Cleaner Production, 142*, 2352–2363.

Barnett, M. L. (2007). Stakeholder influence capacity and the variability of financial returns to corporate social responsibility. *Academy of Management Review, 32*(3), 794–816.

Becchetti, L., Ciciretti, R., Hasan, I., & Kobeissi, N. (2012). Corporate social responsibility and shareholder's value. *Journal of Business Research, 65*(11), 1628–1635.

Beeson, M., & McDonald, M. (2013). The politics of climate change in Australia. *Australian Journal of Politics and History, 59*(3), 331–348.

Begg, K., Van der Woerd, F., & Levy, D. (Eds.) (2018). *The business of climate change: Corporate responses to Kyoto*. New York: Routledge.

Binswanger, H. P., & Townsend, R. F. (2000). The growth performance of agriculture in subsaharan Africa. *American Journal of Agricultural Economics, 82*(5), 1075–1086.

Bordalo, A. A., & Savva-Bordalo, J. (2007). The quest for safe drinking water: An example from Guinea-Bissau (West Africa). *Water Research, 41*(13), 2978–2986.

Branca, G., Arslan, A., Paolantonio, A., Grewer, U., Cattaneo, A., Cavatassi, R., ... Vetter, S. (2021). Assessing the economic and mitigation benefits of climate-smart agriculture and its implications for political economy: A case study in Southern Africa. *Journal of Cleaner Production, 285*, 125161

Brei, V., & Böhm, S. (2014). 'I L = 10L for Africa': Corporate social responsibility and the transformation of bottled water into a 'consumer activist' commodity. *Discourse and Society*, 25(1), 3–31..

Broto, C. V. (2017). Urban governance and the politics of climate change. *World Development, 93*, 1–15.

Brouder, P., & Lundmark, L. (2011). Climate change in Northern Sweden: Intra-regional perceptions of vulnerability among winter-oriented tourism businesses. *Journal of Sustainable Tourism, 19*(8), 919–933.

Calzadilla, A., Zhu, T., Rehdanz, K., Tol, R. S. J., & Ringler, C. (2013). Economywide impacts of climate change on agriculture in Sub-Saharan Africa. *Ecological Economics, 93*, 150–165.

Campbell, J. L. (2007). Why would corporations behave in socially responsible ways? An institutional theory of corporate social responsibility. *Academy of Management Review, 32*(3), 946–967.

Carroll, A. B. (1979). A three-dimensional conceptual model of corporate performance. *Academy of Management Review, 4*(4), 497–505.

Carroll, A. B. (1991). The pyramid of corporate social responsibility: Toward the moral management of organisational stakeholders. *Business Horizons, 34*(4), 39–48.

Carroll, A. B. (1998). The four faces of corporate citizenship. *Business and Society Review, 100–101*(1), 1–7.

Carroll, A. B., & Shabana, K. M. (2010). The business case for corporate social responsibility: A review of concepts, research and practice. *International Journal of Management Reviews, 12*(1), 85–105.

Carter, N. (2014). The politics of climate change in the UK. *WIREs Climate Change, 5*(3), 423–433.

Christiaensen, L., & Demery, L. (2007). *Down to earth: Agriculture and poverty reduction in Africa, directions in development*. Washington, DC.

Clarkson, M. E. (1995). A stakeholder framework for analysing and evaluating corporate social performance. *Academy of Management Review, 20*(1), 92–117.

Collier, P., Conway, G., & Venables, T. (2008). Climate change and Africa. *Oxford Review of Economic Policy, 24*(2), 337–353.

Commission for Africa (2005). *Our common interest: Report of the Commission for Africa*. London.

Craig, C. A., & Feng, S. (2018). A temporal and spatial analysis of climate change, weather events, and tourism businesses. *Tourism Management, 67*, 351–361.

Cranenburgh, K., & Arenas, D. (2014). Strategic and moral dilemmas of corporate philanthropy in developing countries: Heineken in sub-Saharan Africa. *Journal of Business Ethics, 122*(3), 523–536.

Daddi, T., Todaro, N. M., De Giacomo, M. R., & Frey, M. (2018). A systematic review of the use of organization and management theories in climate change studies. *Business Strategy and the Environment, 27*(4), 456–474.

Dahir, A. L. (2018). *Africa's fastest-growing cities are the most vulnerable to climate change globally*. World Economic Forum.

de-Graft Aikins, A., Unwin, N., Agyemang, C., Allotey, P., Campbell, C., & Arhinful, D. (2010). Tackling Africa's chronic disease burden: From the local to the global. *Globalization and Health, 6*(1), 5.

Dixon, J., Gulliver, A., & Gibbon, D. (2001). *Farming systems and poverty*. Washington, DC.

Douglas, I., Alam, K., Maghenda, M., Mcdonnell, Y., McLean, L., & Campbell, J. (2008). Unjust waters: Climate change, flooding and the urban poor in Africa. *Environment and Urbanisation, 20*(1), 187–205.

Driscoll, C., & Starik, M. (2004). The primordial stakeholder: Advancing the conceptual consideration of stakeholder status for the natural environment. *Journal of Business Ethics, 49*(1), 55–73.

Dubash, N. K. (2013). The politics of climate change in India: Narratives of equity and cobenefits. *WIREs Climate Change, 4*(3), 191–201.

Eberlein, B., & Matten, D. (2009). Business responses to climate change regulation in Canada and Germany: Lessons for MNCs from emerging economies. *Journal of Business Ethics, 86*(2), 241–255.

El Zein, A. L., & Chehayeb, N. A. (2015). The effect of greenhouse gases on earth's temperature. *International Journal of Environmental Monitoring and Analysis, 3*(2), 74–79.

Evangelinos, K., Nikolaou, I., & Leal Filho, W. (2015). The effects of climate change policy on the business community: A corporate environmental accounting perspective. *Corporate Social Responsibility and Environmental Management, 22*(5), 257–270.

Fassin, Y. (2009). The stakeholder model refined. *Journal of Business Ethics, 84*(1), 113–135.

Food and Agricultural Organization (FAO) (2011). FAO emergency and rehabilitation assistance in Kenya. Retrieved from http://www.fao.org/fileadmin/user_upload/emergencies/docs/CAP2011_Kenya.pdf (assessed 21/01/21).

Friedman, M. (1962). *Capitalism and freedom.* Chicago, IL: University of Chicago Press

Galarraga, I., Gonzalez-Eguino, M., & Markandya, A. (2011). The role of regional governments in climate change policy. *Environmental Policy and Governance, 21*(3), 164–182.

Galbreath, J. (2011). To what extent is business responding to climate change? Evidence from a global wine producer. *Journal of Business Ethics, 104*(3), 421–432.

Glass, R. I., Blake, P. A., Waldman, R. J., Claeson, M., & Pierce, N. F. (1991). Cholera in Africa: Lessons on transmission and control for Latin America. *Lancet, 338*(8770), 791–795.

Gleditsch, N. P. (2012). Whither the weather? Climate change and conflict. *Journal of Peace Research, 49*(1), 3–9.

Groves, C., Frater, L., Lee, R., & Stokes, E. (2011). Is there room at the bottom for CSR? Corporate social responsibility and nanotechnology in the UK. *Journal of Business Ethics, 101*(4), 525–552.

Gupta, J. (2010). A history of international climate change policy. *WIREs Climate Change, 1*(5), 636–653.

Hale, S. (2010). The new politics of climate change: Why we are failing and how we will succeed. *Environmental Politics, 19*(2), 255–275.

Hamilton, B., & Hoch, D. (1997). Ethical standards for business lobbying: some practical suggestions. *Business Ethics Quarterly, 7*(3), 117–129.

Hawkins, E., Ortega, P., Suckling, E., Schurer, A., Hegerl, G., Jones, P., et al. (2017). Estimating changes in global temperature since the preindustrial period. *Bulletin of the American Meteorological Society, 98*(9), 1841–1856.

Hendrix, C. S., & Salehyan, I. (2012). Climate change, rainfall, and social conflict in Africa. *Journal of Peace Research, 49*(2), 387–388.

Hillman, A. J., & Hitt, M. A. (1999). Corporate political strategy formulation: A model of approach, participation, and strategy decisions. *Academy of Management Review, 24*(4), 825–842.

Hochstetler, K., & Viola, E. (2012). Brazil and the politics of climate change: Beyond the global commons. *Environmental Politics, 21*(5), 753–771.

Hopkins, M. (2005). Measurement of corporate social responsibility. *International Journal of Management and Decision Making, 6*(3–4), 213–231.

Howard-Grenville, J., Buckle, S. J., Hoskins, B. J., & George, G. (2014). Climate change and management. *Academy of Management Journal, 57*(3), 615–623.

Hulme, M., & Mahony, M. (2010). Climate change: What do we know about the IPCC? *Progress in Physical Geography, 34*(5), 705–718.

Idemudia, U., Liedong, T., Agbiboa, D., & Amaeshi, K. (2019). Exploring the culture and cost of corruption in Nigeria: Can Africapitalism help? In U. Idemudia & A. Kenneth (Eds.), *Africapitalism: Sustainable business and development in Africa* (1st ed., pp. 91–110). London: Routledge.

Ihlen, Ø. (2009). Business and climate change: The climate response of the world's 30 largest corporations. *Environmental Communication, 3*(2), 244–262.

Jeswani, H. K., Wehrmeyer, W., & Mulugetta, Y. (2008). How warm is the corporate response to climate change? Evidence from Pakistan and the UK. *Business Strategy and the Environment, 17*(1), 46–60.

Johnson, H. L. (1971). *Business in contemporary society: Framework and issues.* Belmont, CA: Wadsworth.

Jones, C. A., & Levy, D. L. (2007). North American business strategies towards climate change. *European Management Journal, 25*(6), 428–440.

Kabubo-Mariara, J., & Karanja, F. K. (2007). *The economic impact of climate change on Kenyan crop agriculture: A Ricardian approach.* The World Bank.

Kahn, M. E., & Kotchen, M. J. (2011). Business cycle effects on concern about climate change: The chilling effect of recession. *Climate Change Economics, 02*(03), 257–273.

Kassas, M. (1995). Desertification: A general review. *Journal of Arid Environments, 30*(2), 115–128.

Kilcullen, M., & Kooistra, J. O. (1999). At least do no harm: Sources on the changing role of business ethics and corporate social responsibility. *Reference Services Review, 27*(2), 158–178.

Kiriga, M. J., & Barry, S. P. (2008). Health challenges in Africa and the way forward. *International Archives of Medicine, 1*(1), 27. doi:10.1186/1755-7682-1-27

Kolk, A., & Pinkse, J. (2004). Market Strategies for climate change. *European Management Journal, 22*(3), 304–314. doi:10.1016/j.emj.2004.04.011

Kolk, A., & Pinkse, J. (2008). A perspective on multinational enterprises and climate change: Learning from "an inconvenient truth"? *Journal of International Business Studies, 39*(8), 1359–1378.

Kotler, P., & Lee, N. (2005). Best of breed: When it comes to gaining a market edge while supporting a social cause, "corporate social marketing" leads the pack. *Social Marketing Quarterly, 11*(3–4), 91–103.

Koubi, V. (2019). Climate change and conflict. *Annual Review of Political Science, 22*(1), 343–360. doi:10.1146/annurev-polisci-050317-070830

Kühn, A.-L., Stiglbauer, M., & Fifka, M. S. (2018). Contents and determinants of corporate social responsibility website reporting in sub-Saharan Africa: A seven-country study. *Business and Society, 57*(3), 437–480. doi:10.0.4.153/0007650315 614234

Kumssa, A., & Jones, J. F. (2010). Climate change and human security in Africa. *International Journal of Sustainable Development and World Ecology, 17*(6), 453–461. doi:1 0.1080/13504509.2010.520453

Lakshman, C., Ramaswami, A., Alas, R., Kabongo, J. F., & Pandian, J. R. (2014). Ethics trumps culture? A cross-national study of business leader responsibility for downsizing and CSR perceptions. *Journal of Business Ethics, 125*(1), 101–119.

Lash, J., & Wellington, F. (2007). Competitive advantage on a warming planet. *Harvard Business Review.*

Lee, S.-Y. (2012). Corporate carbon strategies in responding to climate change. *Business Strategy and the Environment, 21*(1), 33–48. doi:10.1002/bse.711

Leong, S., Hazelton, J., & Townley, C. (2013). Managing the risks of corporate political donations: A utilitarian perspective. *Journal of Business Ethics, 118*(2), 429–445.

Liedong, T. A. (2017). Combating corruption in Africa through institutional entrepreneurship: Peering in from business-government relations. *Africa Journal of Management, 3*(3–4), 310–327. doi:10.1080/23322373.2017.1379825

Liedong, T. A., & Frynas, J. G. (2018). Investment climate constraints as determinants of political tie intensity in emerging countries: Evidence from foreign firms in Ghana. *Management International Review, 58*(5), 675–703. doi:10.1007/s11575-018-0354-2

Liedong, T. A., Rajwani, T., & Mellahi, K. (2017). Reality or illusion? The efficacy of nonmarket strategy in institutional risk reduction. *British Journal of Management, 28*(4), 609–628. doi:10.1111/1467-8551.12229

Liedong, T. A. (2021). Responsible firm behaviour in political markets: Judging the ethicality of corporate political activity in weak institutional environments. *Journal of Business Ethics*, 172, 325-345.

Liedong, T. A., Aghanya, D., & Rajwani, T. (2020). Corporate political strategies in weak institutional environments: A break from conventions. *Journal of Business Ethics, 161*(4), 855–876. doi:10.1007/s10551-019-04342-1

Liedong, T. A., Peprah, A. A., Amartey, A. O., & Rajwani, T. (2020). Institutional voids and firms' resource commitment in emerging markets: A review and future research agenda. *Journal of International Management, 26*(3), 100756.

Linnenluecke, M., & Griffiths, A. (2010). Beyond adaptation: Resilience for business in light of climate change and weather extremes. *Business and Society, 49*(3), 477–511.

Lischinsky, A. (2015). What is the environment doing in my report? Analysing the environment-as-stakeholder thesis through corpus linguistics. *Environmental Communication, 9*(4), 539–559.

Masipa, T. S. (2017). The impact of climate change on food security in South Africa: Current realities and challenges ahead. *Jàmbá: Journal of Disaster Risk Studies, 9*(1), 1–7.

Mason, N., Nalamalapu, D., & Corfee-Morlot, J. (2019). *Climate change is hurting Africa's water sector, but investing in water can pay off.* Washington, DC: World Resources Institute Report.

Maystadt, J.-F., & Ecker, O. (2014). Extreme weather and Civil War: Does drought fuel conflict in Somalia through livestock price shocks? *American Journal of Agricultural Economics, 96*(4), 1157–1182.

Mbah, E. N., Ezeano, C. I., & Soror, S. F. (2016). Analysis of climate change effects among rice farmers in Benue State, Nigeria. *Current Research in Agricultural Sciences, 3*(1), 7–15.

Mbalyohere, C., Lawton, T., Boojihawon, R., & Viney, H. (2017). Corporate political activity and location-based advantage: MNE responses to institutional transformation in Uganda's electricity industry. *Journal of World Business, 52*(6), 743–759.

McIntyre, J. R., Ivanaj, S., & Ivanaj, V. (Eds.). (2018). *CSR and climate change implications for Multinational Enterprises.* Edward Elgar Publishing, Cheltenham, UK.

McWilliams, A., & Siegel, D. (2001). Corporate social responsibility: A theory of the firm perspective. *Academy of Management Review, 26*(1), 117–127.

Mengel, M. A., Delrieu, I., Heyerdahl, L., & Gessner, B. D. (2014). Cholera outbreaks in Africa. *Current Topics in Microbiology and Immunology, 379*, 117–144.

Michaelowa, K., & Michaelowa, A. (2017). Transnational climate governance initiatives: Designed for effective climate change mitigation? *International Interactions, 43*(1), 129–155.

Milder, J. C., Hart, A. K., Dobie, P., Minai, J., & Zaleski, C. (2014). Integrated landscape initiatives for African agriculture, development, and conservation: A region-wide assessment. *World Development, 54*, 68–80.

Morsing, M., & Schultz, M. (2006). Corporate social responsibility communication: Stakeholder information, response and involvement strategies. *Business Ethics: A European Review, 15*(4), 323–338.

Mukasa, A. N., Woldemichael, A. D., Salami, A. O., & Simpasa, A. M. (2017). Africa's agricultural transformation: Identifying priority areas and overcoming challenges. *Africa Economic Brief, 8*(3), 1–16.

Nejat, P., Jomehzadeh, F., Taheri, M. M., Gohari, M., A. b. d., & Majid, M. Z. (2015). A global review of energy consumption, CO2 emissions and policy in the residential sector (with an overview of the top ten CO2 emitting countries). *Renewable and Sustainable Energy Reviews, 43*, 843–862.

Neron, P. Y. (2016). Rethinking the ethics of corporate political activities in a post-citizens united era: Political equality, corporate citizenship, and market failures. *Journal of Business Ethics, 136*(4), 715–728.

Newell, P., Pattberg, P., & Schroeder, H. (2012). Multiactor governance and the environment. *Annual Review of Environment and Resources, 37*(1), 365–387.

Nikolaou, I., Evangelinos, K., & Leal Filho, W. (2015). A system dynamic approach for exploring the effects of climate change risks on firms' economic performance. *Journal of Cleaner Production, 103*, 499–506.

Nordas, R., & Gleditsch, N. P. (2007). Climate change and conflict. *Political Geography, 26*(6), 627–638.

Okereke, C., Wittneben, B., & Bowen, F. (2012). Climate change: Challenging business, transforming politics. *Business and Society, 51*(1), 7–30.

Oluwatayo, I. B., & Ojo, A. O. (2016). Is Africa's dependence on agriculture the cause of poverty in the continent? An empirical review. *Journal of Developing Areas, 50*(1), 93–102.

Osobajo, O. A., Ajide, O. E., & Otitoju, A. (2019). Fostering sustainable development: A corporate social responsibility approach. *Journal of Management and Sustainability, 9*(2), 142–166.

Pesonen, H.-L., & Horn, S. (2014). Evaluating the climate SWOT as a tool for defining climate strategies for business. *Journal of Cleaner Production, 64*, 562–571.

Phillips, R. A., & Reichart, J. (2000). The environment as a stakeholder? A fairness-based approach. *Journal of Business Ethics, 23*(2), 185–197.

Pinkse, J., & Kolk, A. (2009). *International business and global climate change*. New York: Routledge.

Porter, M. E., & Kramer, M. R. (2006). The link between competitive advantage and corporate social responsibility. *Harvard Business Review, 84*(12), 78–92.

Porter, M. E., & Reinhardt, F. L. (2007). A strategic approach to climate. *Harvard Business Review, 85*(10), 22–26.

Preston, B. L. (2013). Local path dependence of US socio-economic exposure to climate extremes and the vulnerability commitment. *Global Environmental Change, 23*(4), 719–732. doi:10.1016/j.gloenvcha.2013.02.009.

Rabe, B. G. (2007). Beyond Kyoto: Climate change policy in multilevel governance systems. *Governance, 20*(3), 423–444.

Raleigh, C., & Kniveton, D. (2012). Come rain or shine: An analysis of conflict and climate variability in East Africa. *Journal of Peace Research, 49*(1), 51–64.

Ramanathan, V., & Feng, Y. (2009). Air pollution, greenhouse gases and climate change: Global and regional perspectives. *Atmospheric Environment, 43*(1), 37–50.

Revelle, R. (1982). Carbon dioxide and world climate. *Scientific American, 247*(2), 35–43. Retrieved from www.jstor.org/stable/24966657 (Accessed 12 Aug. 2020).

Rivoli, P., & Waddock, S. (2011). "First they ignore you…": The time-context dynamic and corporate responsibility. *California Management Review, 53*(2), 87–104.

Roman Pais Seles, B. M., Lopes de Sousa Jabbour, A. B., Jabbour, C. J. C., de Camargo Fiorini, P., Mohd-Yusoff, Y., & Tavares Thomé, A. M. (2018). Business opportunities and challenges as the two sides of the climate change: Corporate responses and potential implications for big data management towards a low carbon society. *Journal of Cleaner Production, 189*, 763–774.

Rosen, A. M. (2015). The wrong solution at the right time: The failure of the Kyoto Protocol on climate change. *Politics and Policy, 43*(1), 30–58.

Salehyan, I. (2008). From climate change to conflict? No consensus yet. *Journal of Peace Research, 45*(3), 315–326.

Salehyan, I., Hendrix, C. S., Hamner, J., Case, C., Linebarger, C., Stull, E., & Williams, J. (2012). Social conflict in Africa: A new database. *International Interactions, 38*(4), 503–511.

Schwartz, M. S., & Carroll, A. B. (2008). Integrating and unifying competing and complementary frameworks: The search for a common core in the business and society field. *Business and Society, 47*(2), 148–186.

Shen, L., Ochoa, J. J., Shah, M. N., & Zhang, X. (2011). The application of urban sustainability indicators – A comparison between various practices. *Habitat International, 35*(1), 17–29. doi:10.1016/j.habitatint.2010.03.006.

Shepard, D. (2018). Global warming: Severe consequences for Africa. *Africa Renewal*. Retrieved from https://www.un.org/africarenewal/magazine/december-2018-march-2019/global-warming-severe-consequences-africa

Shiferaw, B., Tesfaye, K., Kassie, M., Abate, T., Prasanna, B. M., & Menkir, A. (2014). Managing vulnerability to drought and enhancing livelihood resilience in sub-Saharan Africa: Technological, institutional and policy options. *Weather and Climate Extremes, 3*, 67–79.

Sissoko, K., van Keulen, H., Verhagen, J., Tekken, V., & Battaglini, A. (2011). Agriculture, livelihoods and climate change in the West African Sahel. *Regional Environmental Change, 11*(1), 119–125.

Slegers, M. F. W., & Stroosnijder, L. (2008). Beyond the desertification narrative: a framework for agricultural drought in semi-arid East Africa. *Ambio, 37*(5), 372–380.

Sorgho, R., Quiñonez, C. A. M., Louis, V. R., Winkler, V., Dambach, P., Sauerborn, R., & Horstick, O. (2020). Climate change policies in 16 West African countries: A systematic review of adaptation with a focus on agriculture, food security, and nutrition. *International Journal of Environmental Research and Public Health , 17*(23), 2–21.

Starik, M. (1995). Should trees have managerial standing? Toward stakeholder status for non-human nature. *Journal of Business Ethics, 14*(3), 207–217.

Steynor, A., Leighton, M., Kavonic, J., Abrahams, W., Magole, L., Kaunda, S., & Mubaya, C. P. (2020). Learning from climate change perceptions in southern African cities. *Climate Risk Management, 27*, 100202.

Steynor, A., & Pasquini, L. (2019). Informing climate services in Africa through climate change risk perceptions. *Climate Services, 15*, 100112.

Tacoli, C. (2009). Crisis or adaptation? Migration and climate change in a context of high mobility. *Environment and Urbanization, 21*(2), 513–525.

Tencati, A., Perrini, F., & Pogutz, S. (2004). New tools to foster corporate socially responsible behavior. *Journal of Business Ethics, 53*(1–2), 173–190.

Thistlethwaite, J. (2011). The ClimateWise principles: Self-regulating climate change risks in the insurance sector. *Business and Society, 51*(1), 121–147.

Toulmin, C. (2009). *Climate change in Africa.* Zed Books: London .

Tumwine, J. K., Thompson, J., Katua-Katua, M., Mujwajuzi, M., Johnstone, N., Wood, E., & Porras, I. (2002). Diarrhoea and effects of different water sources, sanitation and hygiene behaviour in East Africa. *Tropical Medicine and International Health,* 7(9), 750–756.

United Nations Development Programme (UNDP) (2021). Climate change adaptation. Retrieved from https://www.adaptation-undp.org/explore/africa/south-africa (assessed 25/9/20)

van Baalen, S., & Mobjörk, M. (2018). Climate change and violent conflict in East Africa: Integrating qualitative and quantitative research to probe the mechanisms. *International Studies Review, 20*(4), 547–575.

van Weezel, S. (2020). Local warming and violent armed conflict in Africa. *World Development, 126,* 104708.

Vesa, J., Gronow, A., & Ylä-Anttila, T. (2020). The quiet opposition: How the pro-economy lobby influences climate policy. *Global Environmental Change, 63,* 102117.

Wei, Y., & Fang, Y. (2012). Impacts and adaptation of climate change on urban economic system: A perspective from the urban planning. *Applied Mechanics and Materials,* 2270–2277, 1740177. doi:10.4028/www.scientific.net/AMM.174-177.2270.

Werther Jr., W. B., & Chandler, D. (2010). *Strategic corporate social responsibility: Stakeholders in a global environment.* Sage: Thousand Oaks, CA

Winn, M., Kirchgeorg, M., Griffiths, A., Linnenluecke, M. K., & Günther, E. (2011). Impacts from climate change on organizations: A conceptual foundation. *Business Strategy and the Environment, 20*(3), 157–173.

Witsenburg, K. M., & Adano, W. R. (2009). Of rain and raids: Violent livestock raiding in Northern Kenya. *Civil Wars, 11*(4), 514–538.

Wittneben, B. B. F., & Kiyar, D. (2009). Climate change basics for managers. *Management Decision, 47*(7), 1122–1132.

Wocke, A., & Moodley, T. (2015). Corporate political strategy and liability of foreignness: Similarities and differences between local and foreign firms in the South African Health Sector. *International Business Review, 24*(4), 700–709.

Wright, C., & Nyberg, D. (2016). An inconvenient truth: How organizations translate climate change into business as usual. *Academy of Management Journal, 60*(5), 1633–1661.

Wright, C., & Nyberg, D. (2017). An inconvenient truth: How organisations translate climate change into business as usual. *Academy of Management Journal, 60*(5), 1633–1661.

Yang, D., He, Y., Wu, B., Deng, Y., Li, M., Yang, Q., … Liu, Y. (2020). Drinking water and sanitation conditions are associated with the risk of malaria among children under five years old in sub-Saharan Africa: A logistic regression model analysis of national survey data. *Journal of Advanced Research, 21,* 1–13.

7

CORPORATE SOCIAL RESPONSIBILITY AND INSTITUTIONAL STRENGTHENING

A RARE Model for Anti-corruption in Africa

Tahiru Azaaviele Liedong

Introduction

Corruption is a significant barrier to socio-economic development in Africa. It is highly endemic across the diverse echelons of society, from the political elite to the ordinary citizen (Liedong, 2017; Mishra & Maiko, 2017). It has evolved into an institution of its own (van den Bersselaar & Decker, 2011; Teorell, 2007) and has become a 'normal' way of life (Hasty, 2005; Apter, 2005; Smith, 2007). It is unlikely for one to live or work in the African region without encountering corruption on a daily basis (van den Bersselaar & Decker, 2011). Corruption manifests through a myriad of behaviours, such as making informal payments to public officials and embezzling or misappropriating public funds. While corruption is not an Africa-only problem, it is widely acknowledged to be highly prevalent in the region.

Concerns about the ramifications of corruption have caused scholars to write much about the canker (e.g. Abdulai, 2009; Albert, 2016; Mishra & Maiko, 2017; Okogbule, 2006; Idemudia, Liedong, Agbiboa, & Amaeshi, 2019; Idemudia, Cragg, & Best, 2010). Similarly, considerable professional work has been done at local and global levels to curb corruption. For instance, the United Nations Convention against Corruption outlines universal provisions for preventing corruption and enforcing anti-corruption regulations. Transnational laws such as the U.S. Foreign Corrupt Practices Act (FCPA) and UK Bribery Act, which make it unlawful to pay bribes to foreign government officials, prevent corporate involvement in corruption. Further, within African countries, several measures have been taken and implemented to address corruption, including the enactment of decrees and laws, the setting up of corruption inquiry committees, the signing up for global anti-corruption initiatives, and the creation of specific anti-corruption institutions. For example, the Economic and Financial Crimes

DOI: 10.4324/9781003038078-8

Commission (EFCC) in Nigeria and the Economic and Organized Crime Office (EOCO) in Ghana were established and mandated to prevent, detect, and investigate crimes such as bribery and money laundering. Freedom of information (FOI) laws have also been passed in African countries such as Angola, Ethiopia, Liberia, Rwanda, Zimbabwe, South Africa, and Uganda.

Despite the myriad of anti-corruption measures, the canker has not abated. There is still widespread corruption in Africa. Data from Transparency International and the World Economic Forum show that most African countries continue to perform poorly in global corruption rankings. The ineffectiveness of existing efforts is borne out of the poor alignment between corruption causes and anti-corruption measures. In Africa, corruption is deeply entrenched in formal and informal institutions (Olaleye-Oruene, 1998; Mishra & Maiko, 2017; Liedong, 2017; Kong & Volkema, 2016), yet the campaigns against corruption are mostly symbolic or focused on macro-economic management (Kolstad & Soreide, 2009; Akume, 2016; Akume & Okoli, 2016). Hence, these campaigns hardly build, strengthen, or change the fundamental institutions that promote or facilitate corruption.

In addition, there is limited participation in anti-corruption campaigns in African countries. The efforts are mostly championed by governments and civil society bodies, with little to no contribution from the private sector (Liedong, 2017). Businesses are both complicit and affected by corruption. On the one hand, bribery is an additional tax that increases uncertainty, raises transaction costs, and reduces business competitiveness (Doh, Rodriguez, Uhlenbruck, Collins, & Eden, 2003; Luiz & Stewart, 2014; Adeyeye, 2017). On the other hand, businesses are parties to bribery transactions, sometimes as the initiators (Bahoo, Alon, & Paltrinieri, 2020; Ufere, Perelli, Boland, & Carlsson, 2012). These realities should make the private sector interested in fighting corruption. Yet, the sector's involvement is abysmal.

A few studies have reported the strategies and tactics used by businesses, especially multinational firms, to deal with corruption (Doh et al., 2003; Hess, 2009a; Mishra & Maiko, 2017; Valentine & Fleischman, 2004; Adam & Rachman-moore, 2004). Though most of the tactics show how businesses are ethically managing bribery, they are inadequate for buffering external institutions to eradicate corruption. In this sense, businesses may recognize anti-corruption as a corporate social responsibility (CSR), but the extent to which their CSR initiatives are targeted at changing the institutions that facilitate corruption is low. Against this backdrop, this chapter addresses how CSR can be used to strengthen anti-corruption institutions. The goal is to present a model of how CSR could bring about institutional change.

Corruption: Causes and Mitigating Efforts

Corruption is a complex social phenomenon whose meaning is confusing. It is not an objective reality, because what some perceive to be corruption might not be corruption to others (Tignor, 1993; Mbaku, 2010; Mbaku, 2000). Hence, corruption is both a concept and a practice that has been defined differently by scholars across varied disciplines ranging from sociology to management. Corruption has also been categorized into types, such as public corruption (Sartor & Beamish, 2019), private corruption (Argandoña, 2003), pervasive corruption, and arbitrary corruption (Rodriguez, Uhlenbruck, & Eden, 2005). Further distillation of these types of corruption yields four sub-types, namely petty versus grand corruption (Nystrand, 2014) and organized versus unorganized corruption (Shleifer & Vishny, 1993). Synthesizing the different connotations of corruption, I define corruption as an illegal activity entailing the misuse of power and authority by private and public officeholders for private gain. This definition captures three important things. First, corruption is an illegal activity and any benefit derived from it is an illegal benefit that is subject to legal recovery. Second, the individuals involved in corruption behave illegally and should be punished within the confines of the law. Third, corruption is inclusive of diverse forms of illegality, including bribery, fraud, money laundering, abuse, falsification, cronyism, nepotism, manipulation, misrepresentation, and misappropriation.

The prevalence of corruption in Africa is overwhelmingly attributed to the failure of formal institutions (Liedong, 2017). Formal institutions are the rules and legal stipulations that regulate human behaviour and socio-economic exchange in society through legal incentives (punishments) to encourage (discourage) acceptable (unacceptable) conduct (North, 1990). Absent or inefficient formal institutions underlie the ubiquitous misappropriation, bribery, and graft in African countries (Liedong, 2017; Mbaku, 2010). For instance, mass looting of the State in Nigeria under the military regimes of Ibrahim Babangida and Sani Abacha was possible because of institutional degradation and poor accountability. A survey conducted by the African Capacity Building Foundation (AFBF) in 2007, cited by Agbiboa (2012), noted how Africans lack confidence in the ability of public institutions to combat corruption. Afrobarometer's 2019 Corruption Barometer also reported how African citizens think corruption is getting worse and governments are doing a bad job at tackling it.

Formal institutional rot in Africa is a result of low political will among Africa's polity (Abdulai, 2009; Lawal, 2007). Politicians have the power to ensure that formal institutions work for the betterment of societies and whole countries. However, they show little interest, arguably because they are the largest beneficiaries of corruption. They control the public purse and oversee macro-economic policies, which puts them in positions to loot public funds or demand kickbacks for public contracts. Visionless political leaders use their position power to appropriate public resources to enrich themselves (Lopez-Claros, 2014) or allow their countries to be exploited by their cronies (Mishra & Maiko, 2017). As Nigerian novelist Chinua Achebe (1983) once argued 'corruption goes with power … therefore to hold any useful discussion of corruption; we must first locate it where it properly belongs – in the ranks of the powerful'. The lack of political will towards anti-corruption can be illustrated in an African proverb 'you do not bite the hands that feed you'. Strengthening institutions to combat corruption may close the loopholes that allow politicians' personal aggrandizement.

It is no secret that across Africa, politicians exploit immunity clauses and provisions to evade the ramifications of their corrupt practices (Markovska & Adams, 2015; Akume, 2016). The irresponsible actions of elites in the highest echelons of government cascade down to the bureaucrats in the lowest levels of public service who, in the steps of their leaders, also use their offices for self-enrichment (Mbaku, 2000; Achua, 2011). Consequently, measures to stem the canker have yielded insignificant results due to a classic problem of endogeneity – i.e. those with the power and authority to stop corruption are the ones with vested stakes to protect the status quo for their personal benefit (Otusanya, Lauwo, Ige, & Adelaja, 2015; Olaleye-Oruene, 1998).

Corruption in the upper echelons of government has far-reaching consequences that permeate and reinforce corruption in society at large (Liedong, 2017). For instance, low public sector salary, a major cause of corruption in Nigeria (Agbiboa, 2012), has pushed public sector workers to draw from public coffers or abuse their offices. Police extort from motorists, utility providers demand 'extra' payments to render services, and civil servants expect 'financial appreciation' from citizens when they discharge their duties. There is a strong entitlement among public workers to ask for or expect informal payments. Consequently, corruption has become deeply engrained in national culture (Olaleye-Oruene, 1998; Scholl & Schermuly, 2020). It has become a way of life for the people (Marquette, 2012). In their everyday activities, they bribe others or make 'facilitation payments' to get things done.

Having evolved into an institution of its own, corruption has become 'acceptable' in Africa (van den Bersselaar & Decker, 2011). There is enormous pressure to indulge in it, because 'when a system has become corrupt – for whatever historical reasons – people who do not want to engage in corruption feel compelled to engage in it because it becomes essential to surviving' (Mishra & Maiko, 2017: 4). Hence, mimetic and coercive isomorphism (DiMaggio & Powell, 1983) in African societies compel individuals to conform to 'corrupt' norms or suffer 'illegitimacy' and its associated disadvantages. Even churches and non-governmental organizations, which are perceived to be 'saintly' and are expected to play important roles in socio-economic development (Porter, 2003) through their activities to strengthen institutions and reduce poverty (Gary, 1996), are either corrupt or have become vehicles for corruption in some African countries (Smith, 2010; Lang, 2014; Mohan, 2002).

The foregoing portrays a degeneration of ethical and moral values in Africa. Thus, collectivism, compassion, generosity, caring, and sharing are fundamental values of African ethics (West, 2014; Mishra & Maiko, 2017; Lutz, 2009). As Mbigi (2005: 75) distinctly noted 'although African cultures display awesome diversity, they also show remarkable similarities. Community is the cornerstone in African thought and life'. Turaki (2006: 36) further emphasized that in Africa, 'people are not individuals, living in a state of independence, but part of a community, living in relationships and interdependence'. However, this collectivist ideal breeds greed and corruption. Africa has disparate ethnicities and a history of ethnic clashes (Imuetinyan, 2015) that cause people to feel stronger loyalty to their kinsmen and communities than to the State (Ekeh, 1975). Such stronger loyalties provide a conduit not only for the pursuit of economic marginalization of ethnic zones and regions but also for reciprocity and corruption (Smith, 2014). For example, ex-governor James Ibori of Delta State in Nigeria who was jailed for corruption was reportedly hailed as a 'true son of the soil' by his kinsmen, arguably because they gained from the corruption proceeds and therefore had no regard for the wider consequences of the governor's actions for the country. The thrust here is that a sense of belongingness to the community could adversely affect nationhood (Posner, 2005) and fuel corruption. In sum, corruption in Africa is caused by weak formal institutions that have helped to create a low accountability culture and allow the canker to evolve into an institution of its own.

Business Response to Corruption: Ethics and Social Responsibility

Some scholarly works have recognized corruption to be an ethical and business problem that companies must address (Hauser, 2019; Rabl & Kühlmann, 2008; Doh et al., 2003). Other professional reports by organizations such as the World Bank have acknowledged the role businesses must play in the fight against corruption.[1] These works argue that corruption is unethical and leaves investors without any recourse when the promised proceeds of corruption are not delivered. In this sense, corruption is a waste of corporate resources. Subsequently, these works make a case for ethical corporate practices, ranging from employee ethical training, whistleblowing, and use of codes of conduct to the adoption of good governance principles. While these actions could be impactful against corruption, they are less likely to succeed in places of endemic corruption. In other words, ethical internal governance that is unsupported by external institutions will be ineffective against corruption. Here is why.

Managers will bend their ethical principles to engage in corrupt practices if these practices are 'normal' and prevalent within the contexts they operate. Holding onto ethical values and resisting the pressures of corruption could lead to business failure (Liedong, 2017). Two dynamics are worth highlighting here. First, managers aim to maximize shareholder value by advancing business interests and making profits (Jensen & Meckling, 1976). Second, managers' own remuneration and job security are often tied to firm performance (Kroll, Simmons, & Wright, 1990). The resultant pressures of these dynamics could compel them to indulge in corruption to increase their firms' profitability, especially when every other firm is doing it (Hess, 2009a). This perhaps explains why multinational firms with widely publicized codes of ethics are sometimes caught up in bribery scandals in developing countries. Essentially, systemic corruption might render ethical values less useful.

What is even worse is that in Africa, the recognition of anti-corruption as an ethical and social responsibility of business is low (Schwartz, 2009). This happens even though companies are on the cause-and-effect sides of corruption. First, corruption negatively affects firms (Fisman & Svensson, 2007; Spencer & Gomez, 2011). Evidence shows that corruption reduces economic growth, increases uncertainty, raises the cost of production, and reduces profitability (Gyimah-Brempong, 2002; Svensson, 2005; Luiz & Stewart, 2014; Van-Vu, Tran, Van-Nguyen, & Lim, 2018; Voyer & Beamish, 2004). Second, as bribery is conceived as an exchange relationship whereby 'one person (the briber) provides an inducement to another person (the bribee) that is intended to be in exchange for the bribee doing, or not doing, something that would favour the briber' (Dunfee, Smith, & Ross, 1999: 22), it is clear that firms aid and abet corruption when they succumb to bribery demands or when they initiate bribes to receive preferential treatment. In doing so, they incentivize government officials to create additional hurdles for the purpose of generating more opportunities for bribery, thus accentuating corruption (Shleifer & Vishny, 1993) Unsurprisingly, some of the most repugnant corruption scandals in Africa involve businesses.

Nevertheless, some firms have adopted various initiatives including the C^2 Principles (Hess & Dunfee, 2000; Hess, 2009b), Transparency International's Business Principles for Countering Bribery, African Union's Convention on Preventing and Combatting Corruption, and UN's Convention against Corruption among others. However, these actions have been ineffective, mainly because they are symbolic and do not buffer corruption-supporting institutions (O'Higgins, 2006; Lopez & Santos, 2014; Campbell & Goritz, 2014). Other businesses in Africa have reduced their social responsibility to philanthropy – i.e. making monetary and material donations to communities and organizations (Amaeshi et al., 2016; Kühn, Stiglbauer, & Fifka, 2018). Notwithstanding its good intentions, philanthropy creates unsustainable outcomes (Cranenburgh & Arenas, 2014). It meets emergent needs on a transactional basis but does not address the institutional causes of those needs. For example, donating equipment to a public hospital does not address the formal institutional weaknesses and inefficiencies that cause the equipment shortage. Also, whereas the donation is one-off, the shortages are usually experienced year-round. Thus, philanthropy provides superficial solutions to the perennial problems of Africa and particularly does not address corruption.

For CSR to help anti-corruption efforts, it must attempt to change the institutions that allow corruption to thrive. Institutional theory posits that a country's institutional environment stipulates the 'rules of the game' that affect a firm's scope of action and strategy (North, 1990; Scott, 2001). Hence, a firm's behaviour towards corruption is shaped by the 'normality' of the phenomenon in the environment within which it is embedded. The implication of this within the African context is that firms will be sucked into corruption and will have no choice but to join the bandwagon. However, other scholars have written about 'de-institutionalization' and 'disembeddedness' (Dacin, Ventresca, & Beal, 1999) whereby firms can restructure or change their institutional environments (Dacin, Goodstein, & Scott, 2002). These works provide insights into the ability of firms to use CSR to buffer their institutional environments.

RARE Model: Using CSR for Anti-corruption Institutional Strengthening

Drawing on previous frameworks about how firms can shape institutions to bring about change (e.g., Kwok & Tadesse, 2006), this chapter presents four channels through which CSR can lead to anti-corruption. They are: regulatory channel, archetypal channel, reinforcement channel, and enforcement channel. These four channels, together, constitute the RARE model (see Table 7.1). This model differs from Kwok and Tadesse's (2006) regulatory, demonstration and professionalization effects in two ways. First, whereas Kwok and Tadesse (2006) focus on MNEs as the source of institutional change, the RARE model is encompassing and captures the roles that local firms can play. This is important because local firms make up a large proportion of the private sector in Africa and can therefore exert more influence on the institutions. Also, beyond exploiting markets and resources, MNEs may not have a genuine interest in institutional change in host countries, but local firms most likely would. Second, Kwok and Tadesse are generalists whereas RARE offers a proximate model of how CSR can be used to fight corruption.

Regulatory Channel

While firms may be able to use initiatives and actions to manage or deal with corruption (Doh et al., 2003), those actions do not eradicate or combat corruption. Evading bribery in one instance does not mean that bribery can be evaded every time because the institutions that support the canker will continue to exist. Hence, effective anti-corruption efforts should aim at institutional entrepreneurship in formal institutional domains. Institutional entrepreneurship refers to 'activities of actors who have an interest in particular institutional arrangements and who leverage resources to create new institutions or to transform existing ones' (Maguire, Hardy, & Lawrence, 2004: 657). These actors – institutional entrepreneurs – use their resources and capabilities to change formal and informal institutions (DiMaggio, 1988; Powell & DiMaggio, 1991; Greenwood & Hinings, 1996). This change occurs through a political process that reflects relationships between interests, agency, and institutions (Maguire et al., 2004). Institutional entrepreneurs identify and frame problems, mobilize other stakeholders and spearhead collective attempts to change values, norms, and beliefs in social structures (Fligstein, 1997; Rao, Morrill, & Zald, 2000).

Institutional entrepreneurship has dominantly focused on crafting, transferring, or shaping organizational practices (Canales, 2016; Fortwengel & Jackson,

TABLE 7.1 Summary of the RARE Model

	Regulatory Channel	*Archetypal Channel*	*Reinforcement Channel*	*Enforcement Channel*
Focus	Changing existing laws and advocating new laws	Becoming a role model for others	Celebrating, rewarding, and motivating good anti-corruption behaviour in the public sector	Ensuring that anti-corruption laws are applied, and anti-corruption institutions are effective; ensuring adequate sentencing for corruption
Targets	Policymakers and politicians	Private sector, civil society, and communities	Public sector	Courts and anti-corruption institutions
Key CSR Initiatives	Sponsoring anti-corruption bills; petitioning anti-corruption laws; providing information for anti-corruption policies; sponsoring training programs for politicians and regulators	Being transparent; abiding by laws and regulations; adhering to corporate governance principles	Giving awards for anti-corruption; creating an index for anti-corruption performance	Up-skilling officials in anti-corruption commissions; donating equipment and logistics to facilitate anti-corruption investigations; supporting anti-corruption charities; establishing foundations for anti-corruption
Required Capabilities	Political	Ethical competence; professional leadership	Innovation; financial; public relations	Political; legal; financial
Main Effect	Illegalizing all forms of corruption	Widespread adoption of anti-corruption behaviour	Institutionalizing anti-corruption	Deterring corruption

2016) or advocating multi-stakeholder response to healthcare (George, Rao-Nicholson, Corbishley, & Bansal, 2015; Maguire et al., 2004). Institutional entrepreneurship has rarely been applied in the fight against corruption, even though there is sufficient expectation of its potential efficacy. In business, institutional entrepreneurship can be likened to political CSR (Frynas & Stephens, 2015) whereby firms (mostly multinational firms) play political roles to address sociocultural problems such as famine, healthcare deficiencies, illiteracy, and environmental degradation (Matten & Crane, 2005; Margolis & Walsh, 2003; Scherer & Palazzo, 2011). However, political CSR has yet to go beyond addressing idiosyncratic problems. Combating corruption in Africa will require political influence to create or shape laws that can curb bribery and financial crimes.

Therefore, businesses should engage in political activity not for self-interested benefits as they mostly do (Hillman, Keim, & Schuler, 2004), but for advocating laws and regulations to fight corruption. Research has shown that firms in Africa are politically active (e.g. Liedong & Frynas, 2018; Liedong, Rajwani, & Mellahi, 2017; Liedong, Aghanya, & Rajwani, 2020; Wocke & Moodley, 2015; Mbalyohere, Lawton, Boojihawon, & Viney, 2017). What remains to be seen is for this corporate political activity (CPA) to buffer national regulations in ways that create broad-based prosperity. CPA has been justified as ethical and socially desirable on the grounds that it allows firms to provide valuable information and experience for equitable policymaking, thus helping to avert the adverse consequences of ill-informed policies (Alzola, 2013). This argument is predicated on the reality that regulators often lack the knowledge or information needed to maximize policy welfare (Leong, Hazelton, & Townley, 2013). There is thus a moral opportunity for businesses to use their CSR to pursue utilitarian outcomes in policy arenas, such as sponsoring anti-corruption bills, petitioning for new or amended anti-corruption laws, testifying and providing valuable experiences or data to inform anti-corruption policies, organizing events to sensitize legislators about corruption or sponsoring training programs for stakeholder political education. These activities, though politically oriented, could be the neo-CSR needed to strengthen Africa's regulatory institutions and combat corruption.

Enforcement Channel

Africa does not lack legal regimes to curb corruption. Rather, she lacks enforcement of existing anti-corruption laws (Swanepoel & Meiring, 2018; Boakye, 2020; Adeyeye, 2017). It is one thing to make a law, and it is another thing to put the law to work. The latter is a significant area of deficiency in Africa's formal institutional domain. Right to Information, money laundering, public procurement, and criminal laws, as well as codes of conduct for public and civil service, are abundant, but they are largely white elephants. In Ghana, for instance, most regulations and timeframes in the country exist only on paper. Consequently, to estimate or expect due process as prescribed in policy documents is to dream. On paper, it should take an entrepreneur an average of 14 days to register or start a business (World Bank, 2016). However, in reality, it takes weeks and months. Also, on paper, it takes 79 days to get electricity to a property and 710 days to enforce a contract (World Bank, 2016). These times are misleading as it could take years to get electricity or settle a court case. The bureaucracy and red tape associated with public service provide a fertile ground for businesses to 'grease the wheels of commerce' to speed up procedures (Cuervo-Cazurra, 2006; Cummins & Gillanders, 2020).

Moreover, anti-corruption agencies and ombudsman, such as the Commission for Human Rights and Administrative Justice (CHRAJ) and EOCO in Ghana, EFCC in Nigeria and Kenya Anti-Corruption Commission (KACC) in Kenya, have yielded insignificant results (Doig, 2006; Williams-Elegbe, 2018). Even these anti-corruption institutions are not free of corruption. For example, in January 2015, the president of Ghana suspended the Commissioner of CHRAJ for misappropriation of the Commission's funds (The Presidency, 2015). In Nigeria, EFCC has been incapacitated by rampant political interference (Akume & Okoli, 2016).

Against this background, CSR must aim to strengthen enforcement of the anti-corruption legal regimes in Africa. Responsible initiatives and programs could be targeted at up-skilling officials in anti-corruption commissions. Businesses could also donate equipment such as computers or other logistics to facilitate anti-corruption investigations. More importantly, businesses could support existing anti-corruption charities, or establish their own foundations for advocating enforcement of anti-corruption policies and laws. For example, these foundations could be used to amplify and sue or support the prosecution of corrupt practices in the public sector. They could also push for equitable punishment, because sentencing practices for corruption in Africa are often incommensurable with the crimes (e.g. Swanepoel & Meiring, 2018). As the lack of continuity arising from political interference is one of the challenges faced by anti-corruption commissions (Doig, 2006), businesses and their foundations could legally challenge any violations of the commissions' independence. This could be risky due to the potential for political reprisals, witch-hunt, and discrimination, but working collectively with other businesses will help to attenuate this risk (Liedong, 2017). Collective enforcement also helps to mitigate concerns of individual businesses using their CSR to 'capture' anti-corruption institutions for their own parochial benefits, such as prosecuting competitors or opponents.

Reinforcement Channel

The regulatory and enforcement channels will bring about change, but the changes will revert if they are not institutionalized. Therefore, it is important for businesses to recognize successful players in the fight against corruption. Just as the Sustainable Stock Exchange (SSE)[2] initiative supports and encourages listed companies to provide ongoing communications and disclose information regarding relevant environmental, social, and governance (ESG) indicators, it is imperative that the private sector in African countries also set up initiatives that rank and publicize the performance of public agencies and departments on anti-corruption metrics. For example, a yearly corruption index could be established to highlight the best and worst performers in the public sector. Award events could also be held periodically to celebrate exceptional individuals and organizations that are committed to and championing the fight against corruption.

Recognition will serve two purposes. First, as widely noted in the motivation literature, acknowledgements, celebrations, and rewards reinforce good behaviours (e.g. Hofeditz, Nienaber, Dysvik, & Schewe, 2017; Deci, Ryan, & Koestner, 1999; Selvarajan, Singh, & Solansky, 2018). They stimulate people to continue to uphold acceptable standards and thus facilitate the permanency of desirable attitudes and conduct. Second, recognition shows a clear distinction between good and bad performance, which could either 'shame' and motivate poor performers to strive for improvement or motivate them to seek positive reputations. Therefore, using CSR to highlight anti-corruption performance will not only put pressure on public agencies to be professional, but it will also help to 'de-normalize' corruption. In this sense, recognition could lead to normative isomorphism – i.e. compliance with ethical behaviours promoted by professionals (DiMaggio & Powell, 1983; Beddewela & Fairbrass, 2016).

Archetypal Channel

One of the important things worth highlighting is that businesses must try to be archetypes, role models, or exemplars (Radin, 2004). To be treated or seen as authentic and serious about buffering and enforcing anti-corruption regulations or reinforcing anti-corruption performance, firms themselves must be ethical and anti-corrupt (Kwok & Tadesse, 2006). This is captured in the African proverb that 'the messenger is as important as the message'. Businesses must be transparent, abide by all regulations, have good internal governance, and act with decorum. They must work to set higher standards, or be willing to engage in inter-organizational collaborations to establish industry codes for accountability, or against corruption (Mirvis & Googins, 2018). Despite the prevailing weak formal institutions, the archetype business should self-regulate and not exploit voids. It must invest to develop political capabilities for advocating or negotiating change and for building coalitions to shape formal institutions (Maguire et al., 2004). Being an archetype is a prerequisite for the other components of the RARE model, mainly as businesses must first change before they change others. Simply, businesses must be the change they wish to see.

The spillovers from modelling the right behaviour for anti-corruption will demonstrate to other businesses how corruption can be combatted (Kwok & Tadesse, 2006). This demonstration of ethical professionalism has the potential to not only lead to normative isomorphism but also mimetic isomorphism whereby other businesses imitate the demonstrated professionalism (DiMaggio & Powell, 1983; Meyer & Rowan, 1977). The culmination of these isomorphic

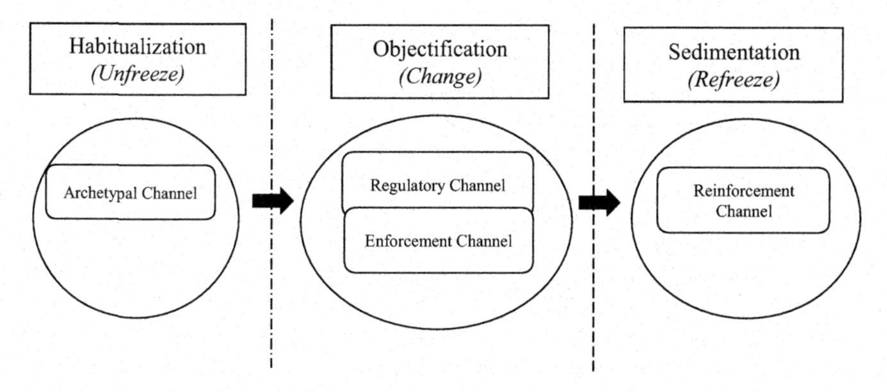

FIGURE 7.1 The RARE Model Process.

pressures will cause a widespread change in attitudes needed to shape the institutions that facilitate corruption in Africa.

Implementing the RARE model requires businesses to go through a process of institutionalization that is similar to Lewin's (1947) unfreeze, change and refreeze process of organizational change. According to Lewin, organizations must unfreeze and prepare to accept change. When change is completed, they must refreeze to institutionalize the changes. Along the same logic, Tolbert and Zucker (1996) argue that the institutionalization process consists of three sequential stages, namely habitualization, objectification, and sedimentation. Habitualization is the development of behaviours or structures to solve problems; objectification is the diffusion or widespread adoption of the structures, and sedimentation is the perpetuation or continuity of the structures. Integrating Lewin's (1947) change and Tolbert and Zucker's (1996) institutionalization processes, I illustrate the sequential relationship among the components of the RARE model (see Figure 7.1).

Conclusion

Corruption is the bane of Africa's socio-economic development. Despite this daunting reality, there has been less success to arrest the canker. This chapter, which calls for Africa's private sector to play a bigger and more effective role in anti-corruption efforts, presented the RARE model to show how businesses can use their CSR to strengthen the weak formal institutions that allow corruption to thrive in Africa. While upbeat about the potency of this model, it must be acknowledged that its implementation could be challenging. In some African countries where checks and balances are often weak, the RARE model could be perilous because politicians – the main beneficiaries of corruption (Idemudia et al., 2019) – may create costs and disadvantages for advocating firms. This especially happens when the firms fail to act through coalitions that are strong and large enough to deter unchecked governments from crashing dissent. Therefore, it is crucial that firms use intra- and cross-industry coalitions, as they will make it difficult for African politicians to persecute, victimize, or discriminate against individual firms. Coalitions will also enable firms to pull their limited resources together for the fight against corruption.

Notes

1 For instance, see http://documents1.worldbank.org/curated/en/494361468333857366/pdf/477910NWP0Focu10Box338866B01PUBLIC1.pdf
2 See https://sseinitiative.org/

References

Abdulai, A. (2009). Political will in combating corruption in developing and transition economies. *Journal of Financial Crime, 16*(4), 387–417.

Achua, J. K. (2011). Anti-corruption in public procurement in Nigeria: Challenges and competency strategies. *Journal of Public Procurement, 11*(3), 323–353.

Adam, A. M., & Rachman-moore, D. (2004). The methods used to implement an ethical code of conduct and employee attitudes. *Journal of Business Ethics, 54*(3), 225–244.

Adeyeye, A. (2017). Bribery: Cost of doing business in Africa. *Journal of Financial Crime, 24*(1), 56–64.

Agbiboa, D. (2012). Between corruption and development: The political economy of state robbery in Nigeria. *Journal of Business Ethics, 108*(3), 325–345.

Akume, A. T. (2016). Combating corruption in Nigeria and the constitutional issues arising. *Journal of Financial Crime, 23*(4), 700–724.

Akume, A. T., & Okoli, F. C. (2016). EFCC and the politics of combating corruption in Nigeria (2003–2012). *Journal of Financial Crime, 23*(4), 725–747.

Albert, A. T. (2016). Combating corruption in Nigeria and the constitutional issues arising. *Journal of Financial Crime, 23*(4), 700–724.

Alzola, M. (2013). Corporate dystopia: The ethics of corporate political spending. *Business and Society, 52*(3), 388–426.

Amaeshi, K., Adegbite, E., Ogbechie, C., Idemudia, U., Kan, K., Issa, M., & Anakwue, O. (2016). Corporate social responsibility in SMEs: A shift from philanthropy to institutional works? *Journal of Business Ethics, 138*(2), 385–400.

Apter, A. H. (2005). *The Pan-African nation: Oil and the spectacle of culture in Nigeria*. Chicago, IL: University of Chicago Press.

Argandoña, A. (2003). Private-to-private corruption. *Journal of Business Ethics, 47*(3), 253–267.

Bahoo, S., Alon, I., & Paltrinieri, A. (2020). Corruption in international business: A review and research agenda. *International Business Review, 29*(4), 101660.

Beddewela, E., & Fairbrass, J. (2016). Seeking legitimacy through CSR: Institutional pressures and corporate responses of multinationals in Sri Lanka. *Journal of Business Ethics, 136*(3), 503–522.

Boakye, J. (2020). Enforcement of logging regulations in Ghana: Perspectives of frontline regulatory officers. *Forest Policy and Economics, 115*, N.PAG–N.PAG.

Campbell, J. L., & Goritz, A. (2014). Culture corrupts! A qualitative study of organizational culture in corrupt organizations. *Journal of Business Ethics, 120*(3), 291–311.

Canales, R. (2016). From ideals to institutions: Institutional entrepreneurship and the growth of Mexican small business finance. *Organization Science, 27*(6), 1548–1573.

Cranenburgh, K., & Arenas, D. (2014). Strategic and moral dilemmas of corporate philanthropy in developing countries: Heineken in sub-Saharan Africa. *Journal of Business Ethics, 122*(3), 523–536.

Cuervo-Cazurra, A. (2006). Who cares about corruption? *Journal of International Business Studies, 37*(6), 807–822.

Cummins, M., & Gillanders, R. (2020). Greasing the turbines? Corruption and access to electricity in Africa. *Energy Policy, 137*, N.PAG–N.PAG.

Dacin, M. T., Goodstein, J., & Scott, W. R. (2002). Institutional theory and institutional change: Introduction to the special research forum. *Academy of Management Journal, 45*(1), 45–56.

Dacin, M. T., Ventresca, M. J., & Beal, B. D. (1999). The embeddedness of organizations: Dialogue & directions. *Journal of Management, 25*(3), 317–356.

Deci, E. L., Ryan, R. M., & Koestner, R. (1999). A meta-analytic review of experiments examining the effects of extrinsic rewards of intrinsic motivation. *Psychological Bulletin, 125*(6), 627–668.

DiMaggio, P. J. (1988). Interest and agency in institutional theory. In L. Zucker (Ed.), *Institutional patterns and culture* (pp. 3–22). Cambridge, MA: Ballinger Publishing Company.

DiMaggio, P. J., & Powell, W. W. (1983). The iron cage revisited: Institutional isomorphism and collective rationality in organizational fields. *American Sociological Review, 48*(2), 147–160.

Doh, J. P., Rodriguez, P., Uhlenbruck, K., Collins, J., & Eden, L. (2003). Coping with corruption in foreign markets. *Academy of Management Executive, 17*(3), 114–127.

Doig, A. (2006). Not as easy as it sounds? Delivering the national integrity system approach in practice - The case study of the national anti-corruption programme in Lithuania. *Public Administration Quarterly, 30*(3), 273–313.

Dunfee, T. W., Smith, N. C., & Ross, W. T. (1999). Social contracts and marketing ethics. *Journal of Marketing, 63*(3), 14–32.

Fisman, R., & Svensson, J. (2007). Are corruption and taxation really harmful to growth? Firm level evidence. *Journal of Development Economics, 83*(1), 63–75.

Fligstein, N. (1997). Social skill and institutional theory. *American Behavioral Scientist, 40*(4), 397–405.

Fortwengel, J., & Jackson, G. (2016). Legitimizing the apprenticeship practice in a distant environment: Institutional entrepreneurship through inter-organizational networks. *Journal of World Business, 51*(6), 895–909.

Frynas, J. G., & Stephens, S. (2015). Political corporate social responsibility: Reviewing theories and setting new agendas. *International Journal of Management Reviews, 17*(4), 483–509.

Gary, I. (1996). Confrontation, co-operation or co-optation: NGOs and the Ghanaian state during structural. *Review of African Political Economy, 23*(68), 149–163.

George, G., Rao-Nicholson, R., Corbishley, C., & Bansal, R. (2015). Institutional entrepreneurship, governance, and poverty: Insights from emergency medical response servicesin India. *Asia Pacific Journal of Management, 32*(1), 39–65.

Greenwood, R., & Hinings, C. R. (1996). Understanding radical organizational change: Bringing together the old and the new institutionalism. *Academy of Management Review, 21*(4), 1022–1054.

Gyimah-Brempong, K. (2002). Corruption, economic growth, and income inequality in Africa. *Economics of Governance, 3*(3), 183–209.

Hasty, J. (2005). The pleasures of corruption: Desire and discipline in Ghanaian political culture. *Cultural Anthropology, 20*(2), 271–301.
Hauser, C. (2019). Fighting against corruption: Does anti-corruption training make any difference? *Journal of Business Ethics, 159*(1), 281–299.
Hess, D. (2009a). Catalyzing corporate commitment to combating corruption. *Journal of Business Ethics, 88*(S4), 781–790.
Hess, D. (2009b). Catalyzing corporate commitment to combating corruption. *Journal of Business Ethics, 88*(S4), 781–790.
Hess, D., & Dunfee, T. W. (2000). Fighting corruption: A principled approach: The C principles (combating corruption). *Cornell International Law Journal, 33*(3), 593-626.
Hillman, A. J., Keim, G. D., & Schuler, D. (2004). Corporate political activity: A review and research agenda. *Journal of Management, 30*(6), 837–857.
Hofeditz, M., Nienaber, A., Dysvik, A., & Schewe, G. (2017). "Want to" versus "Have to": Intrinsic and extrinsic motivators as predictors of compliance behavior intention. *Human Resource Management, 56*(1), 25–49.
Idemudia, U., Cragg, W., & Best, B. (2010). The challenges and opportunities of implementing the integrity pact as a strategy for combating corruption in Nigeria's oil rich Niger Delta region. *Public Administration and Development, 30*(4), 277–290.
Idemudia, U., Liedong, T. A., Agbiboa, D., & Amaeshi, K. (2019). Exploring the culture and cost of corruption in Nigeria: Can Africapitalism help? In U. Idemudia & K. Amaeshi (Eds.), *Africapitalism: Sustainable business and development in Africa* (1st ed., pp. 91–110). London: Routledge.
Imuetinyan, F. (2015). Analysis of options for managing democratic ethnic competition and conflicts: The Nigerian experience. *Journal of Developing Areas, 49*(2), 263–272.
Jensen, M., & Meckling, W. H. (1976). Theory of the firm: Managerial behavior, agency costs and ownership structure. *Journal of Financial Economics, 3*(4), 305–360.
Kolstad, I., & Soreide, T. (2009). Corruption in natural resource management: Implications for policy makers. *Resources Policy, 34*(4), 214–226.
Kong, D. T., & Volkema, R. (2016). Cultural endorsement of broad leadership prototypes and wealth as predictors of corruption. *Social Indicators Research, 127*(1), 139–152.
Kroll, M., Simmons, S. A., & Wright, P. (1990). Determinants of chief executive officer compensation following major acquisitions. *Journal of Business Research, 20*(4), 349–366.
Kühn, A., Stiglbauer, M., & Fifka, M. S. (2018). Contents and determinants of corporate social responsibility Website reporting in sub-Saharan Africa: A seven-country study. *Business and Society, 57*(3), 437–480.
Kwok, C. C. Y., & Tadesse, S. (2006). The MNC as an agent of change for host-country institutions: FDI and corruption. *Journal of International Business Studies, 37*(6), 767–785.
Lang, M. K. (2014). The patterns of corruption in Christian churches of Cameroon; the case of the Presbyterian Church in Cameroon. *Transformation, 31*(2), 132–144.
Lawal, G. (2007). Corruption and development in Africa: Challenges for political and economic change. *Humanity and Social Sciences Journal, 2*(1), 1–7.
Leong, S., Hazelton, J., & Townley, C. (2013). Managing the risks of corporate political donations: A utilitarian perspective. *Journal of Business Ethics, 118*(2), 429–445.
Lewin, K. (1947). Frontiers in group dynamics: Concept, method and reality in social science; social equilibria and social change. *Human Relations, 1*(1), 5–41.
Liedong, T. A. (2017). Combating corruption in Africa through institutional entrepreneurship: Peering in from business-government relations. *Africa Journal of Management, 3*(3–4), 310–327.

Liedong, T. A., Aghanya, D., & Rajwani, T. (2020). Corporate political strategies in weak institutional environments: A break from conventions. *Journal of Business Ethics, 161*(4), 855–876.

Liedong, T. A., & Frynas, G. J. (2018). Investment climate constraints as determinants of political tie intensity in emerging countries: Evidence from foreign firms in Ghana. *Management International Review, 58*(5), 675–703.

Liedong, T. A., Rajwani, T., & Mellahi, K. (2017). Reality or illusion? The efficacy of nonmarket strategy in institutional risk reduction. *British Journal of Management, 28*(4), 609–628.

Lopez, J. A. P., & Santos, J. M. S. (2014). Does corruption have social roots? The role of culture and social capital. *Journal of Business Ethics, 122*(4), 697–708.

Lopez-Claros, A. (2014). What are the sources of corruption? Retrieved from http://blogs.worldbank.org/futuredevelopment/what-are-sources-corruption (accessed 10th March 2017).

Luiz, J., & Stewart, C. (2014). Corruption, South African Multinational Enterprises and institutions in Africa. *Journal of Business Ethics, 124*(3), 383–398.

Lutz, D. (2009). African Ubuntu philosophy and global management. *Journal of Business Ethics, 84*(S3), 313–328.

Maguire, S., Hardy, C., & Lawrence, T. B. (2004). Institutional entrepreneurship in emerging fields: HIV/AIDS treatment advocacy in Canada. *Academy of Management Journal, 47*(5), 657–679.

Margolis, J. D., & Walsh, J. P. (2003). Misery loves companies: Rethinking social initiatives by business. *Administrative Science Quarterly, 48*(2), 268–305.

Markovska, A., & Adams, N. (2015). Political corruption and money laundering: Lessons from Nigeria. *Journal of Money Laundering Control, 18*(2), 169–181.

Marquette, H. (2012). Finding god' or 'moral disengagement' in the fight against corruption in developing countries? Evidence from India and Nigeria. *Public Administration and Development, 32*(1), 11–26.

Matten, D., & Crane, A. (2005). Corporate citizenship: Toward an extended theoretical conceptualization. *Academy of Management Review, 30*(1), 166–179.

Mbaku, J. M. (2000). *Bureaucratic and political corruption in Africa: The public choice perspective.* Malabar, FL: Krieger Publishing.

Mbaku, J. M. (2010). *Corruption in Africa: Causes, consequences and cleanups.* Lanham, MD: Rowman & Littlefield Publishing Group.

Mbalyohere, C., Lawton, T., Boojihawon, R., & Viney, H. (2017). Corporate political activity and location-based advantage: MNE responses to institutional transformation in Uganda's electricity industry. *Journal of World Business, 52*(6), 743–759.

Mbigi, L. (2005). *The spirit of African leadership.* Randburg, South Africa: Knowres.

Meyer, J., & Rowan, B. (1977). Institutional organizations: Formal structure as myth and ceremony. *American Journal of Sociology, 83*(2), 340–363.

Mirvis, P., & Googins, B. (2018). Catalyzing social entrepreneurship in Africa: Roles for western universities, NGOs and corporations. *Africa Journal of Management, 4*(1), 57–83.

Mishra, P., & Maiko, S. (2017). Combating corruption with care: Developing ethical leaders in Africa. *Africa Journal of Management, 3*(1), 128–143.

Mohan, G. (2002). The disappointment of civil society: The politics of NGO intervention in Ghana. *Political Geography, 21*(1), 125–154.

North, D. C. (1990). *Institutions, institutional change and economic performance.* Cambridge: Cambridge University Press.

Nystrand, M. J. (2014). Petty and grand corruption and the conflict dynamics in Northern Uganda. *Third World Quarterly, 35*(5), 821–835.

O'Higgins, E. (2006). Corruption, underdevelopment, and extractive resource industries: Addressing the vicious cycle. *Business Ethics Quarterly, 16*(2), 235–254.

Okogbule, N. S. (2006). An appraisal of the legal and institutional framework for combating corruption in Nigeria. *Journal of Financial Crime, 13*(1), 92–106.

Olaleye-Oruene, T. (1998). Corruption in Nigeria: A cultural phenomenon. *Journal of Financial Crime, 5*(3), 232–240.

Otusanya, O. J., Lauwo, S., Ige, O. J., & Adelaja, O. S. (2015). Sweeping it under the carpet: The role of legislators in corrupt practice in Nigeria. *Journal of Financial Crime, 22*(3), 354–377.

Porter, G. (2003). NGOs and poverty reduction in a globalizing world: Perspectives from Ghana. *Progress in Development Studies, 3*(2), 131–145.

Posner, D. N. (2005). *Institutions and ethnic politics in Africa.* Cambridge: Cambridge University Press.

Powell, W. W., & DiMaggio, P. J. (1991). *The new institutionalism in organizational analysis.* Chicago, IL: University of Chicago Press.

Rabl, T., & Kühlmann, T. (2008). Understanding corruption in organizations – Development and empirical assessment of an action model. *Journal of Business Ethics, 82*(2), 477–495.

Radin, T. J. (2004). The effectiveness of global codes of conduct: Role models that make sense. *Business and Society Review, 109*(4), 415–447.

Rao, H., Morrill, C., & Zald, M. N. (2000). Power plays: How social movements and collective action create new organizational forms. In R. I. Sutton & B. M. Staw (Eds.), *Research in organizational behavior* (pp. 239–282). Greenwich, CT: JAI Press.

Rodriguez, P., Uhlenbruck, K., & Eden, L. (2005). Government corruption and the entry strategies of multinationals. *Academy of Management Review, 30*(2), 383–396.

Sartor, M. A., & Beamish, P. W. (2019). Private sector corruption, public sector corruption and the organizational structure of foreign subsidiaries. *Journal of Business Ethics, 167,* 725–744.

Scherer, A. G., & Palazzo, G. (2011). The new political role of business in a globalized world: A review of a new perspective on CSR and its implications for the firm, governance, and democracy. *Journal of Management Studies, 48*(4), 899–931.

Scholl, W., & Schermuly, C. C. (2020). The impact of culture on corruption, gross domestic product, and human development. *Journal of Business Ethics, 162*(1), 171–189.

Schwartz, M. (2009). "Corporate Efforts to Tackle Corruption: An Impossible Task?" the contribution of Thomas Dunfee. *Journal of Business Ethics, 88*(S4), 823–832.

Scott, W. R. (2001). *Institutions and organizations* (2nd ed.). Thousand Oaks: Sage, 1995.

Selvarajan, T. T., Singh, B., & Solansky, S. (2018). Performance appraisal fairness, leader member exchange and motivation to improve performance: A study of US and Mexican employees. *Journal of Business Research, 85,* 142–154.

Shleifer, A., & Vishny, R. W. (1993). Corruption. *Quarterly Journal of Economics, 108*(3), 599–617.

Smith, D. J. (2007). *A culture of corruption: Everyday deception and popular discontent in Nigeria.* Princeton, NJ: Princeton University Press.

Smith, D. J. (2010). Corruption, NGOs, and development in Nigeria. *Third World Quarterly, 31*(2), 43–258.

Smith, D. J. (2014). Corruption complaints, inequality and ethnic grievances in post-Biafra Nigeria. *Third World Quarterly, 35*(5), 787–802.

Spencer, J., & Gomez, C. (2011). MNEs and corruption: The impact of national institutions and subsidiary strategy. *Strategic Management Journal, 32*(3), 280–300.

Svensson, J. (2005). Eight questions about corruption. *Journal of Economic Perspectives, 19*(3), 19–42.

Swanepoel, A. P., & Meiring, J. (2018). Adequacy of law enforcement and prosecution of economic crimes in South Africa. *Journal of Financial Crime, 25*(2), 450–466.

Teorell. (Göteborg University, Quality of Government Institute) (2007). *Corruption as an institution: Rethinking the origins of the grabbing Han* (unpublished Working Paper Series), Göteborg, Sweden.

The Presidency (2015). *CHRAJ Boss Suspended.* Retrieved from http://www.presidency.gov.gh/node/796 (accessed 27th January 2016).

Tignor, R. L. (1993). Political corruption in Nigeria before independence. *Journal of Modern African Studies, 31*(2), 175–202.

Tolbert, P. S., & Zucker, L. G. (1996). The institutionalization of institutional theory. In S. R. Clegg, C. Hardy, & W. R. Nord (Eds.), *Handbook of organization studies* (pp. 175–190). London: Sage.

Turaki, Y. (2006). *Foundations of African traditional religion and worldview.* Nairobi, Kenya: WordAlive Publishers.

Ufere, N., Perelli, S., Boland, R., & Carlsson, B. (2012). Merchants of corruption: How entrepreneurs manufacture and supply bribes. *World Development, 40*(12), 2440–2453.

Valentine, S., & Fleischman, G. (2004). Ethics training and businesspersons' perceptions of organizational ethics. *Journal of Business Ethics, 52*(4), 391–400.

van den Bersselaar, D., & Decker, S. (2011). 'No Longer at Ease': Corruption as an institution in West Africa. *International Journal of Public Administration, 34*(11), 741–752.

Van-Vu, H., Tran, T. Q., Van-Nguyen, T., & Lim, S. (2018). Corruption, types of corruption and firm financial performance: New evidence from a transitional economy. *Journal of Business Ethics, 148*(4), 847–858.

Voyer, P. A., & Beamish, P. W. (2004). The effect of corruption on Japanese foreign direct investment. *Journal of Business Ethics, 50*(3), 211–224.

West, A. (2014). Ubuntu and business ethics: Problems, perspectives and prospects. *Journal of Business Ethics, 121*(1), 47–61.

Williams-Elegbe, S. (2018). Systemic corruption and public procurement in developing countries: Are there any solutions? *Journal of Public Procurement, 18*(2), 131–147.

Wocke, A., & Moodley, T. (2015). Corporate political strategy and liability of foreignness: Similarities and differences between local and foreign firms in the South African Health Sector. *International Business Review, 24*(4), 700–709.

World Bank (2016). *Doing business 2016: Measuring regulatory quality and efficiency* (12th ed.). Washington DC: World Bank.

8

CSR AND ENVIRONMENTAL SUSTAINABILITY IMPLEMENTATION IN MINING

Perspectives from Ghana

Prince Amoah and Gabriel Eweje

Introduction

While corporate social responsibility (CSR) has a plethora of meanings (Esau & Malone, 2013; Scherer & Palazzo, 2011), the overarching idea involves a voluntary or self-regulatory integration of stakeholder expectations into the operations of companies (Amoah & Eweje, 2020; Deegan & Shelly, 2014; Eweje, 2006a). The rationale for CSR as a fiduciary obligation grew from the inter-dependency and reciprocal relationship between companies and society. Particularly, the impacts of the activities of companies on individuals, groups, and the wider society have placed a special responsibility on corporate managers in the extractive industry (Amoah, Eweje, & Bathurst, 2020; Barkemeyer et al., 2014; Dashwood, 2014). For instance, most studies on CSR within extractive industries have focused on environmental issues, impacts, and frameworks, and the management of the inherent risks associated with the mining process (Mensah et al., 2015; Mudd, 2010). In many ways, it is the concerns about the environmental impacts that have pushed mining companies to embrace CSR as an all-encompassing concept (Eweje, 2005; Hilson, 2012; Vintró, Sanmiquel, & Freijo, 2014). In particular, there are concerns about the extent to which mining companies protect and ensure the environmental rights of people in mining communities (Idemudia, Kwakyewah, & Muthuri, 2020). Additionally, there is a dearth of empirical research examining the environmental CSR practices of large-scale mining companies (Antwi et al., 2017; Fonseca et al., 2014), in developing countries such as Ghana. Beyond this, Essah and Andrews (2016, p. 83) suggest that if mining companies are claiming to be engaging in sustainability practices, 'then there is the need to examine what they mean when speaking of sustainability'.

Moreover, while CSR within mining in Ghana is self-regulatory (Amponsah-Tawiah & Dartey-Baah, 2011), there is a patchwork of policies, laws, and practices that provide a framework for implementation (Oppong, 2016). As such, mining

DOI: 10.4324/9781003038078-9

companies have embraced the concept by striving to implement minimum regulatory requirements (Agyemang, Agyemang, Ansong, & Ansong, 2017), which usually involves investments in community development projects in education, the environment, health, and social entrepreneurship (Oppong, 2016; Yankson, 2010). These areas of CSR investments are usually undertaken by multinational mining companies, as a reputational strategy for social legitimacy and to obtain a social license to operate (Amponsah-Tawiah & Dartey-Baah, 2011; Eweje, 2006b). For example, stakeholder acceptance legitimizes mining activity and facilitates its continuity when companies engage with host communities and conform to wider social values (Parsons, Lacey, & Moffat, 2014).

However, while mining companies in Ghana have a developing environmental responsibility policy (Armah, Luginaah, & Odoi, 2013), Essah and Andrews (2016) refer to CSR implementation in Ghana as disjointed social investment activities. Similarly, Andrews (2016) argues that voluntary CSR practices undermine long-term sustainability within the extractive industry in Ghana. Specifically, CSR initiatives for addressing environmental issues in mining take the form of spillage prevention, reforestation, and land rehabilitation (Oppong, 2016) in relation to the minimum requirements under Ghana's Environmental Assessment Regulations, 1999 (L.I. 1652) and the Minerals and Mining Regulations, 2012 (L.I 2173). However, a study by Amoah and Eweje (2021) indicates that large-scale mining companies in Ghana have embraced voluntary international standards such as the Global Reporting Initiative, the International Cyanide Management Code and International Standard Organisation (ISO) to enhance their environmental CSR practices. Thus, this chapter focuses on the nature of CSR and sustainability implementation in the mining sector and the inherent complexities in addressing environmental issues and impacts within Ghana's institutional context.

The History and Nature of the Mining Industry in Ghana

Mining in Ghana has over a century of history in many forms, including alluvial gold exploration, small-scale and large-scale developments (Jackson, 1992). Particularly, there was gold trading between tribal kingdoms and Arabs merchants from local mines prior to colonization. Yet, significant expansion and commercial growth started in the 1980s during the implementation of the economic recovery programme, as required by the World Bank and the International Monetary Fund (Hilson, 2002; Hilson & Banchirigah, 2009). The economic recovery programme was implemented by the Government of Ghana because of the economic malaise and severe financial stress during this period and included specific mining reforms such as deregulation, privatisation, and tax breaks for significant investments (Hilson, 2002; Hilson & Potter, 2005).

Further, the impacts of the reforms and subsequent initiatives resulted in benefits such as employment, infrastructural development, and foreign direct investment into the economy of Ghana. Indeed, minerals export accounted

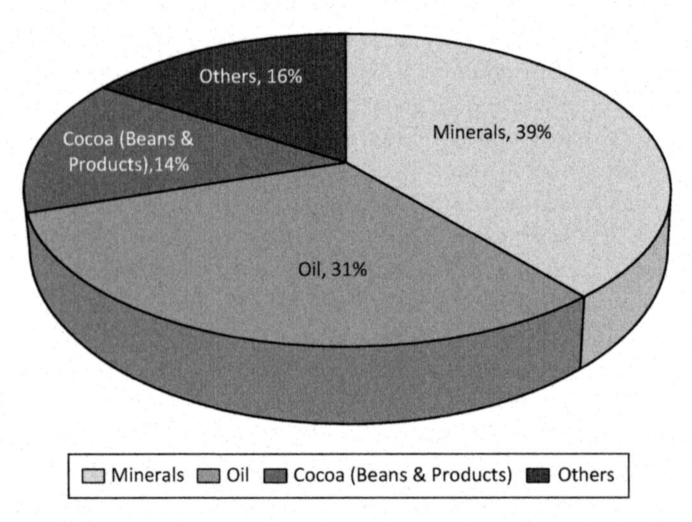

FIGURE 8.1 Share of export commodity in gross merchandise exports. Source: Based on 2019 Bank of Ghana data.

for about 40% of Ghana's gross foreign exchange in 2014 (Mensah et al., 2015) although this is decreasing due to the growth and expansion in the other sectors of the economy (see Figure 8.1). Additionally, while the mining sector directly employed 1.3% of the total labour force of Ghana in 2013 (ICMM, 2015), it also creates 4–28 additional jobs in other sectors (UNDP & UN Environment, 2018). However, 41% of the mining industry's workforce lost their jobs in 2014 (Essah & Andrews, 2016) despite a 400% increase in the price of gold over the past 15 years (Hilson & Hilson, 2017).

Moreover, regarding ownership and natural resource governance, the Government of Ghana by law has pre-emptive rights over minerals deposits and awards concessions, and grants permits and licenses for mining development (Garvin, McGee, Smoyer-Tomic, & Aubynn, 2009). This situation limits large-scale mining companies' accountability to local actors and erodes the effects of stakeholder pressures on corporate behaviour (Amoah, 2021). Additionally, while relevant mining regulations require large-scale mining companies to engage with stakeholders, especially local communities during the environmental impact assessment stage, the evidence shows that public participation has been low or lacking with respect to major decisions (Amoah, 2021; Betey & Essel, 2013; Essah & Andrews, 2016). These factors have resulted in gaps and weaknesses in the regulatory and governance arrangements leading to a non-enabling institutional context.

Taken together, the burgeoning investments and the expanding mining sector have led to mining concessions occupying about 13.1% of the total landmass of Ghana (Hilson & Banchirigah, 2009). Considering the above, the nature and character of natural resources governance, the institutional context and the environmental sustainability issues are further discussed in the next sections.

The Non-renewable Resource Extraction and the Sustainability Paradox

The focus on non-renewable minerals extraction is significant because of the general scientific consensus of resource exhaustion, although there are increasing data to the contrary. For example, Rodríguez, Arias, and Rodríguez-González (2015) and Dobra and Dobra (2014) present data showing that factors such as mining costs and technical changes are much larger determinants of physical resource exhaustion. This means that the continuous exploitation of non-renewable resources may not in itself lead to physical depletion if the opportunity cost of mining and the available technology does not provide economic incentives. Consequently, Dobra and Dobra (2014) indicate that there is no current evidence of resource exhaustion.

Considering these arguments, the main thrust of this chapter is not about whether the depletion of non-renewable resources is possible or even realistic, but that the continuous expansion in the mining sector in many developing countries raises critical concerns about the social and environmental sustainability of local communities. Additionally, the finitude of mineral resources relating to the continuous reduction in the physical stock as a result of extractive activities and the social and environmental impacts (Hilson, 2012; Owen & Kemp, 2015) have brought mining into the mainstream sustainability discourse. Consequently, there are further discussions about how the depletion of a non-renewable natural resource can be sustainable. For example, Mudd (2007) notes that this apparent contradiction because the non-renewable nature of minerals inherently means that future generations cannot have a supply of the same resources due to depletion.

As mentioned earlier, the common impacts of solid minerals extraction include pollution of surface and underground water, ambient dust and noise pollution, blasting-air overpressure causing ground vibration, and loss of biodiversity after mine closure (Moran, Lodhia, Kunz, & Huisingh, 2014; Söderholm et al., 2015). As a result, mining companies are expected to operate within sustainable limits and account for the impacts of their operations on larger environmental and social processes. Similarly, Fraser (2018) expresses that the mining industry has its fair share of many of the sustainable challenges identified by the sustainable development goals and must be part of the global drive for solutions. However, according to Barkemeyer et al. (2015), while mining is the fifth largest global industry, its potential to contribute to sustainability has not received adequate attention.

Therefore, beyond the debate and paradox, an underlying construct in sustainability relates to the effective management of the environmental and social costs of mining development without transferring the associated risks to future generations. This view is consistent with the Brundtland's report definition of sustainable development and the United Nations' Sustainable Development Goals. For instance, the sustainable development goals envisage an equitable, socially inclusive, and global sustainable development (Yonehara et al., 2017). While equity and inclusiveness may involve fair distribution and consumption, sustainability in non-renewable minerals extraction focuses on managing risks and benefits. For instance, Gordon, Bertram, and Graedel (2006) suggest that addressing the environmental costs of minerals extraction should aim at achieving an ongoing availability of resources and an environment that supports the health and productive capacities of future generations.

Accordingly, Laurence (2011, p. 279) suggests that 'even though it is not possible for a mineral resource to last forever, it is possible for the mining operation and the benefits it provides to be prolonged'. As such, the goal of sustainability is to promote inter-generational justice by maintaining the capacity of the ecosystem to support productive processes without creating a gap between present and future generations. To this end, Rajaram, Dutta, and Parameswaran (2005, p. 3) state that:

> Mining is sustainable when it is conducted in a manner that balances economic, environmental and social considerations, often referred to as the 'triple bottom-line'. Sustainable mining practices are those that promote this balance.

Mining and Sustainable Development

The concept of sustainable development is discussed across different disciplines with roots in the natural sciences but has gained currency within the fields of development and business (Tregidga & Milne, 2006). This chapter utilizes the much-quoted definition according to the World Commission on Environment and Development, which defines sustainable development as 'Humanity has the ability to make development sustainable: to ensure that it meets the needs of the present without compromising the ability of future generations to meet their own needs' (WCED, 1987, p. 8). This suggests that sustainable development aims at achieving intra- and inter-generational equity and the prevention of unnecessary transfer of development risks to future societies.

Additionally, Olawumi and Chan (2018) suggest that sustainable development involves a balance between protecting the ecosystem and meeting human needs, which may be achieved by harmonizing social, environmental, and economic sustainability. The combination of social, environmental, and economic aspects in holistic, sustainable development denotes the triple bottom line or pillars of sustainability. As a result, sustainability and sustainable development are often used interchangeably in the management literature (Ihlen & Roper, 2014).

Further, sustainable development is regarded as a collective societal process towards the vision of sustainability. For instance, according to Hector, Christensen, and Petrie (2014), sustainability is the end-state resulting from the dynamic equilibrium between the triple bottom line whereas sustainable development is the process to achieve a dynamic relationship in the dimensions of sustainability. This view is shared by Diesendorf (2000), and Olawumi and Chan (2018), which indicates the basic relationship between sustainability and sustainable development.

Accordingly, sustainable mining relates to processes that maintain and promote the balance between people, planet, and profit (Rajaram, Dutta, & Parameswaran, 2005). It prioritizes the environmental integrity and the livelihoods and well-being of local communities within the policies and practices of companies. As such, the purpose of sustainable mining may necessarily require the sustainable development of host countries, especially the local communities where mine projects are located (Amoah, 2021). Therefore, sustainable mining that promotes the environmental service capacity of the ecosystem, protect biodiversity and soil quality, and ensure safe and adequate supply of water might contribute to sustainable development in resource-rich developing countries.

Natural Resource Governance and Sustainability Challenges

According to Graham, Amos, and Plumptre (2003), governance refers to the interactions among various structures, processes, and traditions, which distributes power and duties and determines the levels of participation of a community of stakeholders. It includes regulations, monitoring, enforcement mechanisms, norms, societal expectations, and standards (Van Alstine et al., 2014). Particularly, resource governance is increasingly recognized as important to the implementation of sustainability policies and initiatives (de la Torre-Castro, 2012). This broader perspective on governance has permeated the field of environmental management, especially within the mining sector. As such, resource governance as it relates to environmental sustainability includes a set of regulatory and non-regulatory frameworks, policies, and arrangements regarding the extraction and beneficiation of mineral resources.

A study by Amoah (2021) identified regulatory gaps, weak compliance monitoring and institutional voids as the major natural resource governance challenges. First, regulatory gaps constitute a major challenge in the environmental CSR practices of large-scale mining companies in Ghana. Accordingly, the major regulatory gaps are based on conflicting standards and nominal guidelines (Amoah, 2021). In particular, conflicting standards refer to different regulators having contradictory standards for measuring regulatory compliance in the same environmental impact parameter while nominal guidelines are advisory principles, which are not legally enforceable under existing regulations. Regarding weak compliance monitoring, the issue lies with the supervisory and implementation activities of regulatory institutions in the mining industry. Also, the lack of an adequate number of staff and logistics for supervision and compliance monitoring.

Second, regarding institutional voids, Amaeshi, Adegbite, and Rajwani (2016) assert that it may be unavoidable to doubt the effectiveness of CSR in contexts characterized by inefficient markets, poor governance, and weak civil societies. Additionally, studies by Tuokuu et al. (2018) and Helwege (2015) in resource-rich developing countries of Africa and Latin America identify institutional voids such as gaps in monitoring and implementation mechanisms and stakeholder dissonance, which mar the sustainability of local mining communities.

Further, Bebbington et al. (2018, p. 1) posit that the 'disappointing development outcomes in economies with substantial extractive activity have been explained in terms of the 'poor quality' or "weakness" of institutions'. As such, the lack of effective institutions that support sustainability implementation and the combinatory weakness in various institutional arrangements constitute the hallmark of most resource-rich developing countries. Thus, the presence and implications of institutional voids may explain the challenging and non-enabling contexts for environmental sustainability implementation in Ghana (Amaeshi et al., 2016).

Despite this, Amaeshi et al. (2016) in their study on CSR practices of a company in a developing country indicate that corporate managers utilize adaptive mechanisms based on normative values to engage in responsible initiatives despite operating in a weak institutional environment. Similarly, large-scale mining companies operating in Ghana have embraced a policy of sustainability and continuous improvement to address existing and emerging environmental risks despite the natural resource governance gaps (Amoah & Eweje, 2021). Thus, while institutional voids are barriers to sustainability implementation, there is evidence to show that companies may have internal incentives to be socially responsible. For example, Johnston et al. (2021) suggest that CSR practices that internalize environmental and social costs allow companies to appropriately respond to governance deficits or institutional voids.

Resource governance gaps as a major challenge to environmental sustainability practices in the mining industry are interesting because Ghana is recognized to have relatively robust mining and environmental laws among developing countries (Amoako-Tuffour, 2017; Standing & Hilson, 2013). This is based on major policies and regulations guiding licensing, operational, and post-closure activities such as the Environmental Assessment Regulations, 1999 (L.I. 1652), and the Minerals and Mining Regulations, 2012 (L.I 2173). However, while the country's mining regulations have evolved over the years, a recent study by Amoah (2021) agrees with previous research, which has suggested institutional voids in existing policies and governance systems in Ghana (Armah et al., 2011; Ayee, Søreide, Shukla, & Le, 2011). For instance, in the domain of environmental governance, Morrison-Saunders et al. (2016) note that policies for post-closure land planning are less developed in Africa, including Ghana compared to OECD nations. In the same vein, Elbra (2017) has observed poor resource governance in Ghana and other developing countries in Africa, resulting in critical sustainability challenges.

The Nature and Character of Environmental CSR Practices in Ghana

Environmental CSR refers to the maintenance of natural capital which is the preservation of factors and practices that contribute to environmental quality on a long-term basis (Vintró, Sanmiquel, & Freijo, 2014). It involves consideration of physical inputs into productive processes ensuring an environmental service capacity, including environmental life support elements like healthy atmosphere, soil, and water (Morelli, 2011). The literature provides various criteria or indicators in defining environmental sustainability. For instance, Moldan, Janoušková, and Hák (2012) identify the criteria of environmental sustainability to include, regeneration (the use of renewable resources not exceeding long-term rates of natural regeneration); substitutability (non-renewable resources efficiently used and the usage limited to levels, which can be offset by substitution with renewable resources); assimilation (referring to polluting substances not exceeding the assimilative capacity of the environment, and avoiding irreversibility beyond reversible thresholds).

Additionally, Veleva et al. (2003) reviewed environmental sustainability of multinational companies in the same industry and identified regulatory compliance (conformance to regulations and industry standards); eco-efficiency and performance (resource use efficiency measurement such as emissions, by-product, waste, occupational injuries); effect indicators (measure the effect of a firm on the environment, worker health, and safety); supply chain and product life cycle (product distribution, use and disposal, and renewable sourcing, product recycling, and sustainable systems) as necessary for sustainability. Generally, environmental impact categories include climate change, acidification, ozone depletion, chemical pollution, freshwater use, and change in biodiversity (Dong & Hauschild, 2017).

Further, studies on environmental CSR practices are increasingly critical because of the impacts of minerals extraction and the monitoring and implementation challenges in mining and natural resource management in developing countries (Helwege, 2015; Tuokuu et al., 2018). With their greater dependency on mining, resource-rich developing countries exhibit weak governance and enforcement mechanisms. Additionally, even in developing countries with strong legislations governing social and environmental impacts, lack of political will may hinder effective monitoring, adequate investigations of social and environmental concerns, and lack of prosecution for multinational companies which fail to comply with local laws (Wudrick, 2015). Hamann (2003) posits this as resulting from the effect of globalization where the power of governments is diminishing relative to multinational corporations, which then limits the degree to which they can be regulated by legislation.

The nature of CSR implementation by large-scale mining companies in Ghana is focused largely on regulatory compliance, although corporate managers are engaging in sustainability performance disclosures based on global standards as evidence of their environmental responsibility commitments (Arthur, Wu, Yago, & Zhang, 2017). The major parameters for environmental assessment include mining impacts on biodiversity, water quality and quantity, ambient climate, and terrestrial condition (Amoah & Eweje, 2021). Accordingly, environmental challenges including deforestation, pollution, loss of fauna and flora, acid mine drainage, and other harmful ecological exposures are major concerns of mining in developing countries, including Ghana (Eweje, 2006a; Idemudia, 2011; Moran et al., 2014).

A study by Amoah (2021) indicates that large-scale mining companies in Ghana have embraced enhanced environmental CSR practices during the pre-licensing and operational stages, but experience gaps in the post-mine closure rehabilitation phase. For instance, Amoah and Eweje (2021) have observed that current environmental CSR practices in ensuring flora and fauna restoration, as part of land reclamation efforts are inadequate in preserving and maintaining biodiversity and the service quality of the environment. In particular, gaps in the residual mitigation practices, particularly relating to the management of legacy impacts and ambient air and noise pollution continuously present critical risks to the environment in local mining communities (Evangelinos & Oku, 2006; Worrall, Neil, Brereton, & Mulligan, 2009). Laurence (2006) sees legacy environmental impacts associated with abandoned mined lands as a critical challenge to environmental sustainability. In Ghana, legacy impacts associated with rampant chemical seepages continue to pose unacceptable risks to mining communities while current remediation has proven inadequate.

Moreover, proactive mitigation gaps involving accidental exposures constitute a significant barrier to environmental sustainability in Ghana at the operational and post-mining phases. For example, spillages of processed water and cyanide, which are common with surface mining pollute groundwater, posing a serious challenge to post-mine rehabilitation (Laurence, 2006; Mhlongo & Amponsah-Dacosta, 2016). There are also incidents where mining disturbs the aquifer resulting in open pits that pose dangers to residents and may negatively affect water availability in local communities. Indeed, the availability of open pits in communities with closed mining projects is a clear demonstration of the lapses in land reclamation practices and the associated environmental risks (Amoah, 2021). Accordingly, Hitch, Kumar Ravichandran, and Mishra (2014) suggest that CSR policies and practices that address environmental concerns should focus on the different stages of the mine life cycle from exploration, development and production, and closures stages (see Table 8.1). Table 8.1 further indicates that environmental sustainability issues during the operational phase are also focal areas at the mine closure stage.

The CSR mechanism in addressing environmental incidents in Ghana's mining industry largely depends on the capacity and willingness of mining companies

TABLE 8.1 Domains for Environmental CSR Practices

Mine Life Cycle	*Environmental Sustainability*
Operational Phase	**Biodiversity** • Fauna and flora **Water** • Quality and quantity **Ambient climate** • Air pollution • Noise pollution **Tailings storage management** • Chemical pollution/seepages **Energy intensity** • Emission/greenhouse gases
Mine closure phase	**Lands/biodiversity restoration** • Vegetation regeneration potential • Animal species richness/diversity • Plant species richness/diversity • Habit diversity • Decreased forest land area **Water Bodies/Soil** • Destroyed or sedimented water course (surface water) • Underground water sources • Contaminated soil

to share in-time data with regulators. This arrangement is based on regulators' severe shortages of inspectors and testing laboratories. Related to this barrier, is the ineffective compliance monitoring regime of industry regulators, which is a direct outcome of resource governance gaps. Generally, a system of compliance monitoring and enforcement is perhaps the most critical for the success of environmental sustainability implementation in the mining sector of Ghana (Tuokuu et al., 2018). Thus, environmental accidents, including cyanide spillage and percolation of chemical solutions into groundwater systems remain a challenge to proactive mitigation practices because managing and decontaminating hazardous chemical infiltration is extremely difficult and involves higher costs.

Finally, the CSR practices of large-scale mining companies have critical gaps regarding emerging environmental threats such as the unsafe disposal of hazardous materials like dumb heavy-duty tyres (Amoah, 2021). Currently, large-scale mining companies bury the unusable dumb tyres into large pits, which takes hundreds of years to decompose. As a result, a proposed Hazardous Waste Act to help in the efficient disposal of dangerous chemicals and mining equipment is under consideration and might be passed by the parliament of Ghana. Yet, this is an indication of environmental issues, which presents ongoing dangers to the long-term sustainability of local communities. Despite these concerns, the institutionalization and implementation of environmental sustainability by large-scale mining companies are based largely on voluntary and global reporting standards (Arthur et al., 2017). Thus, the next section discusses the major sustainability standards and how they help to address environmental concerns at various stages in mining operations.

Global Reporting Standards and Sustainability

According to Brown, de Jong, and Levy (2009), sustainability reporting, especially relating to CSR emerged over the past two decades as formal voluntary standards in obtaining accreditation and promoting industry self-regulation. Additionally, the growing awareness of the critical organizational role in sustainable development drives companies to report on their CSR practices (Adusei, 2017; Ehnert et al., 2016). Accordingly, Tregidga and Milne (2006) see sustainability reports as the principal mechanism by which companies demonstrate how they embed social and environmental issues into corporate discourses including managerial sensemaking of sustainable development. While companies have long reported on their environmental impacts because of regulatory requirements (Tschopp & Nastanski, 2014), sustainability reporting on social issues is also becoming important to corporate managers (Bice, 2014). Indeed, Brown et al. (2009) posit that the widening of the scope in recent years to include social impact indicators is part of the most important trend in sustainability reporting.

The extractive industry is a sector with an entrenched sustainability reporting practice (Böhling, Murguía, & Godfrid, 2019) due to incessant criticisms and stakeholder pressures. For example, Fonseca, McAllister, and Fitzpatrick (2014) note the efforts by large-scale mining companies to publish their practices in addressing social and environmental challenges associated with the extractive process. As such, large-scale mining companies in Ghana have signed up with many voluntary standards and codes in response to regulatory and stakeholder pressures.

The common sustainability reporting standards employed by large-scale mining companies in Ghana are based on the Global Reporting Initiative (GRI), International Cyanide Management Code (ICMC), International Organization for Standardization (ISO14001), and the International Financial Corporation (IFC) performance standards. For instance, while reporting standards are still evolving, GRI emphasizes stakeholder involvement and provides industry and regional specific guidelines including quantitative indicators for assessment (Tschopp & Nastanski, 2014). Similarly, the ICMC is also a voluntary programme for companies using cyanide in gold leaching, involving a multi-stakeholder process, third-party audit for compliance certification and disclosure of results (Greenwald & Bateman, 2016). The code 'focuses exclusively on the safe management of cyanide that is produced, transported, and used for the recovery of gold, and on cyanidation mill tailings and leach solutions' (Akcil, 2010, p. 137). Particularly, a significant requirement for ICMC certification includes compliance with guidelines regarding cyanide detoxification before discharge into tailings storage facilities and the treatment of decant water before releasing into the environment.

These have resulted in beyond compliance environmental practices, including green sourcing, supply chain management, and circular economy (water recycling), which are critical to the maintenance of the environmental integrity of mining communities. These certified ICMC practices by large-scale mining companies in Ghana have improved their impacts on the environment, enhanced water quality, and prevented fauna mortality. Finally, the use of isotainers instead of briquettes to reduce physical contacts with cyanide and reduce accidental discharges is a major outcome of the ICMC guidelines that protect the environment in local communities.

Further, ISO 14001 promotes environmental management and performance and provides objective measures for assessment (Balzarova & Castka, 2008; Psomas, Fotopoulos, & Kafetzopoulos, 2011). Accordingly, ISO 14001 was designed to help companies to identify and control environmental impacts associated with their activities, products and services, and provide stakeholders with a frame of reference to evaluate practices of firms (Delmas & Montes-Sancho, 2011). Based on the ISO requirement, large-scale mining companies have introduced several initiatives such as digging dam sumps around tailing storage facilities (TSFs) to monitor seepages and recycling processed water to reduce the intensity of groundwater usage. Others include preventing percolation of decant solutions into groundwater systems through the use of liners such as clay and High-Density Poly Ethylene (HDPE) for TSFs. Table 8.2 shows the

TABLE 8.2 Major Reporting Standards and the Main Domains Applied

Reporting Standard	*Application/Scope*	*Sources*
GRI	TBL (social, environmental, and economic)	(Brown et al., 2009; Hedberg & Von Malmborg, 2003; Milne & Gray, 2013)
ICMC	Environmental sustainability	(Akcil, 2010; Greenwald & Bateman, 2016)
IFC Performance Standards	Social and environmental sustainability	(Aizawa, 2006; Conley & Williams, 2011)
ISO 14001	Environmental sustainability	(Balzarova & Castka, 2008; Delmas & Montes-Sancho, 2011; Psomas et al., 2011)

major voluntary reporting standards and the sustainability domain(s) in which they are mostly applied

Therefore, sustainability reporting is improving the environmental impact disclosures of large-scale mining companies in Ghana beyond financial transparency. Finally, while voluntary sustainability standards have been criticized for their selective reporting bias (Moran et al., 2014; Sorensen, 2012), they still provide some important indicators for measuring and reporting on the environmental CSR performance of large-scale mining companies.

Conclusion and Implications

Environmental risks and costs are inherently associated with mining projects in developing countries. The major environmental issues span through the entire mining life cycle and relate to gaps in impact mitigation practices during the development and production, and closure stages. Additionally, while concurrent rehabilitation has enhanced proactive environmental CSR initiatives in Ghana, the lack of specified requirements for fauna reintroduction and inadequate compliance level for flora restoration is an ongoing gap in land reclamation practices (Amoah & Eweje, 2021). Further, the weak monitoring and compliance mechanisms stemming from the under-resourced regulatory institutions impede adequate monitoring, investigation, assessment, and enforcement of regulations in cases of non-compliance. This complexity stems from contradictory and mutually constituted demands due to incompatible prescriptions from competing institutional logics (Amoah, 2021). However, the good news regarding environmental protection lies in corporate managers' embrace of global sustainability standards, resulting in the implementation of beyond compliance and continuous improvement initiatives.

This chapter has implications for theory, policy, and practice. In terms of theory, this chapter suggests that while environmental responsibility is a regulatory compliance issue in Ghana, large-scale mining companies have embraced an industry-led voluntary institutionalized process based on perceived ethical obligation. For example, the use of new methods in water recycling, tailings storage facilities management, and green sourcing and consumption of mining chemicals are evidence of an environmental CSR approach. Thus, this chapter has provided insights into the environmental CSR practices of large-scale mining with regards to promoting sustainability and sustainable mining in a challenging and non-enabling institutional context of Ghana.

Regarding policy implication, the existing Minerals and Mining Policy 2012 (L.I 2173) and the Environmental Assessment Regulation 1999 (L.I. 1652) need to be amended and expanded to address mine closure risks. Particularly, there should be a specified requirement for flora restoration beyond the current 40% in the existing policy and regulation. Therefore, this chapter recommends that the Ministry of Natural Resources working with the Environmental Protection Agency and the Minerals Commission should introduce a policy requiring specified strategies to repopulate rehabilitated mining lands in terms of species diversity and composition. Where restoring the ecosystem of an area is impossible due to the dense concentration, diversity, and nature of biodiversity, the policy should restrict mining activities to the peripheral areas. Such a policy should be part of the existing Environmental Assessment Regulation and the Minerals and Mining Act and required under the scoping reports and impact studies prior to the issuance of permits and licenses.

Finally, in terms of the practical implication, first, the environmental issues and impacts require managers of large-scale mining projects to refocus their sustainability orientation from impact mitigation to prevention strategies, especially during the development and production, and closure stages. This will enhance the effectiveness of environmental CSR implementation, as the effects of some mining impacts are irreversible. For instance, pollution of underground water due to seepages from chemicals is impossible to adequately decontaminate by artificial processes or engineering solutions. Therefore, CSR practices should consider impact mitigation and prevention practices during the development and production stages as part of concurrent mine closure strategies.

Second, the chapter demonstrates that implementing environmental CSR and sustainability initiatives is beneficial in terms of managing regulatory and community pressures. Particularly, because of the increasing pressures leading to the discontinuation of mining projects in countries across Latin America, effective social and environmental practices might contribute to corporate sustainability in this context. Thus, large-scale mining companies may consider investing in emerging technologies and cleaner production methods such as phytoremediation to improve land reclamation because of the better possibilities to regenerate biodiversity.

Third, rethinking environmental sustainability implementation relating to the development and production stage requirements is critical to achieving sustainable outcomes in the closure phases of the extractive process. Beyond this, the environmental impact assessment process should also focus on risk avoidance where mining activities, which present higher risks to the sustainability of local communities are not licensed to operate.

Suggestions for Future Research

First, this chapter provides critical reflections on environmental CSR and sustainability issues in the context of the large-scale mining sector in Ghana. Despite this, further research is needed to understand the nature of the environmental issues and the CSR approaches in addressing them in other resource-rich developing countries. While this chapter covers important environmental issues and CSR responses in Ghana, a similar investigation into other challenging and non-enabling institutional contexts may provide further insights. As such, a more cross-country study may be needed in similar contexts to understand the differences and congruities in the environmental CSR approaches. Therefore, it should be interesting to conduct empirical studies by considering other extractive contexts in countries such as Chile, Peru, South Africa, and Indonesia. Particularly, empirical studies in different regions such as Africa, Latin America, and South-East Asia might provide information regarding the impacts of institutional and resource governance frameworks on environmental CSR practices in mining.

Second, the chapter does not provide a complete picture of the mining industry due to an expanding small-scale mining sector. Particularly, the unit of analysis in this chapter was limited to large-scale mining companies, suggesting the need for studies into the environmental and institutional issues in small-scale mining companies. This is significant because promoting holistic environmental sustainability while ignoring the small-scale mining sector might be just an empty drumbeat.

Third, promoting environmental CSR implementation involves processes in a continuum from production to consumption of beneficiated minerals. Therefore, focusing entirely on the sustainability practices of mining companies may be inadequate. As such, future research is needed in tracing and tracking social and environmental footprints back through the entire mining chain through connecting impacts from production to categories of consumption. This can be done using a quantitative input–output approach, which helps to trace the social and environmental impacts of mineral consumption across nations and sectors.

Fourth and finally, future research should consider investigating the economic aspect of sustainability within the mining industry. In particular, the empirical study should examine the economic contribution of mining companies to the economy and the well-being of both internal and external stakeholders as against the severe environmental costs. This is important because achieving environmental sustainability also involves risk avoidance, which is geared towards driving the risk event to zero by removing the source (Hajmohammad & Vachon, 2016). Thus, where the social and environmental costs of mining outstrip the economic benefits, a better strategy for sustainability and sustainable development may be to completely avoid solid minerals extraction. However, since this has not been investigated in prior studies, future research that examines economic sustainability might provide a true and complete picture of environmental CSR against net benefits and costs.

References

Adusei, C. (2017). Accounting on social and environmental reporting in the extractive industry of Ghana: Perspectives of mining staffs. *American Journal Economics Finance and Management, 3*(3), 20–32.

Agyemang, O. S., Agyemang, O. S., Ansong, A., & Ansong, A. (2017). Corporate social responsibility and firm performance of Ghanaian SMEs: Mediating role of access to capital and firm reputation. *Journal of Global Responsibility, 8*(1), 47–62.

Aizawa, M. (2006). IFC's new sustainability performance standards. *Natural Resources and Environment, 21*(1), 62–70.

Akcil, A. (2010). A new global approach of cyanide management: International cyanide management code for the manufacture, transport, and use of cyanide in the production of gold. *Mineral Processing and Extractive Metallurgy Review, 31*(3), 135–149.

Amaeshi, K., Adegbite, E., & Rajwani, T. (2016). Corporate social responsibility in challenging and non-enabling institutional contexts: Do institutional voids matter? *Journal of Business Ethics, 134*(1), 135–153.

Amoah, P. (2021). *Sustainability in the mining sector of Ghana: An empirical study* (PhD Thesis). New Zealand: Massey University, Auckland Campus.

Amoah, P., & Eweje, G. (2020). CSR in Ghana's gold-mining sector: Assessing expectations and perceptions of performance within institutional and stakeholder lenses. *Social Business, 10*(4), 339–363. doi: 10.1362/204440820X15929907056661

Amoah, P., & Eweje, G. (2021). Impact mitigation or ecological restoration? Examining the environmental sustainability practices of multinational mining companies. *Business Strategy and the Environment, 30*(1), 551–565. doi: https://doi.org/10.1002/bse.2637

Amoah, P., Eweje, G., & Bathurst, R. (2020). Understanding grand challenges in sustainability implementation within mining in developing countries. *Social Business, 10*(2), 123–149. doi:10.1362/204440820X15813359568309

Amoako-Tuffour, J. (2017). Ghana: Mineral policy. In G. Tiess, T. Majumder, & P. Cameron (Eds.), *Encyclopedia of mineral and energy policy* (pp. 1–7). Berlin: Springer. doi:10.1007/978-3-642-40871-7_165-1

Amponsah-Tawiah, K., & Dartey-Baah, K. (2011). Corporate social responsibility in Ghana. *International Journal of Business and Social Science, 2*(17), 107–112.

Andrews, N. (2016). Challenges of corporate social responsibility (CSR) in domestic settings: An exploration of mining regulation vis-à-vis CSR in Ghana. *Resources Policy, 47*, 9–17. doi:10.1016/j.resourpol.2015.11.001

Antwi, E. K., Owusu-Banahene, W., Boakye-Danquah, J., Mensah, R., Tetteh, J. D., Nagao, M., & Takeuchi, K. (2017). Sustainability assessment of mine-affected communities in Ghana: towards ecosystems and livelihood restoration. *Sustainability Science, 12*(5), 747–767.

Armah, F. A., Luginaah, I., & Odoi, J. (2013). Artisanal small-scale mining and mercury pollution in Ghana: A critical examination of a messy minerals and gold mining policy. *Journal of Environmental Studies and Sciences, 3*(4), 381–390.

Armah, F. A., Obiri, S., Yawson, D. O., Afrifa, E. K., Yengoh, G. T., Olsson, J. A., & Odoi, J. O. (2011). Assessment of legal framework for corporate environmental behaviour and perceptions of residents in mining communities in Ghana. *Journal of Environmental Planning and Management, 54*(2), 193–209.

Arthur, C. L., Wu, J., Yago, M., & Zhang, J. (2017). Investigating performance indicators disclosure in sustainability reports of large mining companies in Ghana. *Corporate Governance. International Journal of Business in Society, 17*(4), 643–660.

Ayee, J., Søreide, T., Shukla, G., & Le, T. M. (2011). *Political economy of the mining sector in Ghana*. Washington DC: The World Bank.

Balzarova, M. A., & Castka, P. (2008). Underlying mechanisms in the maintenance of ISO 14001 environmental management system. *Journal of Cleaner Production, 16*(18), 1949–1957.

Barkemeyer, R., Holt, D., Preuss, L., & Tsang, S. (2014). What happened to the 'development'in sustainable development? *Sustainable Development, 22*(1), 15– 32.

Barkemeyer, R., Stringer, L. C., Hollins, J. A., & Josephi, F. (2015). Corporate reporting on solutions to wicked problems: Sustainable land management in the mining sector. *Environmental Science and Policy, 48*, 196–209.

Bebbington, A., Abdulai, A. G., Humphreys Bebbington, D., Hinfelaar, M., & Sanborn, C. (2018). *Governing extractive industries: Politics, histories, ideas* (p. 304). Oxford: Oxford University Press.

Betey, C. B., & Essel, G. (2013). Environmental impact assessment and sustainable development in Africa: A critical review. *Environment and Natural Resources Research, 3*(2), 37–51.

Bice, S. (2014). What gives you a social licence? An exploration of the social licence to operate in the Australian mining industry. *Resources Policy, 3*(1), 62–80.

Böhling, K., Murguía, D. I., & Godfrid, J. (2019). Sustainability reporting in the mining sector: Exploring its symbolic nature. *Business and Society, 58*(1), 191–225.

Brown, H. S., de Jong, M., & Levy, D. L. (2009). Building institutions based on information disclosure: Lessons from GRI's sustainability reporting. *Journal of Cleaner Production, 17*(6), 571–580.

Conley, J. M., & Williams, C. A. (2011). Global banks as global sustainability regulators?: The equator principles. *Law and Policy, 33*(4), 542–575.

Dashwood, H. S. (2014). Sustainable development and industry self-regulation: Developments in the global mining sector. *Business and Society, 53*(4), 551–582.

de la Torre-Castro, M. (2012). Governance for sustainability: Insights from marine resource use in a tropical setting in the Western Indian Ocean. *Coastal Management, 40*(6), 612–633.

Deegan, C., & Shelly, M. (2014). Corporate social responsibilities: Alternative perspectives about the need to legislate. *Journal of Business Ethics, 121*(4), 499–526.

Delmas, M., & Montes-Sancho, M. (2011). An institutional perspective on the diffusion of international management system standards: The case of the environmental management standard ISO 14001. *Business Ethics Quarterly, 21*(1), 103–132.

Diesendorf, M. (2000). Sustainability and sustainable development. In D. Dunphy, J. Benveniste, A. Griffiths, & P. Sutton (Eds.), *Sustainability: The corporate challenge of the 21st century* (Vol. 2, pp. 19–37). Sydney: Allen Press & Unwin.

Dobra, J., & Dobra, M. (2014). Another look at non-renewable resource exhaustion. *Mineral Economics, 27*(1), 33–41.

Dong, Y., & Hauschild, M. Z. (2017). Indicators for environmental sustainability. *Procedia CIRP, 61*, 697–702.

Ehnert, I., Parsa, S., Roper, I., Wagner, M., & Muller-Camen, M. (2016). Reporting on sustainability and HRM: A comparative study of sustainability reporting practices by the world's largest companies. *International Journal of Human Resource Management, 27*(1), 88–108.

Elbra, A. (2017). A history of Gold mining in South Africa, Ghana and Tanzania. In *Governing African gold mining* (pp. 67–103). Berlin: Springer.

Esau, G., & Malone, M. (2013). CSR in natural resources: Rhetoric and reality. *Journal of Global Responsibility, 4*(2), 168–187.

Essah, M., & Andrews, N. (2016). Linking or de-linking sustainable mining practices and corporate social responsibility? Insights from Ghana. *Resources Policy, 50*, 75–85.

Evangelinos, K. I., & Oku, M. (2006). Corporate environmental management and regulation of mining operations in the Cyclades, Greece. *Journal of Cleaner Production, 14*(3–4), 262–270.

Eweje, G. (2005). Hazardous employment and regulatory regimes in the South African mining industry: Arguments for corporate ethics at workplace. *Journal of Business Ethics, 56*(2), 163–183.

Eweje, G. (2006a). Environmental costs and responsibilities resulting from oil exploitation in developing countries: The case of the Niger Delta of Nigeria. *Journal of Business Ethics, 69*(1), 27–56.

Eweje, G. (2006b). The role of MNEs in community development initiatives in developing countries: Corporate social responsibility at work in Nigeria and South Africa. *Business and Society, 45*(2), 93–129.

Fonseca, A., McAllister, M. L., & Fitzpatrick, P. (2014). Sustainability reporting among mining corporations: A constructive critique of the GRI approach. *Journal of Cleaner Production, 84*, 70–83.

Fraser, J. (2018). Mining companies and communities: Collaborative approaches to reduce social risk and advance sustainable development. *Resources Policy*, doi: https://doi.org/10.1016/j.resourpol.2018.02.003.

Garvin, T., McGee, T. K., Smoyer-Tomic, K. E., & Aubynn, E. A. (2009). Community–company relations in gold mining in Ghana. *Journal of Environmental Management, 90*(1), 571–586.

Gordon, R. B., Bertram, M., & Graedel, T. E. (2006). *Metal stocks and sustainability*. Paper presented at the Proceedings of the National Academy of Sciences. Washington, DC.

Graham, J., Amos, B., & Plumptre, T. W. (2003). *Governance principles for protected areas in the 21st century*. Ottawa: Institute on Governance, Governance Principles for Protected Areas.

Greenwald, N., & Bateman, P. (2016). The International Cyanide Management Code: Ensuring best practice in the gold industry. In M. D. Adams (Ed.), *Gold ore processing: Project development and operations* (2nd ed., pp. 191–206). Amsterdam: Elsevier. doi:10.1016/B978-0-444-63658-4.00012-8

Hajmohammad, S., & Vachon, S. (2016). Mitigation, avoidance, or acceptance? Managing supplier sustainability risk. *Journal of Supply Chain Management, 52*(2), 48–65.

Hamann, R. (2003). Mining companies' role in sustainable development: The 'why' and 'how' of corporate social responsibility from a business perspective. *Development Southern Africa, 20*(2), 237–254.

Hector, D. C., Christensen, C. B., & Petrie, J. (2014). Sustainability and sustainable development: Philosophical distinctions and practical implications. *Environmental Values, 23*(1), 7–28.

Hedberg, C. J., & Von Malmborg, F. (2003). The global reporting initiative and corporate sustainability reporting in Swedish companies. *Corporate Social Responsibility and Environmental Management, 10*(3), 153–164.

Helwege, A. (2015). Challenges with resolving mining conflicts in Latin America. *Extractive Industries and Society, 2*(1), 73–84.

Hilson, G. (2002). Harvesting mineral riches: 1000 years of gold mining in Ghana. *Resources Policy, 28*(1), 13–26.

Hilson, G. (2012). Corporate social responsibility in the extractive industries: Experiences from developing countries. *Resources Policy, 37*(2), 131–137.

Hilson, G., & Banchirigah, S. M. (2009). Are alternative livelihood projects alleviating poverty in mining communities? Experiences from Ghana. *Journal of Development Studies, 45*(2), 172–196.

Hilson, G., & Hilson, A. (2017). Mining in Ghana: Critical reflections on a turbulent past and uncertain future. In E. Aryeetey & R. Kanbur (Eds.), *The economy of Ghana sixty years after independence* (pp. 261–278). NY: Oxford University Press.

Hilson, G., & Potter, C. (2005). Structural adjustment and subsistence industry: Artisanal gold mining in Ghana. *Development and Change, 36*(1), 103–131.

Hitch, M., Kumar Ravichandran, A., & Mishra, V. (2014). A real options approach to implementing corporate social responsibility policies at different stages of the mining process. *Corporate Governance, 14*(1), 45–57. doi:10.1108/CG-07-2012-0060

ICMM (2015). *Mining in Ghana – What future can we expect?* (No. 0301-4207). Retrieved from https://www.icmm.com/website/publications/pdfs/social-and-economic-development/161026_icmm_romine_3rd-edition.pdf (Accessed 17 May, 2020).

Idemudia, U. (2011). Corporate social responsibility and developing countries: Moving the critical CSR Research agenda in Africa forward. *Progress in Development Studies, 11*(1), 1–18.

Idemudia, U., Kwakyewah, C., & Muthuri, J. (2020). Mining, the environment, and human rights in Ghana: An area of limited statehood perspective. *Business Strategy and the Environment, 29*(7), 2919 –2926.

Ihlen, Ø., & Roper, J. (2014). Corporate reports on sustainability and sustainable development:'We have arrived'. *Sustainable Development, 22*(1), 42–51.

Jackson, R. (1992). New mines for old gold: Ghana's changing mining industry. *Geography*, 77(2), 175–178.

Johnston, A., Amaeshi, K., Adegbite, E., & Osuji, O. (2021). Corporate social responsibility as obligated internalisation of social costs. *Journal of Business Ethics*, 170, 39-52 –14

Laurence, D. (2006). Optimisation of the mine closure process. *Journal of Cleaner Production, 14*(3–4), 285–298.

Laurence, D. (2011). Establishing a sustainable mining operation: An overview. *Journal of Cleaner Production, 19*(2–3), 278–284.

Mensah, A. K., Mahiri, I. O., Owusu, O., Mireku, O. D., Wireko, I., & Kissi, E. A. (2015). Environmental impacts of mining: A study of mining communities in Ghana. *Applied Ecology and Environmental Sciences, 3*(3), 81–94.

Mhlongo, S. E., & Amponsah-Dacosta, F. (2016). A review of problems and solutions of abandoned mines in South Africa. *International Journal of Mining, Reclamation and Environment, 30*(4), 279–294.

Milne, M. J., & Gray, R. (2013). W(h)ither ecology? The triple bottom line, the global reporting initiative, and corporate sustainability reporting. *Journal of Business Ethics, 118*(1), 13–29.

Moldan, B., Janoušková, S., & Hák, T. (2012). How to understand and measure environmental sustainability: Indicators and targets. *Ecological Indicators, 17*, 4–13.

Moran, C., Lodhia, S., Kunz, N., & Huisingh, D. (2014). Sustainability in mining, minerals and energy: New processes, pathways and human interactions for a cautiously optimistic future. *Journal of Cleaner Production, 84*, 1–15.

Morelli, J. (2011). Environmental sustainability: A definition for environmental professionals. *Journal of Environmental Sustainability, 1*(1), 1–9.

Morrison-Saunders, A., McHenry, M., Rita Sequeira, A., Gorey, P., Mtegha, H., & Doepel, D. (2016). Integrating mine closure planning with environmental impact assessment: Challenges and opportunities drawn from African and Australian practice. *Impact Assessment and Project Appraisal, 34*(2), 117–128.

Mudd, G. M. (2007). Global trends in gold mining: Towards quantifying environmental and resource sustainability. *Resources Policy, 32*(1–2), 42–56.

Mudd, G. M. (2010). The environmental sustainability of mining in Australia: Key mega-trends and looming constraints. *Resources Policy, 35*(2), 98–115.

Olawumi, T. O., & Chan, D. W. (2018). A scientometric review of global research on sustainability and sustainable development. *Journal of Cleaner Production, 183*, 231–250. doi:10.1016/j.jclepro.2018.02.162

Oppong, S. (2016). Corporate social responsibility in the Ghanaian context. In S. Idowu (Ed.), *Key initiatives in corporate social responsibility: Global dimensions of CSR in corporate entities* (pp. 419–442). Cham, Switzerland: Springer.

Owen, J. R., & Kemp, D. (2015). Mining-induced displacement and resettlement: A critical appraisal. *Journal of Cleaner Production, 87*, 478–488.

Parsons, R., Lacey, J., & Moffat, K. (2014). Maintaining legitimacy of a contested practice: How the minerals industry understands its 'social licence to operate'. *Resources Policy, 41*, 83–90.

Psomas, E. L., Fotopoulos, C. V., & Kafetzopoulos, D. P. (2011). Motives, difficulties and benefits in implementing the ISO 14001 Environmental Management System. *Management of Environmental Quality: an International Journal, 22*(4), 502–521.

Rajaram, V., Dutta, S., & Parameswaran, K. (2005). *Sustainable mining practices: A global perspective*. UK: Tailor and Francis Group.

Rodríguez, X. A., Arias, C., & Rodríguez-González, A. (2015). Physical versus economic depletion of a nonrenewable natural resource. *Resources Policy, 46*, 161–166.

Scherer, A., & Palazzo, G. (2011). The new political role of business in a globalized world: A review of a new perspective on CSR and its implications for the firm, governance, and democracy. *Journal of Management Studies, 48*(4), 899–931.

Söderholm, K., Söderholm, P., Helenius, H., Pettersson, M., Viklund, R., Masloboev, V., ... Petrov, V. (2015). Environmental regulation and competitiveness in the mining industry: Permitting processes with special focus on Finland, Sweden and Russia. *Resources Policy, 43*, 130–142.

Sorensen, P. (2012). Sustainable development in mining companies in South Africa. *International Journal of Environmental Studies, 69*(1), 21–40.

Standing, A., & Hilson, G. (2013). *Distributing mining wealth to communities in Ghana: Addressing problems of elite capture and political corruption*. Anti-Corruption Resource Center: Chr. Michelsen Institute.

Tregidga, H., & Milne, M. J. (2006). From sustainable management to sustainable development: A longitudinal analysis of a leading New Zealand environmental reporter. *Business Strategy and the Environment, 15*(4), 219–241. doi:10.1002/bse.534

Tschopp, D., & Nastanski, M. (2014). The harmonization and convergence of corporate social responsibility reporting standards. *Journal of Business Ethics, 125*(1), 147–162.

Tuokuu, F. X. D., Gruber, J. S., Idemudia, U., & Kayira, J. (2018). Challenges and opportunities of environmental policy implementation: Empirical evidence from Ghana's gold mining sector. *Resources Policy, 59*, 435–445.

United Nations Development Program, & UN Environment (2018). *Managing mining for sustainable development: A sourcebook*. Bangkok: United Nations Development Programme.

Van Alstine, J., Manyindo, J., Smith, L., Dixon, J., & AmanigaRuhanga, I. (2014). Resource governance dynamics: The challenge of 'new oil'in Uganda. *Resources Policy, 40*, 48–58.

Veleva, V., Hart, M., Greiner, T., & Crumbley, C. (2003). Indicators for measuring environmental sustainability. *Benchmarking: An International Journal, 10*(2), 107–119.

Vintró, C., Sanmiquel, L., & Freijo, M. (2014). Environmental sustainability in the mining sector: Evidence from Catalan companies. *Journal of Cleaner Production, 84*, 155–163.

WCED (1987). *Our common future*. New York: Oxford University Press.

Worrall, R., Neil, D., Brereton, D., & Mulligan, D. (2009). Towards a sustainability criteria and indicators framework for legacy mine land. *Journal of Cleaner Production, 17*(16), 1426–1434.

Wudrick, H. (2015). *Corporate social responsibility in the Canadian mining sector: Ethics, rhetoric, and the economy* [Masters Dissertation]. Burnaby, British Columbia: Simon Frazer University.

Yankson, P. W. (2010). Gold mining and corporate social responsibility in the Wassa West district, Ghana. *Development in Practice, 20*(3), 354–366.
Yonehara, A., Saito, O., Hayashi, K., Nagao, M., Yanagisawa, R., & Matsuyama, K. (2017). The role of evaluation in achieving the SDGs. *Sustainability Science, 12*(6), 969–973.

9

ACHIEVING SUSTAINABLE DEVELOPMENT GOALS THROUGH CORPORATE SOCIAL RESPONSIBILITY

Uwem E. Ite

Introduction

The concept of sustainable development emerged from global public pressure in the 1980s and ultimately forced itself onto the agenda of governments and international institutions. It is now embraced as the global standard for measuring development objectives and performance in both developed and developing countries. The emergence of the Millennium Development Goals (MDGs) in 2000, and its subsequent replacement by the Sustainable Development Goals (SDGs) in 2015 is a clear indication that the concept has made significant progress by moving from global level rhetoric and debates to local level practice and action. The SDGs aim to address economic, social, and environmental challenges. It is expected that member states of the United Nations will use the SDGs to frame their development agendas, while clearly recognizing that the private sector has an important role to play in this regard.

This chapter provides guidance on how the Nigerian oil and gas industry can contribute across all SDGs through their corporate social responsibility (CSR) strategy and programmes. The next section discusses the evolution, principles, and practice of sustainable development from a global perspective, including the United Nations Millennium Development Goals and the Sustainable Development Goals. The third section provides a brief overview of the Nigerian oil and gas industry as well as CSR within the industry, while the fourth section examines how oil and gas companies in Nigeria can integrate SDGs into their CSR strategies and programmes. In the fifth section, relevant stakeholders for SDG integration into CSR delivery by the oil and gas industry in Nigeria are highlighted. Conclusions are drawn in the sixth section of this chapter.

DOI: 10.4324/9781003038078-10

Sustainable Development: Evolution, Principles, and Practice

Evolution and Definition of Sustainable Development

The history of sustainable development thinking and its subsequent evolution as a globally accepted development paradigm is well documented. As Adams (2009) noted, sustainable development has become a central concept in development studies, building on environmental, social, and political critiques of development theory and practice. There is no simple and single meaning of 'sustainable development' because a wide range of different meanings is attached to the term. However, due to its ability to host divergent ideas, the concept has proved to be very useful, to the extent of becoming dominant ever since the idea of sustainable development gained currency in the 1990s.

Nonetheless, the most widely used and generally known definition by the World Commission on Environment and Development (WCED; 1987:43) defined sustainable development as:

> Development that meets the needs of the present without compromising the ability of future generations to meet their own needs

This definition is based on two fundamental principles of development thinking namely: basic needs and environmental limits. By going beyond the concepts of physical sustainability to the economic context of development, the definition by WCED involves a subtle but extremely important transformation of the ecologically based concept of sustainable development (Jamieson, 1998). Several factors triggered the attention of the international community to intergenerational equity in relation to access to natural resources. These included widespread environmental degradation, the existence of severe poverty around the globe and concerns about achieving and maintaining a good quality of life. As Reed (1996) noted, sustainable development emerged from public pressure, ultimately forcing itself onto the agenda of governments and international institutions. The concept is built on three key principles (i.e. social, economic, and environmental sustainability), and remains the global standard for measuring development objectives and performance in both developed and developing countries.

Principles and Dimensions of Sustainability

The first principle, social sustainability, is rooted in the premise of equity and understanding of the human community's interdependence to achieve an acceptable quality of life, which is the aim of development. Therefore, sustainable social development is concerned with equity in the distribution of wealth, resources, and opportunity to all citizens at all levels. It implies access to minimum standards of security, human rights, social benefits e.g. food, health, education, shelter, and opportunities for self-development. It requires active political participation in decision-making and public accountability (Reed, 1996). In other words, social sustainability places emphasis on distributional and gender equity, provision of social services, population stabilization, as well as political accountability and participation.

On the other hand, the second principle, economic sustainability, require societies to generate an optimal flow of income while maintaining their basic stock of man-made, human, and natural capital. It advocates for the internalization of all external costs, including the societal and environmental costs associated with the production and disposition of goods, thereby implementing the full costs principle (Reed, 1996). Economic sustainability is therefore about sound macroeconomic management, poverty alleviating growth, appropriate agricultural policies, role of the state, and cost internalization.

The third principle, environmental sustainability, is predicated on the maintenance of long-term integrity and productivity of the planet's life-support systems and environmental infrastructure. The inefficient use of natural resources is identified by neoclassical economists as the main reason for environmental problems, and the inefficiency is caused by market failure due to external effects (Rennings & Wiggering, 1997). Therefore, environmental sustainability requires the use of environmental goods and services in such a way that their productive capacities are not reduced, nor their overall contribution to human well-being diminished. In practical terms, environmental sustainability hinges on sustainable use of resources, maintenance of sink functions of environmental processes, ensuring the increase in the quality and quantity of natural capital, adopting the precautionary principle and the establishment of adequate and suitable institutional frameworks for environmental protection.

Walking the Talk from Principles to Practice

Against the background presented in the preceding section, as well as the need to walk the talk by translating the principles of sustainability into practical actions, several initiatives have been developed and implemented at the local, national, continental, and global levels. Two of such initiatives are the United Nations Millennium Development Goals (MDGs) which came to end in 2015, and its immediate successor, the United Nations Sustainable Development Goals (SDGs).

The eight MDGs (see Table 9.1) galvanized a global campaign from 2000 to 2015 to end poverty in its various dimensions. The MDGs focused on the most vulnerable populations and marked a historic and effective global mobilization effort to achieve a set of common societal priorities. The MDGs focused on many dimensions of extreme poverty, including low incomes, chronic hunger, gender inequality, lack of schooling, lack of access to health care, and deprivation of clean water and sanitation, among others (Sustainable Development Solutions Network, 2015). By packaging these priorities into an easy-to-understand set of eight goals, and by establishing measurable, time-bound objectives, the MDGs promoted global awareness, political accountability, improved monitoring, mobilization of epistemic communities, civic participation, and public pressure (Sachs, 2012).

TABLE 9.1 The United Nations Millennium Development Goals (MDGs)

Millennium Development Goal (MDG)
MDG 1 – Eradicate Extreme Hunger
MDG 2 – Achieve Universal Primary Education
MDG 3 – Promote Gender Equality and Empower Women
MDG 4 – Reduce Child Mortality
MDG 5 – Improve Maternal Health
MDG 6 – Combat HIV AIDS Malaria and Other Diseases
MDG 7 – Ensure Environmental Sustainability
MDG 8 – Develop a Global Partnership for Development

On the other hand, the SDGs (see Table 9.2) have been the centrepiece of the 2030 Agenda for Sustainable Development adopted by the United Nations Sustainable Development Summit in September 2015 (Woodbridge, 2015). Building on the accomplishments of the MDGs, the SDGs address the most pressing global challenges and call for collaborative partnerships across and between countries to balance the three dimensions of sustainable development described earlier i.e., economic growth, environmental sustainability, and social inclusion (Sustainable Development Solutions Network, 2015). The 17 SDGs form a cohesive and integrated package of global aspirations the world commits to achieving by 2030.

There are significant differences between the MDGs and SDGs as outlined in Table 9.3. For example, while the MDGs were only applicable to developing countries, the SDGs apply universally to all United Nations member states and are considerably more comprehensive and ambitious than the MDGs. Most importantly, the SDGs adopt sustainable development as the organizing principle for global cooperation. In other words, the SDGs are the combination of economic development, social inclusion, and environmental sustainability, hence, the overarching name 'Sustainable Development Goals', as the key message to the global community (Sustainable Development Solutions Network, 2015).

With specific reference to the oil and gas industry, Table 9.4 provides a mapping of SDGs to key issues which the industry must grapple with in their contributions to sustainable development. However, the recent SDG Roadmap for the oil and gas sector (IPIECA, 2021) noted that although the oil and gas sector has the potential to advance all 17 goals either directly or indirectly, ten SDGs can be considered as priority areas where the sector has the most influence or ability to respond to societal needs by driving innovation and impact in its own operations and across the value chain. These are SDG 3 – Good Health and Well-being; SDG 6 – Clean Water and Sanitation; SDG 7 – Affordable and Clean Energy; SDG 8 – Decent Work and Economic Growth; SDG 9 – Industry, Innovation, and Infrastructure; SDG 12 – Responsible Consumption and Production; SDG 13 – Climate Change; SDG 14 – Life below Water; SDG 15 – Life on Land; and SDG 16 – Peace, Justice, and Strong Institutions. In addition, SDG 17 – Partnerships for the Goals, was identified as cross-cutting and essential to all impact opportunities.

TABLE 9.2 The United Nations Sustainable Development Goals (SDGs)

Sustainable Development Goal (SDG)	*Description of Goals*
SDG 1 – No Poverty	End poverty in all its forms everywhere
SDG 2 – Zero Hunger	End hunger; achieve food security and improved nutrition and promote sustainable agriculture
SDG 3 – Good Health and Well-being	Ensure healthy lives and promote well-being for all at all ages
SDG 4 – Quality Education	Ensure inclusive and equitable quality education and promote lifelong learning opportunities for all
SDG 5 – Gender Equality	Achieve gender equality and empower all women and girls
SDG 6 – Clean Water and Sanitation	Ensure availability and sustainable management of water and sanitation for all
SDG 7 – Affordable and Clean Energy	Ensure access to affordable, reliable, sustainable, and modern energy for all
SDG 8 – Decent Work and Economic Growth	Promote sustained, inclusive, and sustainable economic growth, full and productive employment and decent work for all
SDG 9 – Industry, Innovation and Infrastructure	Build resilient infrastructure, promote inclusive and sustainable industrialization and foster innovation
SDG 10 – Reduced Inequalities	Reduce inequality within and among countries
SDG 11 – Sustainable Cities and Communities	Make cities and human settlements inclusive, safe, resilient, and sustainable
SDG 12 –Responsible Consumption and Production	Ensure sustainable consumption and production patterns
SDG 13 – Climate Change	Take urgent action to combat climate change and its impacts
SDG 14 – Life below Water	Conserve and sustainably use the oceans, seas, and marine resources for sustainable development
SDG 15 – Life on Land	Protect, restore and promote sustainable use of terrestrial ecosystems, sustainably manage forests, combat desertification, and halt and reverse land degradation and halt biodiversity loss
SDG 16 – Peace, Justice and Strong Institutions	Promote peaceful and inclusive societies for sustainable development, provide access to justice for all and build effective, accountable and inclusive institutions at all levels
SDG 17 – Partnerships for the Goals	Strengthen the means of implementation and revitalize the global partnership for sustainable development

TABLE 9.3 Comparison of Millennium Development Goals and Sustainable Development Goals

Key Features/Attributes	*Millennium Development Goals*	*Sustainable Development Goals*
Number of Goals	8	17
Number of Targets	18	169
Number of Indicators	48	230
Geographic Coverage	Developing countries only	All countries
Implementation Timeframe	2000–2015	2016–2030
Delivery Focus	Narrow: Poverty reduction	Broad: global development with-and-for sustainability

The Nigerian Oil and Gas Industry

Overview of the Industry

The evolution of the oil and gas industry in Nigeria and its subsequent social, political, and economic impacts on the Nigerian state as well as on state-society relationship in general has been well addressed (see e.g., Obi & Soremekun, 1995; Ikein & Briggs-Anigboh, 1998; Frynas, 2000). In general terms, oil exploration, production, and marketing in Nigeria are undertaken through complex joint venture partnership agreements and production sharing contracts between the federal government and the operating companies. However, since ownership of crude oil is vested in the state, taxes and royalties accrue to the federal government directly. Hence, the federal government is in effect both a direct 'stockholder' and a stakeholder in the Nigerian oil and gas industry (Idemudia & Ite, 2006a).

The Nigerian National Petroleum Corporation (NNPC) was established in 1977 and charged with the responsibility for regulating the activities of all oil and gas companies on behalf of the Nigerian government. The NNPC has therefore been the sole superintendent of the oil sector, dictating the pace and direction of activities in the industry. As the federal government's proxy in the oil business, the NNPC holds an average of 57% in the joint venture partnership arrangements with several multinational oil exploration and production companies in Nigeria (Idemudia & Ite, 2006a).

The private sphere of the Nigerian oil and gas industry is largely dominated by major international oil companies. They can be relatively classified into first and second-generation oil companies, based on the date they went into full independent concessional agreement with the federal government of Nigeria (Idemudia & Ite, 2006a). The first-generation of oil companies account for about 90% of the total crude oil production in Nigeria. Frynas, Beck, and Mellahi (2000) argued that the first-generation oil companies in Nigeria have been able to maintain their dominance in the oil industry through 'first

TABLE 9.4 Mapping Sustainable Development Goals to Key Issue Areas for the Oil and Gas Industry

Sustainable Development Goals	*Key Issue Areas for Oil and Gas Industry*
SDG 1 – No Poverty	• Local Development • Climate Change • Energy Access
SDG 2 – Zero Hunger	• Alignment of Activities • Climate Change • Shared-use Infrastructure
SDG 3 – Good Health and Well-being	• Health Impact Assessment • Road Safety • Worker and Community Protection
SDG 4 – Quality Education	• Local Content Strategy • Workforce Education • Technology Training
SDG 5 – Gender Equality	• Gender-Sensitive Policies • Inclusive Decision-Making • Women's Employment Opportunities
SDG 6 – Clean Water and Sanitation	• Water Strategy • Water Use Efficiency • Water Risk Management
SDG 7 – Affordable and Clean Energy	• Natural Gas • Energy Efficiency • Alternative Energies
SDG 8 – Decent Work and Economic Growth	• Skills Assessment • Local Employment • Workforce and Supplier Development
SDG 9 – Industry, Innovation, and Infrastructure	• Sustainable Infrastructure • Shared Use Infrastructure • Technology Transfer
SDG 10 – Reduced Inequalities	• Impact Assessments • Transparency • Engagement
SDG 11 – Sustainable Cities and Communities	• Cultural and Natural Heritage Protection • Operational Risk Assessment • Sustainable Urbanization
SDG 12 – Responsible Consumption and Production	• Efficient Waste Management • Supply Chain Sustainability • Product Stewardship
SDG 13 – Climate Change	• Resilience and Adaptive Capacity • Emissions Mitigation • Strategic Planning
SDG 14 – Life below Water	• Accident Prevention and Response • Environmental Assessments • Ocean Acidification Minimization
SDG 15 – Life on Land	• Ecosystem Management • Mitigation Hierarchy • Biodiversity Offsets

(*Continued*)

TABLE 9.4 (Continued)

Sustainable Development Goals	*Key Issue Areas for Oil and Gas Industry*
SDG 16 – Peace, Justice and Strong Institutions	• Community Engagement • Anti-Corruption • Human Rights
SDG 17 – Partnerships for the Goals	• Dialogue and Coordination • Government Capacity • Sustainable Energy

Source: Compiled from IPIECA, IFC and UNDP (2017)

mover advantage'. On the other hand, the second-generation oil companies (i.e. indigenous and marginal field operators) are confined to areas either left behind by the first-generation oil companies or newly discovered oil blocks in the country.

The host communities also constitute an important group of stakeholders in the Nigerian oil and gas industry. Agim (1997) divided the host communities into three principal groups, each of which claims equal rights to the social investment programmes provided by the oil companies. These groups are:

(a) Producing communities: These are communities in which onshore oil exploration takes place;
(b) Terminal communities: These are coastal communities on whose territory port or terminal facilities are sometimes located because oil exploration takes place offshore; and
(c) Transit communities: These are communities whose territory transit pipelines pass through.

However, it is important to note here that there are other groups of communities (i.e. neither producing, terminal, nor transit) who are also laying similar claims to the social investment programmes provided by the oil companies since they are generally situated in the oil-producing region of the Niger Delta in Nigeria. Such claims and agitation have been known to result in conflict, dependency culture, and feelings of alienation (see Ite, 2004; Ite, 2005; Idemudia & Ite, 2006a; Idemudia & Ite, 2006b; Musa, Yusuf, McArdle, & Banjoko, 2013).

Corporate Social Responsibility in the Nigerian Oil and Gas Industry

As a business strategy, CSR is driven by globalization, deregulation, and privatization. Proponents are keen to demonstrate that business has responsibilities beyond the production of goods, services, and profit-making and that socially responsible business can help to solve important social and environmental problems. On the other hand, counterarguments on CSR attempt to show that CSR distorts the market by deflecting business from its primary role of profit generation (Ite, 2004).

With about 37 billion barrels of oil reserves and about 179 trillion cubic feet of discovered natural gas (the world's 11th and 9th largest volumes, respectively), Nigeria has the resource base to remain a leading hydrocarbon economy for the long term. The upstream oil and gas industry has played a pivotal role in the Nigerian economy for over four decades, accounting for a predominant proportion of its export earnings and driving economic activity at various levels of government and Nigerian society.

In Nigeria, the proactive pursuit of CSR discourse and subsequent implementation as a business strategy is a relatively new and emerging practice. The good news is that CSR thinking has firmly taken strong roots in the Nigerian oil and gas, banking, and telecommunications sectors. This is evident in the variety of projects and programs designed and implemented over time. Table 9.5 provides a summary of typical CSR initiatives within the oil and gas industry. A cursory look shows that several of these initiatives have been widely embraced and implemented by operators in the Nigerian oil and gas industry. In addition, some companies have also gone further to demonstrate significant commitment and interest in CSR delivery by increasing their CSR budgets and expenditure. Similarly, others have adopted different CSR policy approaches to complement their stakeholder relations strategy. These range from corporate philanthropy, corporate foundations, strategic CSR to partnership schemes (see Ite 2007; Idemudia, 2009; Musa et al., 2013; Idemudia, 2014a).

The prominence of adoption and implementation of CSR strategy in the Nigerian oil industry is not entirely surprising. Oil production remains core to the Nigerian economy and the negative social and environmental impacts associated with oil extraction are always at the centre of public scrutiny (Egbon, Idemudia, & Amaeshi, 2018). The industry plays a pivotal role in the Nigerian economy, accounting for a predominant proportion of its export earnings and driving economic activity at various levels of government and the wider society. Within the context of sustainable development, the overarching goal of the Nigerian oil and gas industry players has been to do business responsibly, contribute to society, minimize risks and avoid harm to the environment (Ite, 2018).

Nevertheless, the pursuit and focus of CSR by oil and gas companies operating in the Niger Delta goes beyond the need to secure or maintain their social license to operate – it also emanates from corporate commitment to support sustainable development in the Niger Delta region. As such, one of the key drivers of CSR practices in the Niger Delta has been a failure of government (i.e. local, state, and federal) to discharge its constitutional responsibility of economic, social, and environmental development in the region. To some extent, this explains the prevailing demands and agitations by local communities for increased levels of CSR activities from oil and gas companies operating in the area (see Ite, 2004; Ite, 2005; Musa et al., 2013).

TABLE 9.5 Typical CSR Initiatives in the Oil and Gas Industry

S/No	*Thematic Area*	*Description*
1	Art and Culture	Funding for cultural organizations such as museums, theatres, cultural centres, dance/music groups, and heritage foundations.
2	Community Welfare	Unspecified community contributions that cannot be labelled as housing, infrastructure and energy investments e.g. volunteer initiatives to renew parks, community events, supporting vulnerable community members such as foster children or the elderly citizens.
3	Disaster Relief	Investments to support those affected by extreme weather events e.g. earthquakes, floods, fires, hurricanes, tsunamis.
4	Education	Primary and secondary education, university funding, scholarships and fellowships, vocation-based skills, teacher training programs.
5	Enterprise Development	Supporting entrepreneurs to start or maintain small- to medium-sized businesses. Often focused on empowering female entrepreneurs helping to lift families out of poverty.
6	Environment	Efforts to protect or enhance the environment, ecological initiatives, such as water conversation, waste management, recycling programs, clearing litter, planting trees.
7	Food and Agriculture	Food donations such as meals for school children, agricultural inputs such as seeds, training farmers in new techniques, initiatives aimed at improving crop yields.
8	Health	Funding programs to eliminate diseases such as cancer, HIV, or malaria, increase access to existing treatments and medicines, improve healthcare infrastructure, improve hygiene, encourage exercise, improve well-being.
9	Housing, Infrastructure and Energy	Community infrastructure initiatives e.g. building houses, roads, access to water and energy.
10	Poverty Alleviation	Investments aimed at most disadvantaged members of society, programs to meet basic needs such as food and clothing or improving financial situation of those in poverty and increasing financial literacy.
11	Safety	Initiatives to improve community safety, most often road safety.
12	Science and Innovation	Grants or funding to further science, innovation, technology, and learning through established or new research institutes.
13	Sports and Recreation	Support for sporting and recreational activities, often focused on children's access to sport.

Source: KPMG International (2014)

As Ite (2018) observed, despite the best efforts in delivery, many CSR initiatives have been known to fail shortly after completion or handing over to beneficiaries. This is partly due to the initial failure to incorporate a robust set of sustainability criteria into CSR design and implementation process. Furthermore, from a project perspective, evidence shows that in many cases, beneficiaries often have a proprietorial sense of the projects but fail to take actual or full ownership and responsibility for the sustainability of the completed projects, thus leading to the rise of dependency and entitlement culture. On the other hand, attempts to measure project impacts after completion sometimes do not yield the desired results for effective CSR communication due to the deployment of poorly designed methodology for data collection and analysis (Ite, 2018).

The need for objective and credible assessment of the impacts and outcomes of CSR initiatives in the oil and gas industry has received considerable attention. External stakeholders have increased their demand for significant evidence of the developmental outcomes and impact of CSR efforts. In addition, internal stakeholders have requested stronger evidence of the contributions of CSR to the business bottom line to justify the annual budget allocations and subsequent CSR expenditure. This creates the impetus for measuring the effectiveness of CSR initiatives by the oil and gas industry (Ite, 2018).

To derive maximum value from CSR initiatives, operators within the oil and gas industry need to communicate with certainty, the direct and indirect impact of their contributions to sustainable development. As Ite (2019) noted, there is a need to move beyond the annual reporting on the number of completed projects and amount of money spent (i.e. quantity delivered), to effective CSR communication which focuses on the outcomes and impact of projects and programs as well as the macroeconomic, social and environmental effects (i.e. quality and value-added).

Towards Integration of Sustainable Development Goals into Corporate Social Responsibility Strategy and Programmes

Contemporary debates on CSR in developing countries of Africa is currently focusing on how best to maximize business contribution to sustainable development (see Idemudia, 2014b), and the SDGs therefore provide ample opportunity in this regard. The scope and nature of typical oil and gas activities point to some SDGs where there are particularly strong opportunities to contribute. As such, there are ample opportunities for oil and gas companies in Nigeria to integrate SDGs into their CSR strategies and programmes, especially with respect to SDG 3 – Good Health and Well-being; SDG 6 – Clean Water and Sanitation; SDG 7 – Affordable and Clean Energy; SDG 8 – Decent Work and Economic Growth; SDG 9 – Industry, Innovation and Infrastructure; SDG 12 – Responsible Consumption and Production; SDG 13 – Climate Change; SDG 14 – Life below Water; SDG 15 – Life on Land; SDG 16 – Peace, Justice and Strong Institutions and SDG 17 – Partnerships for the Goals. This will involve proactive alignment of the SDGs with the CSR strategy and programmes of individual companies within the industry. Table 9.6 provides a

TABLE 9.6 Integrating SDGs into Corporate Social Responsibility Strategy and Programmes

Oil and Gas + SDGs	*CSR Issues for Action*	*Collaborate and Leverage*
SDG 1 – Ending Poverty	• Increase access to energy • Contribute to fiscal sustainability • Address climate change • Invest in local development	• Community development agreements • Reduce gender inequality
SDG 2 – Ending Hunger	• Align co-located agricultural and oil and gas development activities • Shared-use infrastructure to enhance agricultural productive capacity • Address climate change	• Increase efficiency in oil and gas-based agricultural products
SDG 3 – Good Health	• Conduct health impact assessments to strengthen capacity to manage health risks • Reduce occupational risks • Protect workers and community members against infectious diseases • Protect workers and community members against non-communicable diseases • Address mental health and substance abuse • Design benefits programmes • Prevent and mitigate the health impacts of air emissions and effluent discharges • Improve road safety	• Strengthen public health systems' response to potential health risks and epidemics
SDG 4 – Quality Education	• Establish a company strategy for local content to promote sustainable development • Invest in workforce education, training and technical programmes • Invest in education and training in responsible energy use and new technologies	• Support in-country education and skills development efforts

(Continued)

TABLE 9.6 (Continued)

Oil and Gas + SDGs	*CSR Issues for Action*	*Collaborate and Leverage*
SDG 5 – Gender Equality	• Develop gender-sensitive local content policies • Support full and effective participation of women at all levels of decision-making • Increase employment opportunities for women and female representation in management	• Address negative social impacts including all forms of violence • Enhance the use of STEM (science, technology, engineering and mathematics) to empower women in the oil and gas industry
SDG 6 – Clean Water	• Develop a company water strategy • Understand water scarcity risk management • Substantially increase water use efficiency • Manage produced water and wastewater	• Improve understanding of the water-energy nexus • Participatory approach to water management • Shared-use water infrastructure
SDG 7 – Clean Energy	• Improve access to energy through shared infrastructure • Grow the share of natural gas in the energy mix • Increase the share of alternative energies and technologies in the global energy mix • Improve energy efficiency in operation and production	• An integrated, multi-stakeholder approach to energy poverty
SDG 8 – Economic Growth	• Conduct skills assessment and communicate reasonable expectations • Foster full and productive local employment and workforce development • Encourage local procurement and supplier development	• Support economic diversification to achieve higher levels of economic productivity • Multi-stakeholder dialogue to promote development-oriented policies
SDG 9 – Infrastructure	• Upgrade infrastructure and technology to make them sustainable • Evaluate potential opportunities for shared use infrastructure	• Enhance technological capabilities and knowledge transfer

(*Continued*)

TABLE 9.6 (Continued)

Oil and Gas + SDGs	*CSR Issues for Action*	*Collaborate and Leverage*
SDG 10 – Reduced Inequalities	• Ensure full and transparent tax payments • Assess inequality impacts in project planning • Set expectations and communicate with local communities • Mitigate the impacts of climate change • Provide access to energy	• Enhance revenue management and improved local governance
SDG 11 – Sustainable Communities	• Protect and safeguard the world's cultural and natural heritage • Address risks related to operations in urban environments • Support inclusive and sustainable urbanization in communities near operations	• Coordinate planning for urban and regional development
SDG 12 – Responsible Consumption	• Integrate product stewardship approach • Introduce environmentally sound and efficient chemical and waste management • Improve supply chain sustainability	• Coordinate approaches to sustainability
SDG 13 – Climate Action	• Plan strategically for a net-zero emissions future • Self-assess carbon resiliency • Strengthen resilience and adaptive capacity to climate change impacts • Mitigate emissions within oil and gas operations	• Partner in research and development and education outreach • Support effective policy measures • Help consumers lower their emissions
SDG 14 – Life below Water	• Incorporate environmental assessments into management plans • Minimize and address the rate of ocean acidification • Accident prevention, preparedness and response	• Transfer and share marine technology • Coordinate biodiversity research

(*Continued*)

TABLE 9.6 (Continued)

Oil and Gas + SDGs	*CSR Issues for Action*	*Collaborate and Leverage*
SDG 15 – Life on Land	• Effective biodiversity and ecosystem management • Implement the mitigation hierarchy • Minimize impacts through new technologies • Biodiversity offsets	• Multi-stakeholder knowledge sharing • A landscape-wide conservation approach
SDG 16 – Peace	• Integrate human rights perspective in impacts assessments • Community engagement and consent • Integrate anti-corruption systems	• Improve institutions through national oil companies • Increase effective, accountable and transparent institutions
SDG 17 – Partnerships	• Build government capacity • Develop and disseminate sustainable energy technologies	• Participate in dialogue • Strengthen coordination between initiatives • Incorporate SDs into policies • Apply the SDG indicators

Source: Compiled from IPIECA, IFC and UNDP (2017)

summary of specific actions oil and gas companies can take to ensure effective results and sustainable outcomes. This can be achieved by increasing the robustness levels of existing business processes and systems including corporate policies and standards; sustainability reporting; risk assessment and management; stakeholder engagement as well as project due diligence.

Corporate Policies and Standards

Company governance and management systems, standards, and strategies that address areas such as environment, health and safety, compliance, anti-bribery, gender, and supply and procurement can be used to set goals and monitor progress towards integrating the SDGs into CSR strategy of oil and gas companies. Over time, the industry, at local, national, and global levels, has used lessons learned across all geographies to develop good CSR practices and introduced standards and practices that, in many places, go beyond regulatory requirements. In Nigeria, several oil and gas companies have drawn up clearly defined and well-articulated policy, mission, and vision statements which demonstrate their commitment to the general principles of sustainability (i.e. social, economic, and environmental) described earlier in the section 'Principles and Dimensions of Sustainability'. Many have also gone beyond these statements and have proactively 'walked the talk' by developing and implementing action plans and specific projects, programmes, and initiatives to address some of the SDG key issue areas for the oil and gas industry as outlined earlier. It is therefore important for the companies to continue to fine-tune and update their governance and management systems as well as standards and CSR strategies, taking into consideration the changing global narratives and thinking on sustainable development, as well as the local and national realities of delivery.

Sustainability Reporting

Sustainability reporting can help organizations to understand, measure, and communicate their economic, environmental, social, and governance performance. To enhance stakeholder understanding of company contributions towards the SDGs, companies can map and report on the SDGs in their sustainability disclosures (IPIECA, IFC, & United Nations Development Program, 2017). Sustainability reporting, as promoted by the Global Reporting Initiative (GRI) Standards, is an organization's practice of reporting publicly on its economic, environmental, and/or social impacts, and hence its contributions (positive or negative) towards the goal of sustainable development (Global Sustainability Standards Board, 2016). Through this process, an organization identifies its significant impacts on the economy, the environment, and the wider society and discloses these in accordance with a globally accepted standard, such as the GRI Standards.

The GRI Standards create a common language for organizations and stakeholders, with which the economic, environmental, and social impacts of organizations can be communicated and understood. The Standards are designed to enhance the global comparability and quality of information on these impacts, thereby enabling greater transparency and accountability of organizations (Global Sustainability Standards Board, 2016). Sustainability reporting based on the GRI Standards provides a balanced and reasonable representation of an organization's positive and negative contributions towards the goal of sustainable development. The information made available through sustainability reporting allows internal and external stakeholders to form opinions and to make informed decisions about an organization's contribution to the goal of sustainable development (Global Sustainability Standards Board, 2016).

Given that the oil and gas sector is the mainstay of the Nigerian economy, the need for sustainability reporting by the industry cannot be over-emphasized. Several international oil companies are using the GRI standards in their global sustainability reports. However, the operating units of these companies in Nigeria do not necessarily publish such reports locally with a specific focus on their business operations in Nigeria. Interestingly, an indigenous oil and gas company in Nigeria, Oando Plc, published its first and second Sustainability Reports in 2012 and 2013, respectively, using the GRI Sustainability Reporting Guidelines G3.1. The company's third sustainability report published in 2014 was based on GRI

Sustainability Reporting Guidelines G4, thus demonstrating Oando's awareness of the changing discourse and focus on sustainability reporting.

Risk Assessment and Management

Several risks are associated with the oil and gas business. These include financial; regulatory, and political; project (e.g. exploration and drilling, major facilities, construction practices, contracts, and costs) health, safety, and environment; design as well as operation and maintenance risks. Therefore, good decision-making within the business requires proactive and robust assessment of both technical (e.g. reservoir porosity and permeability) and non-technical risks (e.g. safety, health, and environmental issues). Unfortunately, there are several examples, experiences, and lessons which clearly point to the fact that non-technical risks are most likely to be underestimated and overlooked, with significant implications for value erosion at the project level and, in extreme cases, significant portfolio value erosion at the corporate or industry level (see Ite, 2017).

Risk assessments are crucial to identifying and predicting potential risks and implementing preventative measures. There are opportunities for SDGs to be incorporated into companies' risk assessment procedures (IPIECA et al., 2017). Qualitative risk assessment is commonly based on experience or expertise and results in categorical estimates of risk. Quantitative risk assessment leverages empirical data to determine and assign numerical values to risks. Risk assessment activities are used to identify sources of risks, their causes, and consequences. Therefore, appropriate risk assessment techniques (qualitative or quantitative) should be selected to help decision-makers better understand the risks associated with each phase of the oil and gas project development.

On the other hand, risk management activities include the principles, framework, and processes for managing risks effectively. Risk events are characterized as a combination of both the probability and consequences of undesired events. As such, risk management efforts in the oil and gas industry should be focused on a combination of eliminating/reducing the probability of occurrence of an undesired event as well as reducing or mitigating the consequences of the undesired event when it occurs.

Within the context of integrating the SDGs into CSR strategies by the Nigerian oil and gas industry, risk management must involve achieving an appropriate balance between realizing opportunities for gains by the industry and wider society, while also minimizing losses as well. Therefore, identification, assessment of technical and non-technical risks should be given high priority as an integral part of good project management practice, as well as an essential element of corporate governance within the Nigerian oil and gas industry.

Stakeholder Engagement

Proactive engagement and consultation with stakeholders, including local communities, local and national governments, and civil society, are vital to establishing and maintaining trust, understanding concerns and perspectives, and securing and maintaining a company's social license to operate. This approach is mutually beneficial to both oil and gas companies and their stakeholders (IPIECA et al., 2017). The approach and strategy of stakeholder engagement adopted by oil and gas companies in Nigeria have been a subject of debate, criticism, and controversy. However, there is no doubt that companies have deployed various frameworks to manage relationships with their stakeholders (see e.g., Waritimi, 2012). It is pertinent to note here that stakeholder engagement strategies employed by each oil and gas company depend on the prevailing circumstances and issues at hand, as well as the stakeholder groups involved. Within the context of achieving SDGs in Nigeria through CSR, the oil and gas industry must engage proactively with relevant stakeholders to support economic diversification at the local, state and national level with a view to achieving higher levels of economic productivity as well as promoting sustainable development-oriented policies, projects and programmes for the general benefit of all stakeholders.

Project Due Diligence

It is clear from Table 4 that different aspects of oil and gas projects have different impacts on different SDGs. Identifying the social, economic, and environmental baselines of the local area and the potential impacts of operations will inform engagement, contribution, and mitigation measures (IPIECA et al., 2017). Other baseline assessments for due diligence include human rights, health, lifecycle assessments, and landscape-scale plans. The relevant regulatory agencies for the Nigerian oil and gas industry (e.g. Federal Ministry of Environment, Department of Petroleum Resources, etc.) have established guidelines and procedures as part of the due diligence required for oil and gas exploration and production in Nigeria. For example, the Environmental Impact Assessment (EIA) Act No. 86 of 1992 mandates the Federal Ministry of Environment to regulate EIA in Nigeria. The Act specifically requires an EIA for any oil and gas project that involves:

(a) Seismic exploration activities,
(b) Drilling operations (exploratory, appraisal, and development wells) in onshore, near-shore and offshore locations,
(c) Construction of crude oil production, tank-farm, and terminal facilities,
(d) Laying of crude oil and gas delivery lines, flowline and pipeline more than 50km in length, and
(e) Hydrocarbon processing gas plant.

Stakeholders for Integrating Sustainable Development Goals into Corporate Social Responsibility Programs

The SDG Roadmap for the oil and gas sector aligns the industry around the SDGs, providing a platform to foster collaboration throughout the supply chain to accelerate SDG action, and amplify impact (IPIECA, 2021). Therefore, individual oil and gas companies should not aim to achieve the SDGs alone. Various forms of partnerships and dialogues are necessary, as well as a critical assessment of the possibility of obtaining inputs from various key stakeholders (Kolk, Kourula, and Pisani (2017). Within the context of Nigeria, the stakeholders include the government at various levels; oil and gas industry groups; civil society/advisory groups; development partners; as well as contractors, suppliers, and local communities.

Government

The primary responsibility for the implementation of SDGs rests with the government. However, businesses are expected to be proactive in understanding the priorities of their various host nations and seek to align with the priority SDGs they feel they can make strong and meaningful contributions (IPIECA et al., 2017). It is also the government responsibility to establish an enabling environment, including building accountable and inclusive institutions and governance mechanisms, and developing and steering national SDG action plans. They are also expected to draft, implement and enforce the policies, legislation, and regulations governing society, including the oil and gas industry. This includes establishing environmental and human rights protections, and responsible and transparent management of oil and gas revenues through national oil companies (NOCs). This invariably means that NOCs do not only regulate the industry but also conduct oil and gas operations and partner with other companies. As a result, NOCs are therefore important contributors to the achievement of SDGs through CSR.

The federal government of Nigeria ratified and adopted the SDG Agenda for implementation in September 2015 and proceeded to undertake data mapping of the SDGs. The view was to identify government agencies and other stakeholders who could provide relevant and sustained data for tracking the implementation of the SDGs. Consequently, the National Bureau of Statistics, in collaboration with the Office of the Senior Special Assistant to the president on SDGs (OSSAP-SDGs) liaised with other stakeholders to establish a baseline for the SDG indicators that are domesticated in Nigeria (see Federal Government of Nigeria, 2016). This was a good attempt to avoid the challenge of generating the required baseline data which manifested during the implementation of MDGs in Nigeria.

Clearly, Nigeria has the basic institutional framework and relevant benchmark data for monitoring and evaluating progress with SDG implementation and delivery. In this respect, the Nigerian oil and gas industry, and other key stakeholders in the sector including the Nigerian National Petroleum Corporation (NNPC), and the Nigerian Content Development Monitoring Board (NCDMB) have ample opportunity to collaborate with the OSSAP-SDGs towards implementing the SDGs in Nigeria, taking into consideration the available baseline information and institutional support.

Oil and Gas Companies/Industry Groups

The Oil Producers' Trade Section (OPTS) is the umbrella body for the private upstream oil and gas companies in Nigeria under the Lagos Chamber of Commerce and Industry (LCCI). As the oldest advocacy group for the industry, OPTS has a rich heritage of promoting the best interests of the upstream oil and gas sector of the Nigerian economy. There is no doubt that OPTS member-firms have been key to oil and gas production activity in Nigeria, accounting for over 90% of total output. OPTS members have also contributed significantly to employment generation, technological development, community development, and investment in corporate social responsibility on a scale matched by no other sector in Nigeria. Given the significance of SDGs to national development, the OPTS and other groups/associations in the oil and gas sector e.g. Petroleum Technology Association of Nigeria (PETAN), should encourage their members to take effective steps towards the operationalisation and implementation of SDGs in Nigeria.

Civil Society Organizations and Advisory Groups

Civil society organizations are important stakeholders in the Nigerian oil and gas industry. They have the capacity to monitor the implementation of SDGs; provide input from under-represented segments of society on the strategies for achieving the goals; disseminate information to the public and help to form multi-stakeholder partnerships. In 2017, the Private Sector Advisory Group (PSAG) Nigeria was constituted by the Office of the Senior Special Assistant to the President on SDGs (OSSAP-SDGs) and inaugurated on 28 February by the vice president of the Federal Republic of Nigeria. Nigeria was the first United Nations member state to establish PSAG. The aim of PSAG Nigeria is to bring together the private sector in Nigeria to address the common objective of implementing the SDGs. In specific terms, PSAG Nigeria seeks to:

(a) Facilitate broad awareness of the SDGs and mobilize private sector and other stakeholder ownership towards the adoption of the SDGs;
(b) Build capacity and core competency with the private sector for effective SDG intervention through cluster mapping and ownership;
(c) Coordinate disciplined action on SDGs within the private sector and operate results-oriented management; and
(d) Create and embed across the private sector a system for data capturing, tracking, reporting, impact, learning, and continual improvement around SDG interventions.

The involvement of the Nigerian Presidency through OSSAP-SDGs is a clear indication of the premium placed on PSAG Nigeria initiative. The founding members of PSAG are drawn from a cross-sector of critical sectors of the Nigeria economy including oil and gas, civil society organization; non-governmental organization; academia, economic think-tank; management consulting/financial audit, international development organization, telecommunications, food and beverage, banking, engineering and construction, and broadcast media. Given that the oil and gas sector in Nigeria does not exist or operate in isolation, it is imperative for members of the oil and gas industry to forge partnership, collectively or as individual firms, with PSAG Nigeria with a view to supporting implementation of SDGs in the country through their CSR strategy and programmes.

Development Partners

Development partners, including multilateral institutions and bilateral donors can provide financial, technical, managerial, and capacity-building support to other stakeholders. Development partners can also play an important convening role, facilitating information-sharing and coordination, and harnessing synergies between the other stakeholders (IPIECA et al., 2017). In Nigeria, the United Nations Development Programme (UNDP) has been foremost in contributing towards SDG domestication and delivery in the country. For the purposes of achieving SDGs through their CSR deliverables, it would be very beneficial for the oil and gas industry group under the auspices of the Oil Producers Trade Section (OPTS) of the Lagos Chamber of Commerce and Industry to strengthen their current working relationship with the Niger Delta Development Commission (NDDC).

The NDDC was established in 2000 with a broad mandate including the provision of infrastructural development and catalyzing socio-economic development in the Niger Delta region. The vision was to offer a long-lasting solution to the socio-economic difficulties of the Niger Delta, with a view to transforming the Niger Delta into a region that is economically prosperous, socially stable, ecologically regenerative, and politically peaceful. Given that the OPTS members have the opportunity to nominate community development projects for consideration and inclusion in NDDC annual budget proposal and plans for approval by the National Assembly (see Ite, 2007), it is imperative that such projects are jointly designed and implemented by both OPTS and NDDC for the general benefit of the oil-producing communities in the Niger Delta region of Nigeria. In doing so, there is a need for proactive consideration of the principles of sustainability (see the section 'Principles and Dimensions of Sustainability'); the key SDG issues relating to the oil and gas sector (see Table 9.5) and the priority SDGs as suggested by IPEICA (2021).

Contractors, Suppliers, and Local Communities

Contractors and suppliers who are often in direct contact with local communities have an opportunity to align their operations with local SDG priorities (IPIECA et al., 2017). These companies are usually expected to meet the same environmental and social standards as their clients. On the other hand, local communities are the major stakeholders most directly affected by the impacts the SDGs seek to address. As a result, the active participation and perspectives of all community members, including young people, and women can inform the planning, decision-making, and implementation of policies and initiatives that contribute to achieving the SDGs (IPIECA et al., 2017). Communities also provide feedback on the impacts of those efforts. Based on the above, it is imperative for the oil and gas industry to collaborate and work with the relevant contractors, suppliers, and local community stakeholder groups in their effort to integrate the SDGs into CSR strategies and programmes.

Conclusions

Sustainable development requires an understanding of how the SDGs interact with economic, social, and environmental realities at the local, national and global levels. Consequently, effective contribution to the SDGs requires the actors to manage complex interactions between the SDGs and the sub-targets. Given that companies interact with the SDGs through operations as well as goods or services they produce, their contributions to sustainable development can be significantly improved if the focus is fixed on nexuses of integrated SDGs, rather than treating the SDGs as isolated silos (see van Vanten & van Tulder, 2021).

There is no doubt that the oil and gas industry is central to sustainable development in many countries. The industry also serves as a key pillar of the global energy system as well as a critical driver of economic and social development. In Nigeria, the upstream oil and gas industry has played pivotal role in the Nigerian economy for over four decades, accounting for a predominant proportion of Nigeria's export earnings and driving economic activity at various levels of government and society. Although the oil and gas industry already contributes to sustainable development in several ways including CSR programmes, its operations and products potentially have negative impacts on a range of areas covered by the SDGs, including communities, ecosystems, and economies. As such, there is ample opportunity for Nigerian oil and gas companies to fully integrate SDGs into their CSR strategy and programmes through collaboration with other stakeholders. Achieving an individual SDG will often rely on or have implications for some or all other SDGs and the related supporting conditions. Similarly, CSR initiatives designed and implemented to achieve the SDGs may also cut across and have impacts on the economic, environmental, and social spheres or dimensions of sustainability.

Clearly, the primary responsibility for the implementation of SDGs rests with the government. However, businesses are expected to be proactive in understanding the priorities of their various host nations and seek to align with the priority SDGs they feel they can make strong and meaningful contributions. Given that the SDGs are frequently interlinked and indivisible, they require approaches that ensure synergies and manage trade-offs. Given the existence of the basic institutional framework for SDG delivery in Nigeria, effective collaboration and partnership between the oil and gas industry and other relevant stakeholders would be a step in the right direction for achieving the SDGs through the CSR strategy and programmes of the Nigerian oil and gas industry.

References

Adams, W. M. (2009). *Green development: Environment and sustainability in a developing world* (3rd ed.). London, United Kingdom: Routledge.

Agim, C. (1997). Understanding community relations in Nigeria's oil industry. In V. E. Eremosele (Ed.), *Nigerian petroleum business: A handbook* (pp. 129–139). Lagos, Nigeria: Advert Communications.

Egbon, O., Idemudia, U., & Amaeshi, K. (2018). Shell Nigeria's Global Memorandum of Understanding and corporate-community accountability relations. *Accounting, Auditing and Accountability Journal, 31*(1), 51–74.

Federal Government of Nigeria (2016). Nigeria: Sustainable Development Goals (SDGs) *indicators baseline report* 2016, The Office of the Senior Special Assistant to the President on SDGs (OSSAP-SDGs) and The National Bureau of Statistics (NBS), FCT, Abuja, Nigeria.

Frynas, J. G. (2000). *Oil in Nigeria: Conflict and litigation between oil companies and village communities.* Munster-Hamburg, Germany: LIT Verlag.

Frynas, J. G., Beck, P. M., & Mellahi, K. (2000). Maintaining corporate dominance after decolonization: The 'first mover advantage' of Shell–BP in Nigeria. *Review of African Political Economy, 27*(85), 407–425.

Global Sustainability Standards Board (2016). *Consolidated set of GRI sustainability reporting Standards 2016.* Amsterdam, The Netherlands: Global Reporting Initiative.

Idemudia, U. (2009). Assessing corporate-community involvement strategies in the Nigerian oil industry: An empirical analysis. *Resources Policy, 34*(3), 133–141.

Idemudia, U. (2014a). Corporate-community engagement strategies in the Niger Delta: Some critical reflections. *Extractive Industries and Society, 1*(2), 154–162.

Idemudia, U. (2014b). Corporate social responsibility and development in Africa: Issues and possibilities. *Geography Compass, 8*(7), 421–435. doi:10.1111/gec3.12143

Idemudia, U., & Ite, U. E. (2006a). Corporate-community relations in Nigeria's oil industry: Challenges and imperatives. *Corporate Social Responsibility and Environmental Management, 13*(4), 194–206.

Idemudia, U., & Ite, U. E. (2006b). Demystifying the Niger Delta conflict: Towards an integrated explanation. *Review of African Political Economy, 109,* 391–406.

Ikein, A. A., & Briggs-Anigboh, C. (1998). *Oil and fiscal federalism in Nigeria: The political economy of resource allocation in a developing country.* Aldershot, United Kingdom: Ashgate Publishing Limited.

IPIECA (2021). Accelerating action: An SDG *roadmap for the oil and gas sector.* London, United Kingdom: The Global Oil and Gas Industry Association for Environmental and Social Issues (IPIECA).

IPIECA, IFC, & United Nations Development Program (2017). Mapping the Oil and Gas Industry to the Sustainable Development Goals: An Atlas. The Global Oil and Gas Industry Association for Environmental and Social Issues (IPIECA), London, UK; International Finance Corporation – World Bank Group (IFC), Washington DC, USA and United Nations Development Programme (UNDP), New York, USA.

Ite, U. E. (2004). Multinationals and corporate social responsibility in developing countries: A case study of Nigeria. *Corporate Social Responsibility and Environmental Management, 11*(1), 1–11.

Ite, U. E. (2005). Poverty reduction in resource-rich developing countries: What have multinational corporations got to do with it? *Journal of International Development, 17*(7), 913–929.

Ite, U. E. (2007). Partnering with the state for sustainable development: Shell's experience in the Niger Delta, Nigeria. *Sustainable Development, 15*(4), 216–228.

Ite, U. E. (2017). Non-technical risk quantification: A value improvement process for maximizing returns and increasing value, SPE-189100-MS. Paper presented at the SPE Nigeria Annual International Conference and Exhibition, Lagos, Nigeria, 31 July–2 August 2017.

Ite, U. E. (2018). Embedding and operationalizing sustainable development goals in the Nigerian oil and gas industry. SPE-193396-MS. Paper presented at SPE Nigeria Annual International Conference and Exhibition, Lagos, Nigeria, 6-8 August 2018.

Ite, U. E. (2019). Sustainability assurance and evaluation for effective corporate social responsibility communication. SPE-198776-MS. Paper presented at SPE Nigeria Annual International Conference and Exhibition, Lagos, Nigeria, 5-7 August 2019.

Jamieson, D. (1998). Sustainability and beyond. *Ecological Economics, 24*(2–3), 183–192.

Kolk, A., Kourula, A., & Pisani, N. (2017). Multinational enterprises and sustainable development goals: What do we know and how to proceed? *Transnational Corporations, 24*(3), 9–32.

KPMG International (2014). *Sustainable insight: Unlocking the value of Social investment.* KPMG International.

Musa, A., Yusuf, Y., McArdle, L., & Banjoko, G. (2013). Corporate social responsibility in Nigeria's oil and gas industry: The perspective of the industry. *International Journal of Process Management and Benchmarking, 3*(2), 101–135.

Obi, C., & Soremekun, K. (1995). Oil and the Nigerian state: An overview. In K. Soremekun (Ed.), *Perspectives on the Nigerian oil industry* (pp. 5–20). Lagos, Nigeria: Amkra.

Reed, D. (1996). Sustainable development. In D. Reed (Ed.), Structural *adjustment, the environment and sustainable development* (pp. 25–45). United Kingdom: Earthscan Publications.

Rennings, K., & Wiggering, H. (1997). Steps toward indicators of sustainable development: Linking economic and ecological concepts. *Ecological Economics, 20*(1), 5–36.

Sachs, J. D. (2012). From Millennium Development Goals to sustainable development goals. *Lancet, 379*(9832), 2206–2211.

Sustainable Development Solutions Network (2015). *Getting started with the sustainable development goals: A guide for stakeholders.* Paris: Sustainable Development Solutions Network Secretariat.

van Zanten, J. A., & van Tulder, R. (2021). Improving companies' impacts on sustainable development: A nexus approach to the SDGs. *Business Strategy and the Environment*, May 2021, 1–18. doi:10.1002/bse.2835

Waritimi, E. (2012). *Stakeholder management in practice: Evidence from the Nigerian oil and gas industry.* Durham Theses, Durham University. Available at Durham E-Theses Online. Retrieved from http://Etheses.Dur.Ac.Uk/3558/

Woodbridge, M. (2015). *From MDGs to SDGs: What are the sustainable development goals?* ICLEI briefing sheet – Urban issues, No 01, November 2015. Bonn, Germany. Retrieved from www.iclei.org/briefingsheets

World Commission on Environment and Development (1987). *Our common future.* United Kingdom: Oxford University Press.

INDEX

Note: **Bold** page numbers refer to tables; *italic* page numbers refer to figures and page numbers followed by "n" denote endnotes.